The
Wisdom
of
HARRY
POTTER

The Wisdom of HARRY POTTER

What Our Favorite Hero Teaches Us about Moral Choices

Edmund M. Kern

Prometheus Books

59 John Glenn Drive
Amherst, New York 14228-2197

Published 2003 by Prometheus Books

Inquiries should be addressed to
Prometheus Books
59 John Glenn Drive
Amherst, New York 14228–2197
VOICE: 716–691–0133, ext. 207
FAX: 716–564–2711
WWW.PROMETHEUSBOOKS.COM

07 06 05 04 03   5 4 3 2

Library of Congress Cataloging-in-Publication Data

Kern, Edmund M., 1963–
        The wisdom of Harry Potter : what our favorite hero teaches us about moral choices / Edmund M. Kern.
                p. cm.
        Includes bibliographical references and index.
        ISBN 1–59102–133–2 (pbk. : alk. paper)
        1. Rowling, J. K.—Ethics. 2. Didactic fiction, English—History and criticism. 3. Children's stories, English—History and criticism. 4. Fantasy fiction, English—History and criticism. 5. Rowling, J. K.—Characters—Harry Potter. 6. Potter, Harry (Fictitious character) 7. Ethics in literature. I. Title.

PR6068.O93Z735 2003
823'.914—dc21

2003014240

Printed in the United States of America on acid-free paper

For Stephanie, upon whom I rely,

and Lukas and Rowan, who rely upon me

Contents

Acknowledgments

I must recognize the assistance of more than a few people whose help and insights have served me well. Paula Dragosh of *The Chronicle of Higher Education* offered spot-on suggestions early during my work on the Harry Potter books. Both Philip Nel and William O. Stephens took time out of their busy schedules to look over parts of my manuscript and to offer important corrections or advice. Conversations and correspondence with Mary Lenard and Todd Peperkorn, as well as Christine and Zach Tutlewski also proved rewarding. I especially want to thank Zach for sending me his written comments on morality in the Harry Potter books. A number of my colleagues at Lawrence University read portions or discussed aspects of my project in particularly helpful ways, especially Peter Fritzell, Beth Haines, Catherine Hollis, Gervais Reed, Terry Rew-Gottfried, Thomas

Ryckman, Gerald Seaman, and Timothy Spurgin. Again, at Lawrence, Joanne Johnson, Jeanne Martens, and Linda Unke provided exceptional assistance during different stages of my project. In the library, Corinne Wocelka, Gretchen Revie, and Michael May were incredibly helpful.

Although I am tempted, following Voldemort's example, to blame any negligence of mine upon others, I shall instead follow Dumbledore and speak honestly. Invariably, others' comments and assistance improved my work. Any remaining omissions and errors, as well as interpretive deficiencies, are entirely my own.

At Prometheus Books, Steven L. Mitchell and Christine Kramer were thoughtful, encouraging, and patient in moving the project through various stages of editing and production. I especially want to thank them for the extra effort entailed by the addition of my afterword on *Harry Potter and the Order of the Phoenix* late in the process.

I wish finally to thank my family. My wife, Stephanie, first encouraged me to pursue my thoughts on the topic of Harry's morality and to put them into a book. She paid a price, reading every word almost as it was written and discussing topics and themes with me at length. Her help was invaluable. As I was writing, my son, Lukas, read and discussed the stories with me, with both of us perched atop his bunk bed. Too young to engage Harry's adventures on his own, he nevertheless provided me with both keen observations and comical relief. My daughter, Rowan, spent the first year of her life with a Potter-obsessed father. By getting up with me every morning an hour or two before the rest of the household, she allowed me to forget about Harry and to become baby-obsessed instead. I dedicate this book to each of them.

Preface

The *Wisdom of Harry Potter* is primarily for adults with Potter-struck children in their lives. Still, I hope that its readership will be broader and include many others—especially adolescents or young adults—who have taken an interest in Harry's adventures. The book is about the morality of J. K. Rowling's exceptionally popular Harry Potter books. As many readers are no doubt aware, some people have found the books' values disturbing. For example, religious critics have challenged their depictions of witchcraft as potentially demonic and damaging to religious faith. Likewise, a number of social critics see them contributing to consumerism and offering questionable portraits of political, class, ethnic, and gender relations. I offer a reading at odds with writers in both camps. Simply stated, Rowling's wildly imaginative works present an updated Stoic moral system whose primary virtue is old-fashioned constancy—resolution in the face of adversity.

This project bears only a loose relationship to my research as a professional historian who specializes in the study of witchcraft and religious culture between 1350 and 1750. However strange it seemed to me early on, I was ultimately driven to see a connection between Harry and my scholarly interests by college students in a course titled Religion, Magic, and Witchcraft in Early Modern Europe at Lawrence University in Appleton, Wisconsin. This book thus grew out of questions from my students—and, at times, their visiting parents—who wondered if I had any opinions about Rowling's books and all the fuss surrounding them. In time, I wrote a short article for *Lawrence Today*, my university's alumni magazine. It described the stories and advanced the claim that the books' morality was essentially Stoic in character. I eventually developed this line of inquiry further for an essay printed in *The Chronicle of Higher Education* under the title "Harry Potter, Stoic Boy Wonder" on November 16, 2001. By the end of the month, I was a guest on Wisconsin Public Radio, offering my opinions and answering questions from callers around the nation. Without fully realizing it, I, too, had become Potter-struck—a historian of earlier centuries now taking up a twenty-first-century phenomenon.

Nonetheless, I did come to see a historical justification for my madness. Understanding the past led me to a better appreciation of Rowling's creation. Her works offer an exceptionally good example of how historical themes and topics can inform fictional storytelling, even when its setting is contemporary. Her use of the past takes three significant forms: (1) she draws upon history to give her magical world its appearance and customs; (2) she employs her characters' pasts to add to her dramatic portrayal of events; and (3) she develops a moral system that updates ethical principles with a very rich history of their own. In my assessment of Harry's morality, I'll attend to each of these uses of the past but obviously grant priority to the third.

Rowling describes magical practices that have a basis in historical evidence, and she freely makes use of legendary and mythological creatures. But even though many people once believed in the reality of magic and fable, she puts them to use in fanciful literature, set in a near-contemporary present, for an audience that largely does not. I can assure readers that there is nothing remotely demonic in her depictions of magic. Within the context of the stories, even her villain's wizardry bears little resemblance to historical descriptions of demonic invocation, although his motives and actions, and therefore his magic, are certainly evil.

Rowling has a keen historical sensibility and it shows in another way. She creates a *present* that is the result of a *past*. Her characters have interesting histories that continue to shape their lives in the present. They feel the past at work upon them and, through their acts of remembering, self-consciously enter the future.

Ultimately, what is more important for our discussion is Rowling's development of a moral system that has deep historical roots in Stoic philosophy. Fate shapes Harry's life, but his responses to it are not unlike what ancient philosophers such as Zeno, Marcus Aurelius, or Seneca would suggest. His choices and actions are all his own. He meets circumstances beyond his control with resolve and accepts that he must maintain his inner goodness and direct it outward in order to act on behalf of others.

Harry Potter's wisdom is on display in the choices he makes when confronted with troubling circumstances. Although he cannot control events, he can determine his reactions to them. Pursued by fate, he remains virtuous. This book seeks to explain how he accomplishes that feat.

1
Imaginatively Updating an Old-Fashioned Virtue

The Greek and Roman Stoics had no apparent interest in childhood, nor did they ever ask how early experiences shape the mature emotional life. . . . We can see this was an error—that the "geological upheavals of thought" that constitute the adult experience of emotion involve foundations laid down much earlier in life.

—Martha C. Nussbaum, in *Upheavals of Thought*

A Welcome Surprise and a Perilous Burden

In late 1999 three Harry Potter books were found on my doorstep in much the same way that J. K. Rowling's hero is discovered at the beginning of his tale—unexpected and unlooked for. But whereas the books were a welcome surprise from my wife (who couldn't wait until Christmas), the infant Harry is seen as a perilous burden by his thoroughly dislikable aunt and uncle, Petunia and Vernon Dursley (who also can't wait to give him away). My books arrived routinely in Appleton, Wisconsin, via airmail from Amazon.co.uk. Young Harry reaches the Dursleys in the village of Little Whinging via a flying motorcycle ridden by the giant Rubeus Hagrid.

The unanticipated public response to the Harry Potter books has mostly resembled my own happy discovery, but it has also at times approximated the stricken reaction of the Dursleys. This mixed reception of Joanne Rowling's creation has redefined the "literary sensation." No children's books have ever been more popular. If the *New York Times* had not banished the titles to a new children's category, itself the product of Potter-mania, all four would have been on its best-seller list simultaneously. Though plenty of adults were reading the books, purchases made by (or for) children seemed to drive best-seller lists for the first time. But almost as vigorous as the books' sales were frequent (and well publicized) condemnations of them. Mostly through disapproving commentary (but sometimes banning or book burning), critics of the expanding Potter empire have mounted their attacks, claiming all the while to have the best interests of children at heart. They believe that Rowling is (at best) writing clever, but formulaic and conventional, books that contribute to a rampant culture of consumerism and sustain politically reactionary values, or (far worse) composing works that promote dangerous ideas, lead young minds astray, and undermine religious values. What is a concerned adult to do?

Fortunately, attacks on the morality of the Potter series are misplaced, so readers need not worry much at all. Despite the controversy surrounding them, little systematic analysis of the books' ethic has taken place. Critiques dependent upon either unrealistic expectations of social change or overinflated claims of demonic threats do not really engage the morality on display in the stories themselves.

As it turns out, Harry's a terrific role model, if somewhat imperfect, just like the kids who are devouring the books. He comes to grips with moral problems the way most readers would expect: weighing his emotions, considering his options, and discussing issues with friends and mentors. It is true that Harry is neither a social activist nor a religious dogmatist, as some critics would prefer, but these facts do not imply moral depravity. His stories contain a strong ethical dimension. And their author's approach to ethics is so consistent, it's hard to imagine that she arrived at it haphazardly.

Focusing on the books themselves shows that Rowling develops an essentially Stoic moral philosophy through the ethical dilemmas in which she places Harry and his friends, dilemmas requiring them to think in complex ways about right and wrong. In considering her ethic, banish once and for all the common stereotype of the Stoic who is unemotional, tediously puritanical, and blindly indifferent to enjoyment and grief. Although early Stoic works do contribute to this stereotype, Rowling's characters are anything but unfeeling and embrace life to the fullest. Her version of Stoicism is admittedly an updated one, providing full attention to emotional development, but nonetheless one whose chief virtue is old-fashioned constancy. Harry's resolution in the face of adversity is the result of conscious choice and attention to what is and is not within his control. He cultivates himself in order to help others. Harry worries about who he *is*, but realizes that what he *does* matters most. And, I believe, so do the children reading the books. In fact, the stories *focus* on Harry's self-fashioning and the moral decisions that go into it, elaborating, along the way, upon several key Stoic themes such as fatalism, endurance, perseverance, self-discipline, reason, solidarity, empathy, and sacrifice. Rowling's accomplishment, blending imaginative wit and serious contemplation of virtue, is astonishing—an apt term for a work on witchcraft.

But children aren't the only ones absorbed by the adventures of Harry Potter. Adults have been enchanted as well. In some ways, Rowling tells a typical coming-of-age story that recreates age-old understandings of heroism, but in presenting Harry and his friends, she has measured the sensibilities of twenty-first-century kids. They see the constraints placed upon them but value their own decision-making and abilities. Perhaps it is this same formula that so appeals to adults reading the books. The works tap into a philosophy that offers comfort to readers, both kids and adults, as they try to work their way through the instability and uncertainty of the world. An updated Stoicism offers guidance—care of the self and due attention to others—without advancing a new orthodoxy.

Events over the past two years have only intensified the need for comfort. The terrorist assaults of September 11, 2001, on the twin towers of the World Trade Center and on the Pentagon, subsequent attacks with anthrax spores, frequent warnings from governmental officials, additional attacks overseas, and war in Iraq have all replaced vague feelings of insecurity with the promise of future threats. Yet, unease and fear are often being met with calls for resolve, vigilance, patience, and justice—Stoic responses for governing the emotional reactions of anger, panic, rash behavior, and a desire for vengeance.

Harry Potter comes to face similarly intensified threats. His world becomes increasingly uncertain. He finds guidance but no easy way out of his predicament.

Daniel Handler, who writes books for children under the pseudonym Lemony Snicket, has defended the appeal of scary stories, including his own series of books, *A Series of Unfortunate Events*. At the start of the series, he tells his young readers that those looking for happy endings should look elsewhere, and in an op-ed piece for the *New York Times*, he presents a brief in *favor* of *unhappy* stories:

> When children write to me asking if Count Olaf [the villain] is a terrorist, if the Baudelaires [the heroes] were anywhere near the World Trade Center, if the unnamed country where the books are set is in danger of being bombed, it is clear they are struggling with the same issues as the rest of us.[1]

Handler goes on to observe several important things: some people do horrible things; others become victims; threats are pervasive; and it is right to worry about how to respond. Stories that avoid raising such problems will fail to suggest solutions. Stories set in a world of trouble offer more value and less illusion. He continues:

Stories like these aren't cheerful, but they offer a truth—that real trouble cannot be erased, only endured—that is more soothing to me than any determinedly cheerful grin.[2]

It is telling that Handler finds comfort in endurance. It is a feeling with which Harry Potter is only too familiar.

Though it may seem counterintuitive, I believe it is this fact that helps make Harry's stories so appealing, on the one hand, and worthwhile for exploring moral issues, on the other. In the stories, trouble finds Harry, and Harry finds a way through it. Although the stories promise a happy resolution, they make equally clear that getting there will be tough. Harry's old-fashioned ethic of constancy might not strike disquieted readers as all that out of date. How else should he act?

Because of Harry's constancy in response to evil, his adventures offer many opportunities for discussions of morality between adults and children. And parents of a Potter-struck child would be remiss in their duties not to take advantage. In addition to the stories themselves, many critics do raise issues that are worth considering, and thoughtful readers may well want to hear what kids have to say about them. Harry Potter is everywhere. So, too, are an assortment of opinions about him. Forewarned is forearmed.

POPULARITY AND CRITICISM

Bookstores made special efforts in the summer of 2000 to accommodate children's demand for the most recent title in the series, staying open past midnight to release the book and giving out promotional materials. At the Appleton, Wisconsin, Barnes and Noble, I witnessed two children comparing their progress to date. One young boy, wearing a wizard's hat and the round, rubber eyeglasses the store was distributing, earnestly noted that he was nearly through the second book. An adolescent girl, at least a few years older and a full head taller (minus the hat but sporting the glasses), trumped him with her claim of having already completed the third. Both held copies of the newest book and seemed reluctant to leave the store. The time was nearing 1:15 A.M. Such scenes played themselves out at packed bookstores around the nation, and since then similar gatherings have taken place in libraries, schools, and even some churches.

Sales numbers also reverberate with the buzz of excitement. To date sales of the Harry Potter books have topped 175 million worldwide, a fact that puts Rowling among the best-selling authors of all time. A movie based upon the first book had the biggest opening weekend ever, taking in over $90 million in ticket sales. (It's since been ousted from number one by *Spiderman*.) Grossing over $975 million during its first year, the film just misses the number one spot on the all-time box office list, second only to *Titanic*. Sales of the video have only added to its earning power. Barely six weeks into its own opening run, a film based upon the second book had already earned over $222 million. Although hard data on the sale of merchandise are hard to come by, the *Guardian* newspaper in England reports that Rowling now brings in more in royalties from Potter-related items than from books.[3]

Yet, popularity does not guarantee quality, and Rowling's success has been controversial. Some pundits have gainsaid the books' "greatness", or merit, while social critics on the left and champions of religion on the right have questioned their values. Hostile literary critic Harold Bloom denounced the first book, bitterly deriding Rowling's prose as "goo" on *The NewsHour with Jim Lehrer* and as "just slop" on *Charlie Rose*.[4] These sentiments are echoed, if more kindly, by those who imply the books are "only children's literature", falling short of such recognized classics as *Huckleberry Finn*, *The Wind in the Willows*, *The Lord of the Rings*, or *The Chronicles of Narnia*.

Other critics, wisely eschewing the "greatness test", note Rowling's bland politics, along with her failure to challenge accepted norms, her conventional use of folklore and plot, her portrayal of central male and supportive female characters, or questionable aspects of her style— my favorite being her alleged overuse of dashes. They question what Julia Eccleshare, children's books editor at the *Guardian* (London), has described as the works' "cosy model of the world as it might be," finding it too simple out of a preference for more subversive, or at least more demanding, stories. In *Sticks and Stones*, Jack Zipes, an academic expert in folk tales and children's literature, takes aim at a rampant culture of consumerism and sees the books as only the latest formulaic installment, despite the cleverness sometimes on display. Cultural commentator Christine Schoefer at the Internet Web site Salon.com first notes her daughters' love for the books and then asserts, accurately enough, "Harry's fictional realm of magic and wizardry perfectly mirrors the conventional assumption that men do and should run the world." In her essay, "Crowning the King: Harry Potter and the Construction of Authority," Farah Mendlesohn of Middlesex University argues that although Rowling is "not an authoritarian writer," she nonetheless roots her work in a liberalism whose chief feature is its false claim to be non-ideological. By paying only superficial attention to fairness, social mobility, and tolerance, the books serve the status quo through "inherently conservative and hierarchical notions of authority." Although more criticism of this type comes from the left, it is unlikely many parents have limited their children's access to the books because of it. With the exception of Bloom, who should have some fun, most social or literary critics offer something to consider—maybe Rowling does overuse dashes.[5]

A more robust challenge comes from those who would ban the books under the guise of "protecting" children. Why protection? Because the Harry Potter books are anything but comfortable, since they are godless, encourage witchcraft, and pose a demonic threat. Complaints of this sort come from fundamentalist religious circles whose members take umbrage at the absence of an expressly Christian message. It is tempting to dismiss such claims as groundless, and many writing from different religious perspectives have done just that, but such condemnations are common and do have some effect.

Beverley Becker, associate director of the American Library Association's Office for Intellectual Freedom, told me that, by the summer of 2001, challenges to the books had been made in twenty-seven states.

Many others have been recorded since then and in Canada and overseas. (A rather lengthy hiatus between books four and five seems to have diminished some of the controversy.) According to Becker, when books were pulled from shelves by school administrators, those decisions were later rescinded, and "fortunately, most often the books do remain available." Still, fundamentalist critics remain formidable because their actions take books out of the hands of children. As ABC News reported on March 26, 2001, copies of the books were burned in a suburb of Pittsburgh as "ungodly." Although no efforts to ban Harry Potter outright have been successful, Becker believes that repeated calls for removing works from shelves have a broader chilling effect, though "it happens quite subtly, influencing future decisions of teachers, librarians, and publishers."[6]

Controversy over Harry Potter—clearly a cultural phenomenon, beyond a narrowly literary one—will likely continue, at least for some members of the public. As noted, the first movie proved wildly successful, as did the second at the end of 2002, with others due every year or two after that. Rowling has promised three additional volumes in the series, guaranteeing that Harry will stay on kids' radar for some time to come. Potter-related toys, games, and other merchandise—including wallpaper for your children's rooms—can't be avoided. Is Harry Potter only the most recent homogenized manifestation of a bankrupt pop culture? Is he a danger to religious belief? Or is he something else?

WHAT THE BOOKS HAVE TO OFFER

J. K. Rowling inadvertently addresses her critics in an early portrait of several key characters, Harry's adoptive family:

> The Dursleys had everything they wanted, but they also had a secret, and their greatest fear was that somebody would discover it. They didn't think they could bear it if anyone found out about the Potters. . . . The Dursleys knew that the Potters had a small son, too, but they

had never even seen him. This boy was another good reason for keeping the Potters away; they didn't want Dudley mixing with a child like that.

A few pages later, she again seems to have "guardians" of kids' lives and thoughts in mind, writing of Mr. Dursley, "[he] set off for home, hoping he was imagining things, which he had never hoped before, because he didn't approve of imagination."[7]

Imagination, in fact, is the single most important reason the books are so popular, but it also proves to be Rowling's best defense against her adult detractors, regardless of their ideology. Attacks on the works' quality and morality face a stiff challenge from the stories themselves. The creativity on display draws kids' attention and keeps them coming back. Rowling writes a simple, fluid, and clever prose, and she gracefully places Harry and his friends in ethical dilemmas requiring them to *think* in complex ways about right and wrong. Some of her ingeniously drawn characters might "preach," but (as we shall soon see) she never does.

The absence of any overt religious or political messages also distinguishes the books and, I would argue, is the second reason for their success. What can be easily derided as invisible religion and vanilla politics will not offend the majority, after all. Nevertheless, it would be a mistake to believe that the books lack a moral center or social conscience. To the contrary, it is precisely their openness—unburdened by orthodoxy—that contributes to their popularity and provides Rowling so useful a vehicle for advancing a coherent, yet flexible, ethical code. When combined with Rowling's creativity and cleverness, her ease of exposition and clarity make the books irresistible to children. As they read, they get more than they might expect.

This fact, I believe, is the third reason the works have proven so well loved, despite the controversy surrounding them: they are simultaneously imaginatively fun and morally serious. As Rowling herself admitted in response to a fan's query, "I didn't set out to preach to anyone; if people like Harry and identify with him, I am pleased, because I think he is very likeable. But I truly didn't set out to teach morals, even though I do think they are moral books."[8] In fact, creativity and ethics coexist quite easily in Harry's adventures. Rowling offers readers not only an exciting world, but also one troubled by problems; she provides not only the promise of triumph over evil, but also guidance on how to meet it through thoughtful attention to right and wrong. By putting her imagination into play, she also puts her imagination to work. As I shall try to show later, this combination is not lost on most children reading the books.

IMAGINATION AT PLAY

Four books so far, *Harry Potter and the Sorcerer's Stone*, *Harry Potter and the Chamber of Secrets*, *Harry Potter and the Prisoner of Azkaban*, and *Harry Potter and the Goblet of Fire*, are installments in a projected seven-part series.[9] The books unfold Harry's place within the Wizarding World and the Muggle World, presenting him with challenges to overcome in both. In the former, we find witches of various kinds, goblins providing financial services, misunderstood werewolves, envious ghosts, and numerous breeds of dragons, while in the latter, we find everyone else—us "Muggles" with lives shaped by corporate business, electricity, and other prosaic concerns. Wizards know about Muggles, despite an often willful ignorance of their ways. We catch a glimpse of how extensive this ignorance can be when a member of the Ministry of Magic corrects a fellow wizard for wearing a flowery nightgown while trying to pass as a Muggle. ("Muggle *women* wear them, Archie, not men; they wear *these*.")[10] Most Muggles are completely unaware of the world of magic or have their memories modified, should they witness something beyond their ken. (*Obliviate!* is the usual Memory Charm.) Still, the two worlds are alike, with the exciting magical world mirroring the realities of the other: friends and enemies, family, government, eating and sleeping, school, and shopping. The books merge the fantastical and the everyday.

Harry is an orphan whose parents' death at the hands of the arch-villain Lord Voldemort places him with the Dursleys. He is the most famous person in the wizarding world (though he doesn't know it at first), since he alone, while still an infant, survived an attack by "You-Know-Who," who is condemned to a half-life without physical form when his killing spell backfires. Harry spends ten years neglected by his aunt and uncle and tormented by their horrible son, Dudley, before a letter offers escape to Hogwarts School of Witchcraft and Wizardry, where he becomes a student. Although summers return Harry to drudgery, his suffering with the Dursleys and his freer life at Hogwarts both encourage growth.

Harry befriends Ron Weasley, from an ancient if impecunious wizarding family, whose loyalty to Harry and endurance of his fame and fortune waiver but never break, and Hermione Granger, from a family of Muggle dentists, who nonetheless excels at magic and her studies. Ron's a regular guy, and Hermione is the school's best student. They might have a thing for each other. A host of diverse, secondary characters gives Harry's social and academic life its shape.

Harry's foil is the super-rich and bigoted Draco Malfoy, descended from a long line of dark wizards. Oily Professor Severus Snape, also of questionable character, is always looking to catch him out of line. Hovering in the background is the furtive threat of You-Know-Who, who seeks to return to his physical form and the power he once enjoyed. Beginning with his search for the Sorcerer's Stone (really the "philosopher's stone" of medieval history), which will return him to life and give him limitless riches, Voldemort repeatedly challenges Harry in a life-and-death struggle. His return is only a matter of time.

But Harry has his protectors as well. Gamekeeper Rubeus Hagrid alternately gets him into and out of trouble. Headmaster Albus Dumbledore amiably mentors Harry but possesses unequaled power and lore. Professor Minerva McGonagall doles out wisdom or discipline as she sees fit. And Ron's parents become surrogates for Harry's own. In addition, other friends of Harry's parents enter his life. Fully aware of Voldemort's threat, these (at times befuddled, but nonetheless able) adults seek to provide safety and guidance.

Hogwarts is a fabulous castle, filled with great halls and towers, secret chambers, moving staircases, and paintings whose subjects may walk about not only within their own frames but in other paintings as well. Harry's school house is Gryffindor, one of four in addition to Hufflepuff, Ravenclaw, and Slytherin, each with its own insignia, colors, and ethos. The Hogwarts student culture is rich in both adventure and mischief.

Many other books of interest to children offer as much creativity. The authors of the books so frequently placed in comparison certainly imagine exciting worlds but (I would contend) often in language crafted to please well-schooled adults rather than children. Writing from his own experience, Mark Twain hoped "to pleasantly remind adults of what they once were themselves." Kenneth Grahame wrote a number of successful books for adults before *The Wind in the Willows*. J. R. R. Tolkien certainly stopped writing for kids by the second chapter of *The Lord of the Rings*, and one could argue that C. S. Lewis never really intended to do so in his extended allegories.[11]

Philip Pullman's recently completed *His Dark Materials* (1995–2000) belongs in this group in terms of both quality and style. Here he describes (for a full paragraph, without a main clause) the setting of several chapters:

> East along the great highway of the River Isis, thronged with slow-moving brick barges and asphalt boats and corn tankers, way down past Henley and Maidenhead to Teddington, where the tide from the German Ocean reaches, and further down still . . . to where the river, wide and filthy now, swings in a great curve to the south.[12]

Absolutely beautiful. But also the kind of thing many parents *wish* their children would enjoy (and doubtless, many do). This is the language that critics of children's literature love to praise (and it is outstanding), but kids sometimes take a bit longer to warm up to it. At bedtime, I used to like to read to my (then) four-year-old Lukas certain favorites. He was happy (every night, it seemed) to suggest Dav Pilkey's quirky and irreverent *The Adventures of Captain Underpants*.[13] He's every bit as discerning nowadays and a *huge* fan of Harry Potter.

In keeping with her simpler style, Rowling seldom chooses to wander, offering straightforward descriptions of settings central to her story:

> "Yeh'll get yer firs' sight o' Hogwarts in a sec," Hagrid called over his shoulder, "jus' round this bend here."
>
> There was a loud "Oooooh!"
>
> The narrow path had opened suddenly onto the edge of a great black lake. Perched atop a high mountain on the other side, its windows sparkling in the starry sky, was a vast castle with many turrets and towers.[14]

Although the passage is unlikely to impress the editors of the *Horn Book* magazine, who received Rowling's books lukewarmly and editorialized against their popularity,[15] its ordinary language nonetheless works well to convey extraordinary features. Rowling's prose leaves a good deal open to the imagination through telling detail rather than weighty description.

And adding immeasurably to her works' popularity, Rowling revels in their details. She chooses names guaranteed to bring a smile to the attentive reader. Whereas Dudley Dursley attends the elite school Smeltings, his parents would relegate Harry to Stonewall High. Witches travel to Diagon Alley or Knockturn Alley for various goods and services. Similar attention is paid to naming minor characters, whether they are the bureaucratic Minister of Magic Cornelius Fudge; Draco Malfoy's henchmen, Crabbe and Goyle; the yellow journalist, Rita Skeeter; or the ghost Nearly Headless Nick, whose fifteenth-century execution didn't quite come off. Sometimes, punning takes place in French (or other languages) as in Voldemort (theft of death or flight from death) and Malfoy (bad faith). This trend also emerges in the clever mock Latin used for most magical charms such as *Locomotor Mortis* for the Leg-Locker Curse or *Petrificus Totalis* for a Body-Bind.

On nearly every page, Rowling puts the vibrant culture of the wizarding world on display. She invents the song-writing Sorting Hat for placing students in the appropriate school houses, risk-laden Bertie

Bott's Every-Flavor Beans, and the soccer-like game of Quidditch, played on broomsticks above the pitch with balls that sometimes attack the players. Blending the magical and mundane, she is at her best:

> "Help yourself," said Harry. "But in, you know, the Muggle world, people just stay put in photos."
> "Do they? What, they don't move at all?" Ron sounded amazed. "Weird."[16]

Rowling is also adept at structuring her works. Each book relates one year of Harry's life and has its own plot line, but through tantalizing concealment and gradual revelation, the author tells a larger story as well. The first and second books hew closely to the standard formula of children's books. They present a series of episodic chapters, which loosely follow a larger narrative arc, and then offer a rapid climax. Both begin with Harry living with the Dursleys, move the action quickly to Hogwarts, follow his exploits there, and end with his dread return to Little Whinging (sounds like "whining"). Both are no less enjoyable for all this. The longer third book, too, follows this pattern before diverging radically and extending the climactic scenes over its final third. The reader learns a great deal about Harry's history and remains in suspense as the resolution of one threat dissolves into the emergence of another. The twice-as-long fourth book explodes the formula completely, becoming a pivot upon which the series turns. It begins with an episode in which Harry plays no part, has him arriving at Hogwarts a quarter of the way through, and elaborates at length on his "back story." It has an engaging plot, but answers questions raised earlier and poses new ones that lead readers into the unknown.

This aspect of Rowling's shrewd storytelling deserves special attention: each book moves the story both forward and backward. The further we travel into Harry's future, the further we travel into his parents' past. The stories grow darker as the past beckons and the future threatens. In this awareness of the relations among past, present, and future, we see Rowling's keen sense of the importance of history in storytelling. But her sense of the past takes on other forms as well, which add to the overall appeal of her tale.

Sprinkled throughout the books are numerous references to history, legend, and myth. Of course, ample examples of purely fictional events are provided in scenes of Professor Binns's course on the History of Magic, such as eighteenth-century goblin rebellions, or in Hermione's brief, but frequent, know-it-all discourses upon the founding and history of Hogwarts. Just as interesting, however, are details drawn from history, such as the witch-hunts or the alchemical work of Nicolas Flamel, or from legend and myth, such as dragons, centaurs, grindylows, and hippogriffs—all adapted and developed for use in Rowling's imaginative fiction. Though she tends to poke fun at history as an academic subject (Professor Binns is the only ghost teaching at Hogwarts; he just got up one day to deliver a well-worn lecture and left his body behind), she nonetheless employs the past frequently to add depth and context to her descriptions of Harry's adventures.

Though in interviews Rowling claims not to be writing for any particular audience, her brilliance shows most clearly in the authorial voice she adapts for each book, which matures along with Harry. This trend reflects each volume's higher level of difficulty. Harry is eleven in the first book; he is fourteen in the fourth. Also, her voice speaks to children, rather than at them. They thus encounter the chicken blood-and-brandy diet of baby dragons, "bubotuber pus," vomit-flavored candy, and (mildly) off-color jokes, along with occasional drunkenness and violence. Life is not pristine. The death of a likable, righteous character proves that acting morally is hard and that being good does not guarantee being rewarded.

Frankness in the Harry Potter books liberates rather than constrains. Harry is lectured often enough about rules and rule-breaking, but his choices are his own. Subject to unfairness and jealousy, he does not always act with the best of intentions. Not above giving into temptation, breaking the rules, or even acting contrary to explicit instruction, Harry and his friends are no prudes. Yet, empathy and tolerance motivate them, virtues mostly absent, in contrast, from William Bennett's preachy (and unappealing) *Children's Book of Virtues*.[17] Despite occasional misbehavior, they remain steadfast within what is shaping up as an epic battle between good and evil. By refusing to smother her young readers, Rowling crafts an appealing ethical system, one that they can both relate to and think through.

IMAGINATION AT WORK

A foreboding permeates Harry's life. He senses quite accurately that he has some frightful enemies and that he is the target of vengeance. Despite some cheery optimism, Harry has a pronounced sense of fatalism—that is, he recognizes how events unfold around him, drawing him into circumstances not of his own making. As a result, Harry experiences life's ambiguities, the things pulling him in different directions, along with his own conflicting desires.

It is easy to underestimate how appealing this portrayal of foreboding circumstances is to young readers, whose lives turn on the whims of others, and how satisfying it is to follow a character working his own way through them. Even adults, ostensibly more in control of their own lives, have no difficulty identifying with these themes. In Harry's stories, although events are often beyond his control, he is governed ultimately by rules of his own making.

In precisely this way, Rowling introduces the Stoicism so central to the moral system at work in her series. She gives Stoic fatalism a clear voice in the characters mentoring Harry, along with its Stoic antidotes, endurance and perseverance. In the first book we find Dumbledore observing:

> "Nevertheless, Harry, while you may only have delayed his return to power, it will merely take someone else who is prepared to fight what seems a losing battle next time—and if he is delayed again, and again, why, he may never return to power."[18]

By the fourth book, these sentiments are echoed in the plain language of the groundskeeper Hagrid:

"Knew he was goin' ter come back," said Hagrid, and Harry, Ron, and Hermione looked up at him, shocked. "Known it fer years, Harry. Knew he was out there bidin' his time. It had ter happen. Well, now it has, an' we'll jus' have ter get on with it. We'll fight. Migh' be able ter stop him before he gets a good hold."[19]

Commenting particularly upon Voldemort's return, Hagrid also speaks thematically about evil and how to meet it. Harry has become only too familiar with evil by this time, and he has learned how to cope with it—remaining true to what is right regardless of consequence. He remains constant.

Rowling's characterization of Harry recalls a rich history of Stoic thinking on how to confront evil and on the importance of constancy. Though she does not make direct allusions to it, striking resemblances between her treatment of Harry and this historical legacy are there for those who look. A Stoic ethic has often been embraced during times of trouble.

A particularly good historical example is the sixteenth-century commentary of the Dutch philosopher Justus Lipsius (1547–1606). In the midst of violent political turmoil engulfing the Netherlands in 1584, as Spain sought to put down a revolt of the northern United Provinces, Lipsius asked what was the proper response of the thinking person to adverse circumstances. The result became his neo-Stoic classic, *The Book of Constancy.* As his title suggests, Lipsius found the answer in "a right and immovable strength of mind, neither lifted up nor pressed down with external or casual accidents" (that is, unplanned events). Such steadfastness was to stem from sound reason, found internally, but corresponding to the true nature of things. Thinking persons were to make their will correspond to what was right (understood by the Christian Lipsius as the will of God). In adverse circumstances, they endured rather than seeking to flee.[20]

Stoicism has a long history, beginning in the fourth century B.C.E. with the lectures of Zeno of Citium (366–280 B.C.E.) from the "painted porch" (*Stoa Poikile*) in Athens, which gave the school its name. Zeno emphasized the importance of strength of character in moral and political affairs. Soon, Cleanthes of Assos (331–232 B.C.E.) and Chrysippus of Soli (280 B.C.E.) added spiritual enrichment and greater systematic rigor. An important school of thought since then, its most famous proponents are the ancient Romans Seneca (2–68 C.E.), Epictetus (born between 50–60 C.E.), and the Emperor Marcus Aurelius (died 180 C.E.), who each sought to reconcile the Stoic emphasis upon inward tranquility with the likewise important, outward moral values of social duty, education, and good citizenship.

According to the Stoics, living well means living in accord with the world, which divine reason has shaped. Nature (or the divine within it) is thus the standard for the regulation of life; it not only dictates proper action but also shapes the outcome of events. In practical terms, fate (or fortune) consists of things beyond a person's control. Within this scheme, Stoics distinguish among good things (virtues, virtuous acts, good feelings), bad things (vices, vicious acts, and bad feelings), and indifferent things—things beyond one's control, which are further divided into preferred things (e.g., life, beauty, and health) or rejected things (e.g., death, ugliness, and illness). Stoics embrace what is good, deplore what is bad, and either value or discount what is indifferent.

How Stoics understand particular things is dependent upon whether they are "external" or "internal" to the self. External things—whether preferred or rejected—must necessarily be met with indifference, because they cannot be controlled. Stoics may welcome fame, wealth, and life itself, but when fortune takes them away, they should not be surprised or assert that life is unfair. Stoics reconcile themselves to inescapable circumstance. Internal things, in contrast, constitute either the greatest benefit or the greatest evil, because they alone are fully under a person's control and, therefore, the responsibility of the individual. Stoics can maintain honor, honesty, and wisdom in the face of unexpected and horrible events, but they cannot change the uncertainty and imperfectability of existence. Virtue results only from conscious choice and attention to what is within one's control. Stoicism thus seeks to subject desires, feelings, and judgments to restraints that cultivate the self in service of what is good.

The Stoics balance inner tranquility against a strongly egalitarian way of viewing the world. And this cosmopolitan ethic—not bound by local or state or ethnic prejudice—represents the most significant basis for acting morally on behalf of others. Given this view of human equality, it may seem strange that Stoics often repudiate the emotions—and especially compassion—as legitimate motivation for taking action on behalf of others. But they do so in a particular way that nonetheless allows for empathy, the establishment of an imaginative connection to other people. For compassion, as construed by the Stoics, leads a person away from seeing the inherent dignity of *all* human beings and toward recognizing the worth of only *some*. Compassion, in this sense, is an unreliable guide to acting morally. It often as not can lead to cruelty and vengeance. The Stoic distrusts the emotions, because they interfere with an impartial stance toward all individuals, events, and circumstances. A truly cosmopolitan ethic, according to the early Stoics, requires the cultivation of neutrality in the service of justice.

In some sense, then, the stereotype of the Stoic as unfeeling is well deserved. And critics of the original Stoics have been keen to argue that unfeeling neutrality is not only practically impossible but also dehumanizing in its demands. This is particularly so when it finds expression in what the eminent philosopher Martha C. Nussbaum calls its "normative" form, which requires the complete eradication of emotion. But Stoicism is not, after all, a single thing, which one either accepts or rejects in its entirety. It consists, rather, in ways of thinking that require the constant and continuous reassessment of what is right and what is good. In fact, as Nussbaum has shown, Seneca and other Roman Stoics had difficulty maintaining the early Greeks' normative view, interested as they were in exploring the imaginative empathy that seemed so necessary to duty, instruction, and cosmopolitanism.

Despite a skeptical (and healthy) scrutiny that sometimes greeted early Stoic views, the school of thought continued to exert an important influence in subsequent centuries. Many early Christian writers put its ways to good use, as did St. Augustine (354–430), who found much to admire in the philosophy, and Boethius (480–524), who sounded Stoic themes in his early medieval work, *The Consolation of Philosophy*. In the early modern period (between 1350 and 1750), the Stoic worldview engaged Renaissance humanists and Christian reformers alike, shaping the works of such authors as Francesco Petrarca (1304–1374); Desiderius Erasmus (1466–1536); John Calvin (1509–1592), who wrote a lengthy book on Seneca; Michel de Montaigne (1533–1592); and John Milton (1608–1674); not to mention Justus Lipsius (1574–1606). And Benedict Spinoza (1608–1677), Immanuel Kant (1724–1804), and Adam Smith (1723–1790) each gave voice to Stoic moral principles during the Enlightenment of the late seventeenth and eighteenth centuries, extending the philosophy's sway well into the twentieth century and beyond.

Today, we find both Christian thinkers and the more secular-minded often making use of the basic elements of Stoic thinking. The former invoke a transcendent God who is not only all-powerful but caring. They call upon humans to recognize the shaping influence of divine providence without abandoning the uncertain task of conforming their own thought to it. The latter (a more diverse group) reason in a similar, though nonreligious, fashion, seeking to balance the constraints of circumstance against the demands of individual agency. They emphasize the solidarity of all humans, the primacy of reason, the need for self-sacrifice, or the interconnectedness of things, particularly in relation to environmental matters.[21]

In the past few years, Stoicism has begun to experience a renaissance of sorts, finding a place in popular and philosophical works, as well as political culture. As the Creighton University philosopher William O. Stephens has recently shown, both Tom Wolfe's novel *A Man in Full* and Ridley Scott's film *Gladiator* elaborate upon basic Stoic themes. (The latter features Marcus Aurelius played by the late Richard Harris, who also portrayed another great Stoic, Albus Dumbledore, in the first two *Harry Potter* films.) Very recently, best-selling author Alain de Botton sketched several Stoic thinkers (along with their hero Socrates, who predates the school founded by Zeno) in his book *The Consolations of Philosophy*, whose very title is a variation upon Boethius's own. De Botton suggests that philosophy, often in a Stoic guise, can offer ways through problems if not necessarily around them. In 2001, Martha C. Nussbaum offered her own "construction of a contemporary neo-Stoic view" in her magisterial book, *Upheavals of Thought*, whose subtitle, *The Intelligence of Emotions*, provides clues about how emotional insights might find a home within an essentially Stoic framework.[22]

In the aftermath of September 11, policy-makers have sounded Stoic themes in their calls for patience, diligence, and sacrifice in the name of greater goods. Though one might legitimately question their motives (are they meeting a challenge to U.S. hegemony, boosting a sagging economy, spinning events for political gain?), there can be little doubt that the rhetoric has its appeal. If I am right about the moral system in the Harry Potter books, they might just comprise the most visible contribution to Stoicism's reemergence as a viable, practical philosophy offering comfort and guidance in these uncertain times.

Although Rowling is careful not to present my dry-as-dust academic version of Stoicism, she does introduce the basic ideas early on. Her characters may value life and material possessions, but they realize that many things are more important. What is Voldemort's search for the Sorcerer's (philosopher's) Stone, after all, but a lust for the means of living forever and obtaining unlimited riches? Dumbledore explains the folly in such thinking:

> "After all, to the well-organized mind, death is but the next great adventure. You know, the Stone was really not such a wonderful thing. As much money and life as you could want! The two things most human beings would choose above all—the trouble is, humans do have a knack of choosing precisely those things which are worst for them."[23]

A "well-organized mind," accepting the inevitability and certainty of death, it seems, might just find its method in Stoic principles.

But likable characters have fun, often give free reign to their emotions, and get into more than their fair share of trouble. Here, Rowling's depictions of life at Hogwarts echo the neo-Stoic views of

Nussbaum, which seek not to deny the emotions but to harness them to reason—to comprehend "the intelligence of emotions":

> The Greek and Roman Stoics had no apparent interest in childhood, nor did they ever ask how early experiences shape the mature emotional life. Indeed, they appear to have had the implausible view that children, like animals, do not have emotions. We can see this was an error—that the "geological upheavals of thought" that constitute the adult experience of emotion involve foundations laid down much earlier in life.[24]

In Rowling's world, characters thus experience ambiguity in a threatening world and, at times, give in to its temptations. Nonetheless, these tendencies do not preclude acting morally when the stakes are high.

Rowling's characters thus try to assess competing desires and recognize the importance of doing the right thing. Although they rely upon no clearly available divine or objective standards in making their choices, they intuit that the absence of such standards does not allow them to avoid responsibility. Instead, taking the right steps requires the exercise of self-discipline and the use of reason; solidarity grounded in empathy calls for running the risk of sacrifice. While, it is true, Harry and his friends would likely fall asleep during a lesson on Stoicism, as they often do in Professor Binns's classes on the History of Magic, they could recognize within it some of the motivations behind their own decisions.

In presenting Harry and his friends, Rowling follows other works of children's literature. Tolkien, Lewis, and (most recently) Pullman each show how self-discipline, in service of a larger good, is the only sure means of remaining virtuous and securing victory. In each of these authors' works, even though characters never offer up a universal distinction between good and evil, they do not abandon reason in their attempts to discern the difference. They comprehend that the difference depends upon the ability to imagine the suffering of others and the desire to do something about it. An imaginative extension of the self encourages acting for the well-being of all regardless of personal risk. Withdrawal from empathy signals the advent of evil.

Harry Potter's morality is thus not unlike that on display in the works of Tolkien, Lewis, or Pullman, where Stoic constancy is valued. In fact, forms of Stoicism seem to be central to much twentieth-century children's literature. Perhaps this is not surprising. The last century witnessed both extreme mass-violence and the wearing away of objective epistemologies (that is, the notion that the truth is obvious and we always and already know it). As Harry's fans, both young and old, seem to recognize, an updated Stoicism provides guidance without advancing a new orthodoxy in the midst of so much uncertainty. In this postmodern age (distinguished by an uneasy suspicion of universal explanations, stable meanings, and objective truth) the basic Stoic practice of reconciling personal tranquility with strong, cosmopolitan moral commitments may seem especially vital. Harry's adventures appeal to those finding themselves in circumstances not of their own making but hoping to make the right choices when charting their own paths.

Again, the events of September 11 seem germane to assessing the appeal of Rowling's ethical system. A common response to televised horror was shock, prompted not only by the audacity of the attacks, but also by the terrorists' perceived inability to associate their acts with the enormous suffering among both victims and survivors. An outpouring of support—shared grief, volunteerism, and charitable contributions—alleviated the shock and restored an imaginative, empathetic connection to those harmed by the attacks. In the minds of many, even such limited denial of the self (in service of the self) became an opportunity for acting on behalf of an apparent greater good (and for restoring a degree of personal tranquility).

If we recall the observations of Daniel Handler, we should take seriously his claim that children grapple with the same problems confronting the rest of us—along with their own, which are no less serious to them. We should also recognize that thinking carefully about difficult issues is not beyond them. In fact, children are capable of showing amazing canniness in coming to understand how the world works, whether they consider events unfolding in the world or their own growing pains. Furthermore, beginning to cultivate the necessary self-discipline for judicious thought might be especially important during their formative years.

In his foundational works on the psychology of moral development, Lawrence Kohlberg certainly suggests as much. In addition to outlining six progressive stages of moral reasoning, he shows that the period of most productive advancement occurs between the ages of ten and eighteen. Furthermore, he argues, sufficient opportunity to think through ethical dilemmas is essential to children and adolescents developing their own sense of right and wrong. Although a number of other developmental psychologists have since questioned just how discrete each stage of moral advancement might be in actual children (who not only progress but also regress), they nonetheless support the notion that children must actually work through the difficulties of moral conflict to have a better sense of ethical problems and solutions. The nonthreatening conditions of imaginative play allow them to try out different approaches and to adopt different perspectives.[25]

Fantasy literature offers many such opportunities for "serious play." Discerning adults, it seems, can turn Harry Potter into more than just a pop-cultural phenomenon. Making use of what J. K. Rowling has provided, they can help to make it an important learning experience.

THE KIDS IN YOUR LIFE

The Appleton Public Library has hosted a number of special events for children reading the Harry Potter books. In addition to organizing the usual readings, trivia contests, craft projects, and science demonstrations, librarians facilitate discussions of the works among children. According to Children's Librarian Linda DeNell, the kids come to have a good time, but end up speaking earnestly about the characters. "Everybody loves Harry," she said, "though they do identify with all the kids and teachers."

Asked if they ever discuss the morality of the books, DeNell told me, "they pick up on Dumbledore's role and know 'we should listen to what Professor Dumbledore has to say.'" After a moment's thought, she added, "children like the fact that Harry and his friends get to make choices, and they pick up that the choices they make are the right thing to do rather than the easiest." Perhaps only dimly aware of the real-world social issues (such as injustice, prejudice, class antagonism, and bigotry) taken up at times by Rowling, children can nonetheless sense her books' Stoic themes about responsibility. As DeNell told me, kids often point to a key passage in which Harry worries about who he is. When Dumbledore explains, "it's our choices, Harry, that show what we truly are, far more than our abilities," he knows intimately that Harry has already demonstrated as much. The kids reading the books do as well.[26]

Kids experience not only the thrill of Rowling's creation but the values of its moral system as well. Allowing their imaginations to play paves the way for putting their imaginations to work, and they come to see how this combination works its magic upon them. Drawn to his magical world but then won over by his qualities, children want to emulate Harry Potter.

I hope to chart here in some detail just what kids might be emulating. I primarily have in mind the millions of concerned parents who already find themselves and their children in the midst of Potter-mania, but I hope to speak as well to any curious reader (regardless of age) captivated by the books. I avoid the whole question of "great literature," which is an issue that strikes me as beside the point, since children themselves really don't care. Instead, I focus upon how Rowling's vibrant imagination stakes a claim on kids' attention and provides her with opportunities to teach important moral lessons.

In four additional chapters, you will find a progressive defense of the Harry Potter series against some of the complaints made against it and a liberal-minded case for considering it a highly moral work. I claim no professional expertise in childhood development, despite my occasional use of Kohlberg's developmental theories and the views of some of his critics, and my opinions must be understood in light of that fact. Instead, I approach the works as a father whose own children have been and will be swept up by Harry Potter. Although I do bring some academic expertise to my encounter with the books, discerning readers really can understand and assess the issues I raise if they have the right kinds of information available to them.

Chapter 2, "Plot Threads and Moral Fibers," provides synopses of the four books currently available and sketches, along the way, the central moral of each one. It reminds readers of basic plot developments and describes Harry's moral choices, arguing that Rowling's hero becomes more self-conscious as his adventures proceed. They lead him toward greater comprehension of (1) the workings of fate, (2) the significance of inborn proficiencies and shortcomings, (3) the nature of moral ambiguity, and (4) the importance of virtuous intentions—which are the main ethical themes of each subsequent book in the series.

Chapter 3, "Harry Potter's Morality on Display: A Primer on Stoic Virtue," assesses Harry's adventures with both eyes on the rich legacy of Stoic ethics that Rowling gives new shape. I begin with a brief discussion of Stoic self-consciousness and then relate its twin themes of self-reliance and empathy to Harry's stories. I also focus upon some of the moral ambiguities the books raise; Rowling's ethic, after all, is not doctrinaire or prescriptive. The chapter then takes up, in turn, several basic principles of Stoicism and shows how crucial episodes in Harry's adventures give them new life for today's kids. I conclude this chapter by examining how Rowling's ethical system corresponds, in some important ways, to findings in the field of developmental moral psychology. Her stories and the updated Stoicism on display within them offer children opportunities for carefully assessing moral problems, rather than prescribing doctrinaire solutions to them.

Chapter 4, "Greed, Conventionality, Demonic Threat," takes up some of the complaints directed against the Harry Potter series. No book is above criticism, so this chapter offers both descriptions and assessments of some of the more common ones, since a familiarity with them might prove useful in discussions with children. Adults can help shape any lessons that kids take from their imaginative engagement with the books. Put briefly, social critics tend to see the works as not imaginative enough; religious ones see them as too much so. I'm somewhat sympathetic to several of the social critiques on offer, which warn about the dangers of consumerism and acceptance of societal disparities. I'm less so to those from a religious perspective, especially if they rely upon the assumption that any story is worthy of denunciation and is implicitly demonic if it does not convey an expressly Christian message and portrays fanciful witchcraft in a favorable light. Not all religious commentaries, however, have been so narrow, and many writing from a religious perspective have defended Rowling's works. Like those authors, I value a pluralistic society and open inquiry, and my comments in defense of Harry's virtue will not convince anyone who does not. Harry searches for the right things to do; he must look to many places for guidance, since he does not have ready-made solutions to his problems.

Chapter 5, "Imagination, History, Legend, and Myth," confronts head-on the nature of the author's creative imagination. It mixes both familiar aspects of the historical and fantastical details of the legendary or mythical. The chapter first provides numerous examples of both, showing how the admixture creates something new—a world that resembles our own, but isn't quite our own. The chapter next illustrates how Rowling's decision to set a work of fantasy in the real world opens her to criticism. According to the critics, Harry Potter—as a work of *fiction*—fails to protest (enough) everyday institutions, practices, and assumptions that are the *product of history* (irking the social critics) and reintroduces (with gusto) fantastical elements that are *drawn from legend and myth* (frightening the religious critics). She is either too accepting of the status quo or too hostile to it. But Rowling allows the past, in both its fantastic and familiar forms, to serve her larger moral concerns. Harry's magical adventures might be farfetched, but their realistic setting encourages readers to see that his ethical conundrums are like their own. Drawing from the past, Rowling depicts a traditional hero and deploys historically significant symbolism in a story set in the late twentieth century. In blending the familiar and the fantastic, Rowling becomes a literary "alchemist," intermixing realism and fantasy to produce a literary myth rich in Stoic morality. It tells an old story in a new way. The chapter ends with one last personal reflection on the relation between Rowling's uses of the past and her fiction, concluding that her decision to turn the everyday into something fantastical actually increases her work's appeal to so many readers. They find themselves enchanted by imaginary and strange problems whose solutions, it turns out, are not so unfamiliar after all.

Walt Disney used to speak of the "four C's" as essential to realizing dreams: curiosity, confidence, courage, and constancy. Wait a minute. Constancy? Yes. Take a look at Harry Potter and find it anew. The kids in your life already have.

I could end my introduction there—with a glib observation linking Harry Potter's popularity to the Stoic themes manifest in his actions. It's not an uncommon formula after all. But in the shadows cast by the events of September 11, it has taken on a new significance. Simple Stoic fortitude may not be the answer to our current plight, but it is certainly one in which many have found solace. In what follows, I hope to show that Harry Potter has chosen just such a path in his quest to do the right thing.

2
Plot
Threads
and
Moral Fibers

It is our choices, Harry, that show what we truly are, far more than our abilities.
—Headmaster Albus Dumbledore in
Harry Potter and the Chamber of Secrets

LITTLE WHINGING

It is amazing how little whining we hear in Little Whinging—or, to be more precise, how little we hear coming from Harry in the cupboard under the stairs, 4 Privet Drive. There's plenty coming from Dudley Dursley and his parents about pretty much everything. As the Dursleys "shuddered," "yelled," "dashed," "hurried," "snapped," "seized," and "worried" their way around the first chapter of *Harry Potter and the Sorcerer's Stone*, Harry is introduced to us simply, plainly, as "The Boy Who Lived." Early on we see the Dursleys measuring their worth according to their possessions and what others might think, while Harry makes do with little or nothing. In this juxtaposition, Rowling could hardly draw a starker contrast between lives entangled with external concerns and a life relatively free of them. At the risk of reading too much into a pun, I'd like to suggest that "little whining" strikes a kind of keynote in Harry Potter, orienting us to the Stoic moral themes on display throughout the series.[1]

Harry, in fact, could complain about a lot. His treatment certainly amounts to emotional, if not physical, abuse. And he is clearly deprived of adequate material comfort and love. Some critics deride this treatment and Harry's response to it as unrealistic within the context of the stories, suggesting that it should harm and disturb him emotionally. Many more critics rightly note that Harry's extreme circumstances are a ludicrous caricature serving other literary purposes.

And we must not forget that Harry is a literary creation. Harry is an orphan, but Harry is also a hero. These two identities are not unrelated, as numerous age-old legends and more recent literary works make clear. In *The Sorcerer's Stone*, as an orphan, Harry finds himself in conditions that he must surmount in order to make the transition to a richer and fuller life. His isolation, mistreatment, and hand-me-down lot make possible the promise of something else, but they also signal his already formed, self-possessed demeanor in the face of adversity. As a hero, Harry creates a life less obviously controlled by others. His heroic destiny, fully promised at the beginning of his tales, strengthens readers' sense of his growing autonomy and heralds his potential to shape the outcome of larger events as well.[2]

But Harry's journey also becomes an inward one, and it is here that we see most plainly Stoic principles at work. His basic good character remains stable, but he must cultivate it within a world increasingly beyond his control. He must grow into and make sense of the reputation the wizarding world has bestowed upon him, even if he has already established himself as worthy in the loneliness, misery, and deprivation of his initial circumstances. An early exchange between McGonagall and Dumbledore sounds the theme:

> "These people will never understand him! He'll be famous—a legend—I wouldn't be surprised if today was known as Harry Potter day in the future—there will be books written about Harry—every child in our world will know his name!"
>
> "Exactly," said Dumbledore, looking very seriously over the top of his half-moon glasses. "It would be enough to turn any boy's head. Famous before he can walk and talk! Famous for something he won't even remember! Can't you see how much better off he'll be, growing up away from all that until he's ready to take it?"[3]

For even though Harry's moral character remains stable, Harry's self-consciousness does not.

Not only do others test him in the larger world, but he tests himself, as well, arriving at a better understanding of his own inner life. When things are so stacked against him in Little Whinging, he has little reason to assess his worth, because others tell him he has none. And his own instinctive views to the contrary are all he has available. Still, within Rowling's Stoic moral system, instinct is not enough, for it is unthinking. A process of self-examination must lead to greater knowledge of the contingencies of fate.

We can see this process at work in key developments in each book in the series. *The Sorcerer's Stone* outlines Harry's discovery of the realities of fate beyond Little Whinging—including the ultimate reality of death. *Harry Potter and the Chamber of Secrets* takes this process further, revealing Harry's own doubts about his self-worth when confronted with the similarities he shares with the Heir of Slytherin. *Harry Potter and the Prisoner of Azkaban* develops Harry's inner turmoil to extremes in its portrayal of his own mostly hidden anxieties about his lost parents and in its exploration of the ambiguous tensions between rules and larger moral principles. *Harry Potter and the Goblet of Fire* relents a little, but Harry is still made to confront his own inadequacies, as an underage champion in the Triwizard Tournament, and he must see that he needs the assistance of others throughout the competition. Through this self-scrutiny, Harry becomes more resigned to his fate, and better able to cope with it by recognizing the importance of his own virtues and intentions.

Thus, Harry's unenthusiastic return to the Dursleys at the end of every book signals not only his continuing resignation, but also higher levels of self-consciousness. He is both more rebellious and more able to reach accord with his adoptive family, both because of and despite the continuing indignities they heap upon him. Back in Little Whinging each summer, Harry has a better appreciation of what is and is not under his control, even if he must still contend with questions about the uncertain relations between the two.

We see this theme played out on a larger scale in Rowling's construction of a narrative arc that highlights her hero's Stoic struggle with things outside of his control. This tendency can be seen in small things as well as large: his contentment with a cheap lemon ice at the zoo, his determination to return to Hogwarts despite warnings of danger offered by the house-elf Dobby at the beginning of the second book, oft-repeated realizations that trouble seems to find him on its own, and, of course, his resignation in the face of his archenemy Lord Voldemort. Rowling's narrative sustains a threatening and suspenseful atmosphere, but her literary skills do more then merely retain her readers' interest. They also place Harry's struggle with things outside of his control at the heart of his morality.

Assessing the Harry Potter stories in light of ethical questions reveals the importance of balancing desire and constraint in making moral choices. As numerous critics have noticed, Harry is certainly a good role model for children, but few have offered more than superficial explanations of why he is. The answer lies in Rowling's portrayal of uncertainties and ambiguities in her imaginative world and in her call to meet these circumstances with ethical principles that are essentially Stoic in character. Harry cannot avoid problems, but must endure them. An updated Stoicism allows Harry to work his way through circumstances beyond his control.

Harry is familiar with frustration, but he knows that it is within his power to adapt to it. While he cannot escape the unrelenting demands of fate, he sees his many disappointments in light of what he can control. He remains constant only by becoming more self-conscious. As it turns out, we shouldn't be so surprised after all that we hear so little whining coming from Harry.

THE SORCERER'S STONE

The first book of Rowling's series introduces us to her hero. Harry has survived a horrible attack while still only a year old, but both of his parents die at the hands of evil Lord Voldemort. Hagrid rescues the infant Harry from the wreck and ruin of his parents' house and brings him to the Dursleys in Little Whinging, where Professor McGonagall and Professor Dumbledore are waiting. Dumbledore leaves a sleeping Harry, bundled in blankets and disfigured by a strange cut in the shape of a lightning bolt, on the doorstep to await his fate.

The next ten years bring neglect at the hands of the Dursleys. They tell him that his no-good parents died in a car crash and hide his identity as a wizard from him. Although he experiences some inexplicable events while growing up, he really has no sense of his own magical powers. When he is eleven years old, strange letters begin to arrive for him, but his uncle Vernon refuses to hand them over. A flurry of letters arrives, and ultimately the Dursleys flee Little Whinging with Harry to prevent the arrival of still more. Forced eventually into a shack located on an island off the coast of England, they begin to wait out the night in the midst of a terrible storm. Before long, loud booming upon the door and its forced removal from the jamb signal Hagrid's return to Harry's life. He personally delivers a letter from Hogwarts School of Witchcraft and Wizardry and reveals the secret of Harry's identity.

Harry soon enters the world of magic as he and Hagrid head to London in order to pick up his school supplies. Harry can only wonder at the sights and experiences in this strange parallel universe, located within but hidden from the world of Muggles. He learns of the riches that his parents have left him, deep under London in the vaults of a bank run by goblins, where Hagrid also retrieves a special, secret package for Dumbledore. He acquires a magic wand, other assorted magical apparatus, and a pet owl that he soon names Hedwig. Nonetheless, he begins to sense that he doesn't belong, and even Hagrid's protests to the contrary leave him with profound feelings of ignorance and inadequacy as he returns to the Dursleys to finish out the summer.

In a short while, his disorientation increases. The Hogwarts Express, a magical train leaving from King's Cross station, takes him to his new school, which turns out to be a huge and fantastic castle that first-year students reach by boat across a dark lake. Although a quick friendship on the train with Ron Weasley eased his doubts at first, they return full-force when he learns that he will be "sorted" at the welcoming feast into one of four school houses by a magical hat capable of peering into his thoughts.

All students at Hogwarts become members of either Gryffindor, Hufflepuff, Ravenclaw, or Slytherin, named after the four founders of the school, and described by the Sorting Hat, which sings a song at the start of the ceremony. Gryffindor houses the "brave at heart," Hufflepuff, the "just and loyal," Ravenclaw, those of "wit and learning," and Slytherin, "those cunning folk [who] use any means to achieve their ends."[4] The hat has some difficulty placing Harry and considers his assignment to Slytherin, the only house that has produced dark wizards fascinated with using magic for malevolent purposes. Harry's protests secure him a spot in Gryffindor. Harry joins his fellow students at the Gryffindor table and is soon relieved that Ron, too, is sorted into the house. Dumbledore welcomes the assembled students, food magically appears on golden plates, and the feast commences. Before bringing the evening to a close with a rendition of the school song, Dumbledore makes several announcements, including a very strange one: students hoping to avoid a painful death should stay away from an off-limits third-floor corridor.

Soon, Harry finds a home away from home, as he befriends other members of his house and settles into life at Hogwarts. His courses bring him some satisfaction, when he learns that other students do not already excel at magic. Instruction in Charms, Transfiguration, Defense Against the Dark Arts, Herbology, and the History of Magic soon bring him up to speed. His course in Potions, in contrast, is far less enjoyable, because its instructor, Severus Snape, harbors some deep-seated animosities toward Harry and seems to go out of his way to make Harry's life miserable. Harry also rebuffs the early advances of one of Snape's favorites, Draco Malfoy, a member of both Slytherin and a family with a questionable past. This rejection earns him the hatred of Malfoy and much of Slytherin House as well.

Nonetheless, Harry's relationships with Hagrid and Ron continue to grow, and soon he becomes friends with Hermione Granger as well. Confronting a mountain troll, as Harry, Ron, and Hermione do on Halloween, brings them together as fast friends, especially because Hermione fudges the truth to protect Harry and Ron from punishment. Harry learns that he excels at Quidditch and becomes a popular and indispensable member of the Gryffindor team. He and his friends get into and out of trouble both on their own and with the help of an anonymously given Christmas present. Using this gift, an invisibility cloak that had belonged to his father, Harry encounters the Mirror of Erised, in whose reflection he can see not only himself, but also his lost family. He learns from Dumbledore that the mirror shows one's deepest desires. Using the cloak on other occasions, Harry, Ron, and Hermione wander the halls at night, visit Hagrid when they're not supposed to, and help him relocate a contraband baby dragon. This last bit of misbehavior earns Harry and Hermione detention. It also leads to a 150-point deduction from Gryffindor's score in the competition for the House Cup. Because of this infraction, Harry goes from being among the most popular Gryffindors to being the most despised.

All the while, the mystery of what is hidden in the forbidden corridor on the third floor remains unsolved. This question plagues Harry right from the beginning of the term. He recalls the parcel Hagrid retrieved from Gringotts, the goblin bank, and he is sure it must be related to warnings delivered by Dumbledore following the sorting ceremony. Using several clues discovered on their own or delivered up by an indiscreet Hagrid, Harry, Ron, and Hermione piece together that the Sorcerer's Stone is being protected on the third floor by a series of magical obstacles. Discovered by the now six-hundred-sixty-five-year-old Nicolas Flamel, it transforms any metal into gold and produces the Elixer of Life, capable of granting immortality to those who drink it.

A number of events convince them that Voldemort, who lost his own physical form in his attack upon Harry, seeks the Stone. While serving detention on a task in the forbidden forest, Harry and Hermione learn that something has been killing unicorns and that the centaurs have read Voldemort's return in the stars. Harry is threatened by a strange figure found to be drinking silver unicorn blood, but he is saved by the centaur Firenze, who, unlike the other centaurs, is willing to intervene on Harry's behalf. During what remains of the term, Harry, Ron, and Hermione come to believe that Snape must be assisting Voldemort in finding the Stone. When they learn that Hagrid has told a stranger a key piece of information, they conclude that Snape is making his move.

They seek out Dumbledore but realize they don't know how to find him. They turn to McGonagall for help, but once she overcomes her shock, she tells them that Dumbledore is away on ministry business and that everything is under control. Learning of the headmaster's absence, they conspire to prevent Snape from acquiring the Stone. Ignoring McGonagall's instructions to leave matters alone, they incapacitate Neville, a fellow Gryffindor, who objects when they leave the common room after hours. They enter the forbidden corridor.

Confronting the obstacles protecting the Stone, Ron and Hermione prove their worth several times, before Harry enters the last chamber. There he encounters neither Snape nor Voldemort, but Professor Quirrell, the Defense Against the Dark Arts teacher, timid and stuttering no longer, and the last person Harry expected to find. Quirrell stands before the Mirror of Erised, which shows him handing the Stone to Voldemort. Harry is forced to look in the Mirror and feels the Stone slide into his pocket. Soon, sensing that something is amiss, Voldemort himself confronts Harry. As the turban falls from Quirrell's head, he is revealed to have two faces. Voldemort, in possession of Quirrell's body, leers at Harry from the back of the professor's head. Voldemort promises to spare Harry's life if only he will surrender the Stone in his pocket. Harry refuses, and Quirrell seeks to take it by force, but he is unable to touch Harry's skin without it blistering his own hands. Harry as well experiences severe pain, but he comprehends enough of what is happening to grab hold of Quirrell's face. Both become entangled and Harry loses consciousness to Voldemort's screams of "KILL HIM! KILL HIM!"[5]

When Harry recovers in the hospital wing, he learns that he survived because of Dumbledore's timely return to Hogwarts. Voldemort has fled, once again without physical form, leaving Quirrell behind to die. Dumbledore also informs Harry that he survived Voldemort's original attack because his mother died trying to save him. This protection, the result of her love for him and the deepest magic of all, prevented Quirrell, who shared his soul with Voldemort, from touching him. Before long, Harry recovers from the attack, and the year concludes with Dumbledore awarding Harry, Ron, Hermione, and Neville enough points for bravery to secure the House Cup for Gryffindor. Harry boards the Hogwarts express to return to the Dursleys in Little Whinging for the summer.

FLIGHT FROM DEATH

When we catch our first glimpse of Harry, we see him in the hands of fate. The survivor of a brutal attempted murder, he is lifted from the ruins of his family's house by Hagrid. He is then taken by Dumbledore, who leaves him finally in the care of the Dursleys. He is literally scarred by one of his earliest experiences, and his life beyond it is constrained by its lingering effects. It is his fortune (both good and bad) to find himself in circumstances he did not choose. Although he is a hero, he is also a victim.

Yet, within Rowling's universe, fate does not determine everything. It provides both good and bad, but it does not dictate choices or actions. Individuals are *free* to shape their reactions to it, even if they are *compelled* to accept it. They balance desires against insurmountable realities.

Although *The Sorcerer's Stone* develops the workings of fate in a number of ways, most significant is its treatment of everyone's ultimate fate: death. This is a hard question that Rowling asks of her young readers. Yet, she reminds them of the inevitability of death in a number of ways. They know about the murder of Harry's parents. They observe the many dangers in which he finds himself. And, most important, they witness his willingness to risk death against a villain who seeks to avoid it. She goes even further, however, by encouraging them to assess her characters' moral stature in light of their attitudes toward death.

We can see this theme clearly if we consider the nature of the Sorcerer's Stone and Voldemort's interest in it. It is an artificial means of forestalling death against the unrelenting onslaught of time. The Stone can produce the Elixir of Life, which confers immortality upon all those who continue to produce and to drink it. In other words, it allows its possessor to "cheat" fate.

The central moral emerging from *The Sorcerer's Stone* is that this attempt is unwise. Rowling delivers it both chillingly and gently. In both Voldemort's desire for the Stone and Flamel's use of it, we see two different but related views of the problem.

Voldemort's condition, arrived at by seeking to escape fate, graphically illustrates the senselessness and futility of his denial of death. The horrors he both creates and experiences stem from this imprudence. For what motivates this villain if not his refusal to acknowledge death? The name he has chosen for himself expresses it directly: "theft of death" or "flight from death." Yet, what kind of life does this bring him? He is left without shape or body and must wander the world possessed only of his cruel intellect and his festering intentions to reclaim the eternal life that is denied him. Furthermore, he must depend upon the efforts of others, compelled through threat and force, in ways that diminish his own autonomy.

When Voldemort pits himself against fate through his refusal of death, his decision has consequences. After all, the unfettered exercise of power in pursuit of unrealistic desires is only one possible course of action open to him. He ignores the importance of accepting realities beyond his control and of choosing how best to meet them. He has not yet conquered death, and his decisions have denied him almost everything except his malice. When Quirrell speaks Voldemort's philosophy, "there is no good and evil, there is only power, and those too weak to seek it,"[6] he betrays that both he and Voldemort are ignorant of the consequences of their decisions. They forget that their choices make them evil.

But what are we to make of Nicolas and Perenelle Flamel? Their examples seem to suggest that cheating fate might be accomplished benignly. True enough. But Nicolas and Perenelle do come to recognize the folly of their actions, even if they do so belatedly. Dumbledore explains their reaction to the destruction of the Stone:

> "Well, Nicolas and I have had a little chat, and agreed it's all for the best."
>
> "But that means he and his wife will die, won't they?"
>
> "They have enough Elixir to set their affairs in order and then, yes, they will die."
>
> . . . "I'm sure it seems incredible, but to Nicolas and Perenelle, it really is like going to bed after a very, *very* long day."[7]

They could continue to live "a quiet life in Devon,"[8] but they also accept the wisdom behind destroying the Stone and meeting their somewhat delayed encounters with death. Rowling uses their overlong lives as a gentle reminder of the same lesson Voldemort's dementia teaches.

Fate is a strange thing. It both gives and takes away, comforts and distresses. Having survived Voldemort's murderous designs twice,

Harry is left with the example of his parents' own love for him and its relation to their untimely demise. Some things are more important than life itself, particularly the decision to make the ultimate sacrifice when circumstance demands it. Harry's own self-scrutiny and moral choices show that he recognizes as much.

Yet, tempting fate is no better a course of action than denying it. For Harry's amusement, Dumbledore illustrates this lesson to his own chagrin:

> "Ah! Bertie Bott's Every Flavor Beans! I was unfortunate enough in my youth to come across a vomit-flavored one, and since then I'm afraid I've rather lost my liking for them—but I think I'll be safe with a nice toffee, don't you?"
>
> He smiled and popped the golden-brown bean into his mouth. Then he choked and said, "Alas! Ear wax."[9]

Voldemort, of course, will continue to learn the lessons of fate the hard way.

THE CHAMBER OF SECRETS

Rowling's second book of adventures takes up another year of Harry's life. A sign of troubles to come arrives in Little Whinging with Dobby the house-elf, enslaved to a family whose secrets he cannot reveal. He attempts to warn Harry, telling him he must not return to Hogwarts, because unnamed people will be seeking to harm him there. Harry attempts to reason with Dobby, explaining that life at Hogwarts is really all he has. Dobby insists that he not return. He cannot explain further because of his enslavement; only the gift of clothing from his family would release him from service and allow him to speak freely. Events go horribly awry, and the Dursleys, infuriated by the chaos caused by the elf, imprison Harry in his bedroom. He escapes when Ron, Fred, and George Weasley arrive to break him out, flying a turquoise Ford Anglia automobile.

Free of the Dursleys, Harry settles into life at the Weasley home for a short while before the start of the new school year. They take the annual trip to Diagon Alley, traveling by Floo powder from their fireplace to the Leaky Cauldron, but Harry ends up in a shop catering to the dark arts in Knockturn Alley. He witnesses Mr. Lucius Malfoy, the father of Draco, negotiating the sale of some prohibited items, before escaping the shop and running into Hagrid, who is seeking Flesh-Eating Slug Repellent. Later, after he has been reunited with the Weasleys, Harry meets the new Defense Against the Dark Arts teacher, Gilderoy Lockhart, who seems to have a rather high opinion of himself. In Flourish and Blotts, he also witnesses a fracas between Mr. Weasley and Mr. Malfoy, who trade insults and more over whether proper wizards consort with Muggles or Muggle-born witches and wizards.

True to Dobby's warnings, a series of additional unfortunate developments characterize Harry's second year at Hogwarts. Ron and Harry are unable to enter the platform for the Hogwarts Express. After they fly Mr. Weasley's Ford to the school, they are both nearly beaten to death by the Whomping Willow, when they crash land into it. Ron's wand malfunctions repeatedly due to damage it sustained in the wreck. Tensions between Harry and Malfoy reach an all-time high over Hermione's "Mudblood" parentage and on the Quidditch pitch. More ominously, Harry begins to hear a strange and malevolent voice threatening death and mayhem. Soon after, he finds Mrs. Norris, the caretaker Filch's cat, petrified in front of a scrawled message claiming that the Chamber of Secrets is open and warning enemies of the Heir of Slytherin. To make matters worse, suspicions fall upon Harry, who begins to doubt his own moral character. During a Quidditch match, one of the balls used in play, a rogue bludger, breaks Harry's arm, and then Lockhart removes all the bones in it while trying to repair the break. During his recovery from these injuries, Harry learns that Dobby was behind the rogue bludger as well as a number of earlier mishaps, believing he was acting for Harry's own good. Worst of all to this point, Colin Creevey, a Gryffindor student born to Muggle parents, is found petrified, and Dumbledore concludes that the Chamber of Secrets has indeed been reopened.

As Professor Binns explains in class one day, the Chamber is allegedly a room hidden in Hogwarts containing a monster of horrific power. Only the Heir of Slytherin would be able to unleash it. Salazar Slytherin had made no secret of his belief that Muggle-born students were untrustworthy, and eventually he left the school because the other founders did not share his preference for admitting only students from all-magic families. According to legend, the Heir would release the monster to purge Hogwarts of unworthy students.

Shortly after the attack on Colin Creevey, Harry inadvertently reveals to the entire school that he is a Parselmouth—someone capable of speaking with snakes. This episode increases not only others' suspicions of Harry (because Slytherin was a Parselmouth) but his own self-doubt as well. Harry, Ron, and Hermione resolve to settle the mystery of the Chamber and the Heir of Slytherin. Convinced that Malfoy is involved, they use advanced magic in the form of Polyjuice Potion to take on the appearance of members of Slytherin, in order to test their hypothesis. They brew the potion in a girls' bathroom haunted by Moaning Myrtle, who died there a long time ago. But as it turns out, Malfoy is as much in the dark as they are. Hermione, however, takes on the appearance of a cat as a result of using a bit of fur in her own draft of potion, rather than a hair belonging to Millicent Bulstrode, another Slytherin student, and she has to recover in the infirmary for at least several weeks. At roughly the same time, a strange diary comes into Harry's possession. He discovers that its blank pages will write back in response to questions, and that it is capable of allowing him to enter the memories of Tom Riddle, a Hogwarts student some fifty years ago. Harry thus witnesses events linked to when the Chamber was opened for the first time. He learns that Hagrid was expelled from Hogwarts because he had hidden and cared for a huge spider, which was taken to be the monster within. Before he can delve more deeply into the mysteries of the diary, someone with access to Gryffindor Tower steals it from him.

Meanwhile, events at Hogwarts continue to spin out of control as more students are petrified, including Hermione. Cornelius Fudge of the Ministry of Magic sends a fearful Hagrid to a mysterious and distant wizard prison called Azkaban for safekeeping, in light of the suspicions that fell upon him fifty years earlier. At the same time, the school's board of governors, influenced by Mr. Malfoy, suspends Dumbledore as headmaster because of the attacks. Prompted by a hint offered by Hagrid as he is taken away, Harry and Ron go in search of the spiders in the Forbidden Forest, which are thought to have knowledge of the monster in the Chamber. They learn that Hagrid was completely innocent but little else. They barely escape with their lives when the Ford Anglia that they flew to Hogwarts arrives to whisk them away from a large number of very threatening spiders.

Clear of further threats, Ron and Harry deduce that Moaning Myrtle was the first victim of the monster from the Chamber. The next day they head off to speak with her, but McGonagall finds them wandering the halls. They tell her they are off to see Hermione in the hospital wing, and she lets them go to visit her. While there, they discover a piece of paper clasped within her petrified hand. It reveals that she has figured out that the monster in the Chamber is in fact a basilisk, an enormous snake capable of killing its victims with a mere glance. Set to head off to Myrtle's bathroom, they learn that the monster has claimed another victim, Ginny Weasley, who has been taken into the Chamber. All students are sent to their dormitories.

Unable to sit still, Harry and Ron try to enlist the help of the unwilling Defense Against the Dark Arts teacher Lockhart. They learn what they have suspected all along: he is a fraud. He attempts to erase their memories, but they overpower him. Marching Lockhart along, they head to the girls' bathroom, which they believe contains the entrance to the Chamber. After querying Myrtle, they find the entrance and descend into the Chamber. Lockhart grabs Ron's wand, unaware that it has been malfunctioning all year. Yelling *Obliviate!* he caves in the ceiling of the entrance. He loses his memory and he and Ron become separated from Harry. Harry enters the Chamber alone in search of Ginny.

He finds Ginny's nearly lifeless body and encounters a strange boy whom he recognizes as Tom Riddle. Seeking his help, Harry is rebuffed by Tom, who takes his wand. Tom reveals himself to be Voldemort with the appearance he had while still a student at Hogwarts. He tricked Ginny through the diary into opening the Chamber and has been draining the life from her in order to reconstitute himself as more than a mere memory. He orders the basilisk to attack Harry. Defenseless at first, Harry soon receives assistance from Fawkes, Dumbledore's pet phoenix, which arrives carrying the Sorting Hat. Fawkes blinds the basilisk, and Harry is able to retrieve the Sword of Gryffindor from the Hat. He beheads the monster, but is mortally wounded through the arm by its poisonous fang. As Tom Riddle gloats over Harry's demise, Fawkes soothes him and bathes his wound with tears. Riddle suddenly realizes that phoenix tears have incredible healing powers. Before he can act, Harry has regained enough strength to stab the diary with the basilisk's broken fang. Torrents of ink spurt from the diary, flooding the floor; screaming and writhing, Tom Riddle disappears. Ginny soon comes to her senses.

Back through the tunnel and then carried along by Fawkes, Harry and Ginny return to the girls' bathroom with Ron and Lockhart. They follow the phoenix which leads them to McGonagall's office. There they find McGonagall, Dumbledore, and Mr. and Mrs. Weasley. Harry tells what happened, careful to avoid implicating Ginny. Sensing the truth, Dumbledore explains how Voldemort was able to ensnare her. Encouraging the others to leave, he sits down to chat with Harry. He attempts to alleviate Harry's doubts about himself, because of the similarities he shares with Voldemort; he explains that choices make people who they are, not their abilities. Interrupted by Mr. Malfoy, who is accompanied by Dobby, both Dumbledore and Harry recognize his involvement in this year's events. He had secretly given the diary to Ginny in Flourish and Blotts, following his tussle with Mr. Weasley. Dumbledore politely but firmly implies as much, and Malfoy turns to leave. On a whim, Harry wraps the diary in his sock, runs to catch up, and hands the bundle to Mr. Malfoy. He unwraps the diary and carelessly tosses the sock to Dobby—an unthinking action that frees Dobby from his service. Enraged, Malfoy attempts to curse Harry. Dobby quickly blasts Malfoy down a flight of stairs with a curse of his own and commands, "You shall not touch Harry Potter. You shall go now."[10]

In what little time remains in the term, the victims of the basilisk are restored to health by a now-ready mandrake root potion, final exams are cancelled, and Gryffindor earns enough points to win the House Cup. All the students board the Hogwarts Express. And Harry returns, once again, to his miserable life in Little Whinging.

House-Elves and Mudbloods

Fate, once again, plays a prominent role at the beginning of Harry's second tale, when we hear Dobby speak of the ominous threats awaiting him at Hogwarts. But Rowling adds other dimensions to her treatment of it. Fate endows her characters with certain attributes, but it does not dictate what they will do with them. This theme, of course, is not entirely absent in the first book, but Rowling develops it with greater care in the second.

Two related but distinct plot developments introduce readers to the central moral of *The Chamber of Secrets*: persons should be judged by their choices and not by their circumstances. The house-elf Dobby's involvement in Harry's life is the first of these; the reality of prejudice and bigotry toward Muggles and the Muggle-born is the second. In each instance, Rowling explores and explodes stereotypes. She thus begins to illustrate that identity is not the same as destiny.

Dobby's status as a house-elf is described in some detail. We learn that it is the house-elf's fate to be enslaved. Dobby may not speak his family's secrets or act directly against its interests. Its members may abuse him, even very severely, and he has no recourse but to suffer in silence. Still, in Dobby, we find a character aware of his subject status and one willing to work the system, capable of violating the spirit of his servitude if not its letter. We also find in Dobby someone with a keen sense of the rules but with an even keener sense of larger moral obligations.

In Rowling's portrayal of prejudice and bigotry toward Mudbloods in the wizarding world, we see another exploration of status. In the words and attitudes of Lucius and Draco Malfoy, as well as the legacy of Salazar Slytherin, we see graphic examples of ignorant hatred—an overweening concern with identity rather than capacity or potential. The Malfoys are not merely snobs; they are bigots, cruel and vengeful. Neither the Grangers nor Muggles in general do anything to deserve the Malfoys' contempt, and Hermione's skills as a witch (being herself a Mudblood) prove beyond doubt that their bias is unwarranted. Their attitudes and actions must be met with resolve by those who do not share their views.

If these two plot lines introduce readers to the book's central moral, an additional one emphasizes it. I have in mind, of course, Harry's struggle with his own identity. Through much of the book, he believes that he is Slytherin's heir or not so different from Voldemort. In thinking so, Harry is guilty of confusing identity and destiny. He misunderstands the relationship between his abilities and his capacity and potential for using them. An exchange between Harry and Dumbledore makes the point succinctly (as is so often the case):

> "So I *should* be in Slytherin," Harry said, looking desperately into Dumbledore's face. "The Sorting Hat could see Slytherin's power in me, and it—"
>
> "Put you in Gryffindor," said Dumbledore calmly. "Listen to me Harry. You happen to have many qualities Salazar Slytherin prized in his hand-picked students. His own very rare gift, Parseltongue—resourcefulness—determination—a certain disregard for rules," he added, his mustache quivering again. "Yet the Sorting Hat placed you in Gryffindor. You know why that was. Think."
>
> "It only put me in Gryffindor," said Harry in a defeated voice, because I asked not to go in Slytherin. . . ."
>
> "*Exactly*," said Dumbledore, beaming once more. "Which makes you *very different* from Tom Riddle. It is our choices, Harry, that show what we truly are, far more than our abilities."[11]

Harry's on-the-spot *decision* to help downtrodden Dobby serves only to punctuate Dumbledore's claim. If fate gives Harry certain qualities, it does not determine how he will use them.

THE PRISONER OF AZKABAN

Rowling's third book describes yet another year of Harry's passage through childhood. His summer goes by uneventfully as he corresponds with friends and prepares for school. He is gratified to learn that the Weasleys won the *Daily Prophet* Grand Prize Galleon Draw and used the money to visit their eldest son, Bill, in Egypt. An article from the newspaper, complete with a picture of the family, had accompanied one of Ron's letters. Things change one day, when Uncle Vernon gleefully denounces a criminal named Black, along with the televised reporting of his escape, and then announces a visit by Aunt Marge. Harry is informed that she is unaware of his abnormality and that the Dursleys want to keep it that way.

After suffering under Aunt Marge's extreme insults for the better part of a week, Harry finally snaps when she turns her attention to his deadbeat parents:

> "It all comes down to blood, as I was saying the other day. Bad blood will out. Now, I'm saying nothing against your family Petunia"—she patted Aunt Petunia's bony hand with her shovel-like one—"but your sister was a bad egg. They turn up in the best families. Then she ran off with that wastrel and here's the result right in front of us."[12]

A short while further into her discourse on Harry's parentage, she falls silent and begins to swell, popping the buttons on her jacket. As she begins to float into the air, Harry dashes to his room, collects all his things, and runs from the house.

He slows a few blocks away and begins to wonder about his predicament. While considering how the Ministry of Magic might react to this improper use of magic, picturing himself in prison or in exile from Hogwarts, he senses someone or something nearby. Startled by a very large shape with gleaming eyes in a nearby alleyway, he steps back and trips over his trunk, flinging out an arm to break his fall. BANG, a purple triple-decker bus appears, with gold lettering identifying it as The Knight Bus. Unable to see the figure that startled him anymore, Harry considers his options and boards the bus for Diagon Alley. After settling into place, he learns that the convict who had drawn Uncle Vernon's ire is in fact a wizard named Sirius Black. Escaped from Azkaban Prison and responsible for the murders of thirteen people, Black was reportedly a supporter of Voldemort and captured after his fall. After telling the driver and conductor he is Neville Longbottom, Harry is left to rue his own fate as the bus thunders its way across the country.

To Harry's surprise, he is met at the Leaky Cauldron, a pub that serves as the entrance to Diagon Alley, by Cornelius Fudge, the Minister of Magic. Fearing the worst, Harry can't believe his luck when Fudge is clearly glad to see him and allows him to spend the last two weeks of his vacation in Diagon Alley. He fills his days with window-shopping, completing homework for the new term, buying school supplies, and just plain hanging out. The arrival of Hermione and her parents, along with the Weasleys, just back from Egypt, signals his departure for school the next day aboard the Hogwarts Express. While still in Diagon Alley, Ron purchases some tonic for his pet rat Scabbers, who has seen better days, and Hermione obtains an orange cat named Crookshanks that takes an instant dislike to the rodent. That night, after dinner, Harry secretly overhears Mr. and Mrs. Weasley arguing about whether Harry should know the truth about Sirius Black. He learns that Black is after him and that guards from Azkaban will be posted outside of Hogwarts. Before the train leaves in the morning, Mr. Weasley, unaware of what Harry already knows, asks him to promise not to go after Black. He stops short of explaining why.

On the train to Hogwarts at last, Harry, Ron, and Hermione find themselves in a compartment with an unknown adult, Remus Lupin, who, they assume, is the new Defense Against the Dark Arts teacher. The trip is relatively uneventful, except for some animosity between

Crookshanks and Scabbers, until the train halts and a dementor—one of the Azkaban guards—visits the compartment. Everyone feels horrible in the guard's presence, but Harry actually loses consciousness to the sounds of someone's screams in his head. Upon awaking to the worried looks of his friends, he is handed some chocolate by Lupin, who had sent the dementor away with a silver substance emitted from his wand.

Soon after their arrival at Hogwarts, McGonagall summons Harry and Hermione to her office. There Madam Pomfrey examines Harry and prescribes more chocolate. Learning that Lupin had already given Harry some, she muses, "So we've finally got a Defense Against the Dark Arts teacher who knows his remedies?"[13] Harry is allowed to leave, but Hermione remains behind briefly for a private conversation with McGonagall. They finally make it to the feast, having missed the sorting, to hear Dumbledore welcoming the students and warning them about the dementors stationed at all entrances to Hogwarts. He also announces that the new Care of Magical Creatures teacher is Rubeus Hagrid, already known to all.

The year at Hogwarts is filled with the usual activities, including a good deal of mischief. In addition to their usual subjects, as well as Care of Magical Creatures, Hermione, Ron, and Harry find themselves in a divination course taught by Professor Sybill Trelawney, who takes every opportunity to forecast Harry's imminent demise. Hermione, however, seems to be taking every course offered to third-year students, a patently absurd endeavor, since most of the classes overlap with one another. Particularly enjoyable is Professor Lupin's course, since he is teaching practical skills, and the students feel, for the first time, that they are actually learning something in Defense Against the Dark Arts. The course on Care of Magical Creatures does not go as well, when Draco Malfoy, against Hagrid's instructions, insults a Hippogriff named Buckbeak (part eagle, part horse) and is injured in return. As a result, Buckbeak is brought up on charges and Hagrid loses his interest in teaching.

Two related concerns haunt Harry as the school year unfolds. Sirius Black's efforts to find Harry—including an attack upon the Fat Lady in an attempt to gain entrance to Gryffindor Tower—lead him to a fuller understanding of events surrounding his parents' deaths. Likewise, the dementors' presence and Harry's efforts to withstand them release apparently repressed memories of his parents' murder at the hands of Lord Voldemort. The dementors' arrival at a Quidditch match, against Dumbledore's orders, causes Harry, once again, to lose consciousness, a circumstance that leads to Gryffindor's defeat by Hufflepuff and to the demise of his Nimbus 2000, the racing broom that had served him well. Sick of living in fear, Harry takes advantage of an opportunity provided by Fred and George Weasley to visit Hogsmead, an act that is very much against the rules. Because the Dursleys never signed his permission slip, this magical village is off limits to him and patrolled by dementors, but he can reach it via a secret tunnel depicted on the Marauder's Map given to him by Fred and George. He uses his invisibility cloak and meets Ron and Hermione, who had permission to be in the village, along with other students. While in the Three Broomsticks pub, they overhear a group of teachers discussing Black with Cornelius Fudge, and Harry learns more about this villain's role in Voldemort's plans. He had been Lily and James Potter's best friend, their Secret-Keeper intended to protect them from Voldermort, and their betrayer. On the day after Voldemort's own demise, he blasted another friend of theirs, Peter Pettigrew, leaving only a single finger among his bloody remains, and killed twelve innocent Muggles. Worst of all, Black is Harry's godfather.

Disappointments and threats continue. Harry cannot believe that no one told him about Black and he resolves to seek vengeance. At the same time, proceedings against Buckbeak begin and his future looks bleak. The arrival of a Firebolt, the best racing broom in the world, for Harry on Christmas day leads both Hermione and McGonagall to suspect that it might be from Black. Before Harry can use it, Professor Flitwick, the Charms instructor, must inspect it for curses. Left without a broom, Harry worries about Gryffindor's chances in Quidditch. Unwilling to fall victim to the dementors again, Harry begins special lessons with Lupin, who teaches him the *Patronus* charm, the means he used against the dementor on the Hogwarts Express. Lupin uses a boggart—a being that adopts the form of what its victims most fear—to coach Harry. Although he improves his defense over time, he cannot quite surmount the debilitating effects of the boggart/dementor's presence and experiences again and again, in ever greater detail, the last moments of his parents' lives. With the next match looming, Scabbers disappears, the likely victim, at last, of Crookshank's animosity. His disappearance opens a rift in Ron and Hermione's friendship that Harry is clueless to mend. That evening, however, Black is seen again in Gryffindor Tower, in the boys' dormitory, during an apparently mistaken attack upon Ron. Things do look up, however, when Harry's Firebolt is returned to him and Gryffindor defeats Ravenclaw in Quidditch. During the match, Harry produces a first-class *Patronus* when he sees several dementors approaching, although they turn out to be only Draco Malfoy and several other Slytherins in costume. The following week, while unwisely visiting Hogsmead again, Harry is nearly found out by Snape, who is itching to have him expelled. Only lying and the knowing and dissembling intervention of Lupin prevents further inquiry; Lupin confiscates the Marauder's Map and leaves Harry and Ron somewhat relieved but appalled by their own stupidity. Although things look up briefly, when Gryffindor wins the Quidditch Cup and final exams go well, Professor Trelawney's mysterious (and unconscious) prediction disturbs Harry once more: Voldemort will rise again with the help of a servant. If that were not bad enough, Hermione sadly announces the failure of the Hippogriff Buckbeak's appeal and his imminent execution for injuring Malfoy.

Hermione, Ron, and Harry surreptitiously go to Hagrid's cabin, resolved to offer moral support to their distraught friend, who has blamed himself from the start. In doing so, they initiate a particularly strange chain of events. They find Scabbers alive, and the rodent is soon once again in Ron's pocket, but very unhappy about it. They must flee Hagrid's cabin when the executioner arrives to take Buckbeak. Hiding in the forest, they hear the ax swing and fall, but before they can come to grips with their grief, Crookshanks appears out of nowhere, and

Scabbers leaps from Ron and takes off. Ron catches him, barely, but then a huge black dog (which Harry has seen a number of times before, including the night he fled from the Dursleys) grabs hold of Ron, with the rat back in his pocket, and drags him into a secret passage under the Whomping Willow. Hermione and Harry follow, with Crookshanks, and soon find themselves in a house in Hogsmead, which they recognize as the haunted Shrieking Shack. What they encounter there is stranger still.

Ron lies upon a bed in an upstairs room and reveals that the dog is really an animagus, a human magician who can transform into an animal. Black has trapped them. In a fit of rage, Harry overpowers the seriously weakened Black, with the help of Ron and Hermione, and prepares to kill him out of revenge. Muffled footsteps are heard in the hall, and Lupin arrives to disarm Harry and Hermione. Before he can explain himself, Hermione reveals him to be a werewolf, a fact hidden from the students, and accuses him of being in league with Black. He returns their wands and begins to explain. He had seen something very strange on the Marauder's Map: Peter Pettigrew. What's more, Peter accompanied the three friends from Hagrid's cabin. Yes, he admits that he is a werewolf and that he has been since he was a young boy. Dumbledore had made provision for him to spend his periods of transformation in the Shrieking Shack, away from humans. James Potter, Sirius Black, and Peter Pettigrew had been his best friends at Hogwarts, and each had become an animagus, in order to stay with him every month when he became a wolf. They were also the authors of the Marauder's Map, which now shows Pettigrew at Hogwarts, even though that should be impossible. Clearly, Black had not killed him. Pettigrew had become Scabbers.

As Lupin tells his story, they are interrupted by the sudden appearance of Severus Snape. He had seen the Marauder's Map on Lupin's desk and followed him to the Whomping Willow, where he found Harry's invisibility cloak. He binds Lupin and threatens Black with his wand. As he gloats over their predicament and threatens to hand them both to the dementors, Harry attempts to disarm him, while Hermione and Ron each do the same. Snape is blasted into the wall and knocked out cold. Black continues the story from the point Lupin had left it. Voldemort was searching for the Potters, and they decided to use a special kind of magic to hide their location from him. As long as a special Secret-Keeper would not reveal their location, no one would ever be able to find them. Black admits that he was to be the Potters' Secret-Keeper but reveals that he and James had decided to switch to Peter, whom Voldemort was unlikely to suspect. Of course, Sirius and James did not know that Peter had already entered into Voldemort's evil service. Following Voldemort's attack, Black states, he had indeed gone to kill Peter. He failed, however, when Peter faked his own death, cutting off one of his fingers and leaving it in the carnage that he caused. Black had been falsely arrested and thrown in Azkaban Prison without trial. There, on a small island far from the coast, he stayed until he saw the picture of Ron's family in the *Daily Prophet* and recognized Peter. Since his break from prison and his arrival in Hogsmead, he has relied upon the help of Crookshanks, who immediately sensed that Scabbers was not a real rat. Following these revelations, Lupin and Black force Pettigrew to return to human form, much to the surprise and disgust of Hermione, Harry, and Ron. Lupin and Black prepare to kill the traitor, but Harry won't allow it, reasoning that his father wouldn't want his friends to become murderers. They all head back to Hogwarts, with Peter bound and gagged, and with Snape's unconscious body floating among them.

Things go horribly wrong once they pass out of the tunnel at the foot of the Whomping Willow. Lupin transforms into a wolf under the light of a full moon, Pettigrew attacks Ron and turns back into a rat, and Black changes into a large dog in order to follow Lupin and keep him away from the children. In the chaos, Lupin and Pettigrew escape, Ron and Snape remain unconscious by the Whomping Willow, and dementors soon surround Harry, Hermione, and Black, intent upon administering their "kiss," which would suck the souls out of their victims. As Harry loses consciousness, he sees a large, silver animal drive the dementors away and return across the lake to a familiar-looking figure. He awakens in the infirmary to learn what happened next.

Snape had recovered first and returned to the school with the children and Black on stretchers and with Black bound and gagged. Black now awaits a dementor's kiss. Upon learning this, Harry and Hermione object, but no one other than Dumbledore gives them any heed, preferring to believe that Black had bewitched them. Dumbledore insists upon speaking to them alone, while Fudge and Snape head upstairs to await Black's fate. He informs Harry and Hermione that more time is needed, and that they might be able to save two innocent lives tonight if they act quickly. As he closes the door behind him upon leaving the room, Hermione explains what Dumbledore means. All year she has been traveling back in time to complete her lessons; they are now to use her Time-Turner to save both Buckbeak and Sirius. They return to the past at about the time Buckbeak is to be executed. They arrange his escape and wait for events to unfold. After two hours pass, they witness what occurs beside the Whomping Willow, including the convergence of the dementors. Harry, in particular, awaits the appearance of the silver animal that had saved them, only to realize that he, having visited the present from the future, had conjured a Patronus, not his father as he had earlier suspected. He yells *Expecto Patronum* and produces a large, silver stag, the form his father had taken on as an animagus. The dementors depart, and Harry and Hermione return to the castle flying Buckbeak. They rescue Sirius, who flies away with the Hippogriff, and return to the infirmary just in time for Dumbledore to let them in before he locks the door.

The next day, a weary Harry bids farewell to Lupin, who returns the invisibility cloak and the Marauder's Map. Lupin must leave because it is unseemly (and potentially dangerous) for a werewolf to be teaching at Hogwarts. A short discussion with Dumbledore follows, and Harry hears what he already knows: the consequences of any action are so complicated that one cannot really foresee its outcome, and Harry's father really is alive and well, if only in Harry himself. He is surprised to learn that Pettigrew may now be in his debt, because he had spared the villain's life. Exhausted by events, Harry boards the Hogwarts Express. Along the way, a tiny owl enters the compartment, carrying a message from Sirius. He and Buckbeak are now in hiding, and he did in fact send Harry the Firebolt; Ron is free to keep the owl, since Sirius deprived him of his pet rat. Back in London, leaving the station for Little Whinging with Uncle Vernon, Harry fudges the truth about his godfather, "He's a convicted murderer, but he's broken out of wizard prison and he's on the run. He likes to keep in touch with me though . . . keep up with my news . . . check if I'm happy. . . ."[14]

A LAW UNTO HIMSELF

Let's look at Harry's behavior in *The Prisoner of Azkaban*, without considering why he acts the way he does. He rebels against the Dursleys, eavesdrops on the Weasleys, sneaks off school grounds, wanders about after hours, and lies fairly often to everyone from Stan on the Knightbus to Lupin in the classroom. Together with Ron and Hermione, he even attacks a teacher. Furthermore, the entire work ends in a conspiracy, in violation of the law, when Harry, Ron, and Hermione join with Dumbledore himself—a beacon of morality—to conceal the facts of Sirius's escape. In the earlier stories, readers already encounter Harry and his friends lying, disobeying authorities, and violating the rules, but not to the extent that they do so in this third tale.

Has Harry gone rotten? Not quite. To be sure, he is acting more or less the way most thirteen-year-olds behave in asserting their independence. More important, however, his behavior, even if it is not always exemplary, suggests that, in assessing larger moral issues, he has a far keener awareness of how they must be understood in context, in light of particular situations. *The Prisoner of Azkaban* presents Harry with choices far more difficult than the earlier books.

Rowling's third book is thus considerably more complex than her first two. Both *The Sorcerer's Stone* and *The Chamber of Secrets* present good and evil in a fairly straightforward fashion. Although Harry remains constant in his resistance to evil, that resistance is his only real option if he wants to avoid becoming evil himself. In the third book, in contrast, the true nature of things is in doubt: what appears to be evil turns out to be good; what seems to be good turns out to be evil. For Harry, working his way through this conundrum becomes a moral task more difficult to negotiate than the challenges he faced during his first two years at Hogwarts.

In fact, I would argue, *The Prisoner of Azkaban* is a single, extended commentary upon the tensions between rules and the moral principles they are intended to sustain. It pays attention to context. The book's entire plot suggests that truth-telling, submission to authority, and following the rules are not always the moral things to do, particularly when the stakes are high. Appearances can be deceiving.

This tendency can be seen most clearly in the main plot line of the book. Sirius is innocent of the charges against him, but no one knows it, and it can't be proven. Black is white. For Pettigrew, of course, the opposite is true. Making matters worse, the Ministry of Magic is intent upon deepening an already long-standing injustice. Dumbledore explains, while Sirius awaits his fate:

> "*Listen to me, Harry*. It's too late, you understand me? You must see that Professor Snape's version of events is far more convincing than yours."
>
> "He hates Sirius," Hermione said desperately. "All because of some stupid trick Sirius played on him—"
>
> "Sirius has not acted like an innocent man. The attack on the Fat Lady—entering Gryffindor Tower with a knife—without Pettigrew, alive or dead, we have no chance of overturning Sirius's sentence."
>
> "*But you believe us.*"
>
> "Yes, I do," said Dumbledore quietly. "But I have no power to make other men see the truth, or to overrule the Minister of Magic. . . ."[15]

In order to correct this wrong, a whole series of rule violations already begun must continue its course. Such actions serve a higher moral principle, and Harry learns an important lesson. Rules have their place, but, at times, they can serve ends other than what their creators intended.

But this ambiguity does not imply that anything goes, and Rowling makes this clear as well. Often enough, Harry does act contrary to rules and authority—and sometimes without any good reason—but these episodes serve two related literary purposes in Rowling's stories. First, they realistically depict the thought and behavior of teenagers. Second, they make possible higher levels of moral insight. If Harry were always good, he would have no need to learn additional lessons. By the end of the book, he does have a greater awareness of the moral implications of his decisions.

This development can be seen in a pivotal episode in which Harry reacts differently to Snape and to Lupin, when they both discover his second illegal visit to Hogsmead. Snape tells the truth, but he does so in a gloating lecture:

> "So," he said, straightening up again. "Everyone from the Minister of Magic downward had been trying to keep famous Harry Potter safe from Sirius Black. But famous Harry Potter is a law unto himself. Let the ordinary people worry about his safety! Famous Harry Potter goes where he wants to, with no thought for the consequences."[16]

In contrast, once he is alone with Harry and Ron, Lupin makes the same point (that Harry has become "a law unto himself") in a different fashion:

> "I would have thought that what you have heard when the dementors draw near you would have had more effect on you. Your parents gave their lives to keep you alive, Harry. A poor way to repay them—gambling their sacrifice for a bag of magic tricks."[17]

Whereas Harry's response to Snape is greater intransigence, his response to Lupin is stunned silence. He leaves "feeling worse by far than he had at any point in Snape's office."[18] At first blinded by Snape's hatred, but then given insight by Lupin's guidance, Harry experiences the real pangs of conscience and recognizes his foolishness.

Harry's growing awareness of his parents' sacrifice thus provides him with the opportunity to learn another important lesson: their values are alive inside him. Although released memories of their deaths disturb him, this experience—inadvertently caused by the dementors—leads to greater strength and an enhanced moral compass, precisely because they occasion disorientation and suffering. Working through this inner turmoil, Harry recognizes that his parents' example can serve him well.

Later in the book, Harry puts this insight to use in a very serious context, when his heightened conscience allows him to foresee the consequences of his and others' actions. Confronting Sirius, he allows his rage to give way to reason, as he, Hermione, and Ron feel and then think their way through difficult circumstances. Decisive moments must be treated with great care, especially when the issues involved are so complicated. Harry comes to believe Sirius but refuses to allow him and Lupin to kill Pettigrew, even if the action is justified on its face: "I'm not doing this for you. I'm doing it because—I don't reckon my dad would've wanted them to become killers—just for you."[19] Harry realizes that it is not for him to determine Pettigrew's fate; the law must decide. Nonetheless, he rightly believes that it is within his control to prevent his father's friends from acting rashly, as his father would have done. Although events outpace Harry's intentions, he has nonetheless correctly assessed what is necessary and what is possible.

Dumbledore, of course, later confirms the wisdom of these decisions, but Harry remains unconvinced. Earlier the headmaster inadvertently teaches a more important lesson, when he reveals his own fallibility to Harry: "I have no power to make other men see the truth, or to overrule the Minister of Magic."[20] Although *The Prisoner of Azkaban* concludes with the expected "debriefing" by Dumbledore, it is important to note just how little he says in this third book. To be sure, he reminds Harry of the contingencies of life and assures him that his father is alive inside him, but he offers only one new insight: Pettigrew may now be in Harry's debt. More so than in previous books, Dumbledore simply confirms what Harry already knows. Still, Harry remains confused—as he should be, as Dumbledore expects.

For by the end of the book Harry really is "a law unto himself," not in the sense that Snape implies, but in a more meaningful way. Some moral questions demand that he exercise his prerogative. Rules provide guidance, but they do not always provide solutions. It is up to Harry to decide how best to apply them in particular contexts. He cannot avoid this responsibility.

If we return to the litany of Harry's misconduct in *The Prisoner of Azkaban*, we can begin to sort through minor infractions and major ones. Ethical violations occur along a spectrum of right and wrong and do not fit neatly into discreet categories of "good" and "evil." Furthermore, we can begin to assess the justifications for each of Harry's misdeeds. When we sort and assess his mischievous actions in this fashion, we find that most are rather frivolous. We also find that he *mostly* commits major violations with very good reasons. Harry is imperfect but he is developing a higher moral sensibility.

Rowling reveals this growth gradually. *The Sorcerer's Stone* makes plain that Harry must respond to circumstances beyond his control. *The Chamber of Secrets* goes a step further and makes clear that he did not choose his own strengths and weaknesses. *The Prisoner of Azkaban* shows how he becomes more conscious of both of these constraints: the contingent nature of life and the extent of his own abilities. It also asks tougher questions of him by portraying competing claims to what is true and what is right. Ultimately, because of its greater ambiguity, the third book provides a fuller depiction of how Harry's *consciousness* informs his *conscience* in meeting circumstances beyond his control. As he grows, he becomes more aware.

THE GOBLET OF FIRE

Rowling's fourth book takes up the tale of Harry's life in an unexpected way. Voldemort murders an old man who discovers him and Pettigrew in an abandoned house. He also reveals a plan to kill Harry. Clear across England, Harry awakes to a searing pain in his head and a clear vision of what has just happened. Desiring adult advice about the meaning of this experience, he regrets the deaths of his parents, remembers his godfather, and dispatches a letter with Hedwig to Sirius, who is still on the lam but staying in touch. Harry fails to mention the threat on his life. Not sensing any further threat to himself, he shrugs off the dream.

Better able to work his influence upon the Dursleys now that he is fourteen, Harry arranges a short visit to the Weasleys at their home, the Burrow. Although the Weasleys' arrival in Little Whinging to collect Harry creates nothing short of a disaster for Harry's adoptive family, when they must blast apart the boarded-up fireplace in which they arrive (using Floo powder to travel), Harry is relieved that he'll spend the rest of the summer away from Little Whinging. Later, departing for the Quidditch World Cup, he travels along with Hermione and some of the Weasleys via a Portkey: in this case, an old boot that magically transports all who touch it to a prearranged location. Also accompanying them are Cedric Diggory, captain of the Hufflepuff Quidditch team, and his father. They arrive safely and find that the site of the Cup is buzzing with tens of thousands of wizards from around the world, a scene that puzzles a few dazed and confused Muggles.

There, Harry takes in the spectacle, runs into old friends, and meets several of Mr. Weasley's colleagues from the Ministry of Magic, including Bartemious Crouch, Percy Weasley's boss and head of the Department of International Magical Cooperation and Ludo Bagman, head of Magical Games and Sports. The contest itself is an unusual and exciting one, with Ireland defeating Bulgaria, even though the Bulgarian seeker captures the Snitch. Viktor Krum, the best player in the world and also the youngest, decides to end the match on his own terms, before it could become a rout.

The Cup's aftermath proves to be even more exciting, even if it becomes an ominous portent of things to come. A rowdy gang of hooded wizards abducts the campground manager and his family, magically suspending them high in the air. Seeking safety, Harry, Ron, and Hermione flee into the woods, and Harry realizes that he no longer has his wand. They soon encounter Draco Malfoy, who hints that his father, along with other former supporters of Voldemort, planned the disturbance. They then witness the nearby conjuring of the Dark Mark, a huge sparkling skull, entwined with a snake, used in previous years by Voldemort to mark his kills. Wizards and witches from the ministry soon descend upon the spot and nearly stupefy the children, before finding Barty Crouch's house-elf Winky in possession of Harry's wand, which had been used to summon the Mark. Crouch runs into the forest to investigate further, but upon his return, Winky is unable to explain what happened beyond protesting her innocence. Crouch threatens to release her from his service, causing her even greater anguish. Things eventually calm down at the site once the crowd is dispersed. The manager's family is safely returned home, their memories modified. Harry, Ron, and Hermione return to their tents, and early the next day they travel back to the Burrow.

The previous night's events bring chaos to the ministry, and Mr. Weasley and Percy must pull double shifts to sort out the aftermath. Although Mrs. Weasley is disturbed by news of events at the Cup, she nonetheless keeps everything in order over the following week, picking up everyone's school supplies in Diagon Alley and packing them up for school. Harry eventually reveals to Hermione and Ron what he had dreamed before the Cup, choosing not to mention the designs Voldemort has upon his life. On the morning of their departure for Hogwarts, Mr. Weasley must get Mad-Eye Moody out of a jam and leaves the house early. Mad-Eye, a former Auror who had ruthlessly pursued the followers of Voldemort, caused an uproar in his neighborhood the night before, believing himself to be under attack by dark wizards.

The trip aboard the Hogwarts Express proves to be uneventful, even if a smirking Malfoy taunts Harry, Ron, and Hermione over their ignorance of a major event to take place at school this year. Later, at the opening feast Dumbledore explains. Hogwarts is to host the Triwizard Tournament, a magical competition among three champions representing Hogwarts and two other wizarding schools, Durmstrang and Beauxbatons. Entrants will have to be at least seventeen years old. Dumbledore's magic will prevent underaged contestants from submitting their names, but everyone should enjoy the tasks set for the champions. Along with glory, the winner will receive one thousand galleons in prize money. Dumbledore's comments are interrupted by the appearance of a stranger: Mad-Eye Moody, the new Defense Against the Dark Arts teacher.

The year's courses begin pretty much the way Harry expects, with the exception of Moody's. Making his point that constant vigilance is required to keep practitioners of the dark arts at bay, he instructs his students on the first day of class about the unforgivable curses. The Imperious Curse allows the spell-caster to control completely the actions of the victim. The Cruciatus Curse causes its victim extreme pain. *Avada Kedavra* kills its victim instantaneously. The Imperious Curse can be resisted, while the latter two cannot. Only one person has ever survived *Avada Kedavra* and he sits right in front of Moody— namely, Harry Potter. Both excited and disturbed by Moody's demonstration of each curse upon three spiders, the students shuffle out of the class talking animatedly and eager to learn more. Only Neville Longbottom remains silent.

Soon the school is swept up by the coming tournament and the arrival of contenders from Beauxbatons and Durmstrang. Students from the first reach Hogwarts flying in a large blue carriage pulled by gigantic horses that drink only single-malt whiskey. Hagrid soon takes a liking to the school's headmistress, Madam Maxime, who just happens to be about as tall as he is. Students from the second come in a large ship that appears out of the depths of the lake. Their headmaster is Professor Karkaroff, a rehabilitated follower of Voldemort, accompanied by Viktor Krum, the world-famous seeker. After hopeful contestants submit their names and schools written on a piece of parchment, the Goblet of Fire chooses the champions to represent each of the three schools. Fleur Delacour will represent Beauxbatons, Viktor Krum will represent Durmstrang, and Cedric Diggory will represent Hogwarts. Before the three champions can be given instruction, the Goblet emits Harry Potter's name as well. Someone had tricked it into naming a fourth champion, and the resulting magical contract compels Harry to compete. The judges for the competition—Dumbledore, Maxime, Karkaroff, Bagman, and Crouch—are all stunned, because nothing like this has happened before.

The fallout is intense. Members of the other schools cry foul. Snape suspects Harry of bending the rules yet again. Even Dumbledore seems annoyed. Ron, in particular, is incensed. He is convinced that Harry found a way over Dumbledore's age line and that he chose not to share his secret. Hermione is concerned, recognizing immediately how this circumstance places Harry in great danger. Other Gryffindors are elated, but the rest of the school begins to despise Harry. They are convinced that he seeks more fame and glory. Making matters worse, Rita Skeeter, a reporter for the *Daily Prophet*, buzzes around and writes a goopy article about Harry, which becomes a source of humiliation. Harry is left to face the first task without Ron's friendship and with most of his school against him. He has no idea what is in store for him.

Hagrid provides a clue. Harry will have to face a dragon with only his wand. Moody likewise helps, hinting that Harry must play to his strengths—namely, his flying skills. Hermione teaches Harry the necessary spell to get his Firebolt at the beginning of the task. Harry warns Cedric about what's in store, convinced he's the only champion still in the dark. On the day of the competition, Ludo Bagman, one of the tournament's judges, offers to help Harry, but Harry rejects the offer and succeeds on his own, capturing the golden egg guarded by a Hungarian Horntail in record time and tying for first place with Krum. Awed by what he witnesses and coached by Hermione into seeing the dangers confronting Harry, Ron overcomes his jealousy. Harry is relieved; talking about Quidditch really is more fun than hanging out in the library with Hermione.

The golden egg is a clue for the next task, but Harry puts it out of his mind, going into denial and concerning himself with other issues. The knowledge that Sirius is worried about him both consoles and disturbs Harry. Communication is highly anticipated, but Harry feels that Sirius is placing himself in unnecessary danger. Before the first task, Sirius had warned Harry to watch out for Karkaroff; it is highly likely that Voldemort is behind his participation in the tournament. Harry is also drawn into Hermione's plans. From the first day of the term, she has been outraged that house-elves do most of the work at Hogwarts. She begins to organize on their behalf, and Ron quickly dubs her Society for the Promotion of Elfish Welfare "spew." Wheedling information from Fred and George Weasley, she learns how to enter the kitchens at the school. There, she, Ron, and Harry encounter happy elves who give no thought to their condition. They also encounter Dobby, hired by Dumbledore and paid a wage to work at Hogwarts. He still wears the sock Harry used to end his service to the Malfoys. Of greater concern to Harry is the fact that, as a school champion, he must ask a date to accompany him to the Yule Ball. He finally screws up the courage to ask Cho Chang, only to learn that she will accompany Cedric. He ends up going with Parvati Patil, but can't overcome his jealousy of Cedric and is further annoyed that Percy is in attendance on behalf of his boss, Mr. Crouch, who is ill and unable to travel to Hogwarts. Hermione accompanies Viktor Krum, and Ron's jealousy knows no bounds, even though he can't quite understand why. Harry finds himself in the middle. Ron and Harry learn to their surprise that Hagrid and Maxime are descended from giants, while overhearing a private conversation between them. At the end of the evening, Cedric tells Harry to take a bath with the golden egg—a tip to repay him for information about the dragons.

Still in a state of denial and foolishly unwilling to heed advice coming for Cedric, Harry persists in delaying his preparations for the second task. He even forgets to consult with Sirius. Rita Skeeter strikes again with an exposé revealing that Hagrid is a half-giant, the son of Fridwulfa who probably left England in the aftermath of Voldemort's demise. Hagrid is devastated. Even more disturbing to him is Madame Maxime's refusal to admit her own descent from giants. Hermione lambastes Skeeter one day in the Three Broomsticks, and Ron warns her that she'll be Skeeter's next target. All three friends finally coax Hagrid out of his depression with some help from Dumbledore.

Harry finally follows Cedric's advice and takes a bath with the egg.

Moaning Myrtle provides moral support, having witnessed Cedric do the same. Harry learns that something will be taken from him and hidden in the lake among the merpeople who live there. While returning to Gryffindor Tower under his invisibility cloak, Harry notices on the Marauder's Map that Bartemious Crouch is rummaging around Snape's office, and he goes to investigate. His foot get stuck in a trick stair, and he drops the egg, which opens and emits piercing shrieks. First Filch and then Snape come to investigate. Only the intervention of Moody protects Harry, who is hiding under his cloak, from discovery. Harry tells him about Crouch, and Moody asks Harry if he can borrow the Map. It might be useful in keeping an eye on things.

Relieved, Harry returns to his bed, but there's still a problem confronting him; he has no idea how to survive underwater, a skill he will have to master for the second task. Despite Hermione and Ron's help, Harry still hasn't found a solution by the eve of the task. After sneaking off to the library to continue his research, he falls asleep. He awakens in a panic minutes before the task is to begin. Dobby prods him and hands over the magical Gillyweed that Harry will need to breathe underwater; he had overheard McGonagall and Moody discussing it. Harry runs to the event.

He arrives by the lake and is set to the task without explanation from the judges—Percy once again taking the place of Mr. Crouch. He chews and swallows the Gillyweed and enters the lake. Underwater, he really has no idea where he must go until Moaning Myrtle points him in the right direction. He soon comes upon a settlement of merpeople and finds Ron, Hermione, Cho, and a young girl tied to a large statue. He soon frees Ron, but is prevented from loosening the other hostages. Cedric frees Cho, and Krum frees Hermione, but Harry waits for the arrival of Fleur. With time running out, he threatens the merpeople with his wand until they let him take the girl. He returns with her and Ron to the surface. Soon feeling humiliated when he realizes Dumbledore would not have allowed any of the hostages to be harmed, he curses himself for being so stupid. Nonetheless, he receives close to full marks for moral fiber and finds himself tied for the lead with Cedric.

The third task awaits him in several months, but other distractions take up his time. First, Harry and Hermione become targets of Skeeter's acid quill. Second, Harry sees an agitated Karkaroff showing a distressed Snape a spot on his arm, and overhears him asking the potions master if he has noticed the same change. Third, Sirius returns to Hogsmead and meets with Harry, Ron, and Hermione to discuss the year's strange events. They ruminate over Snape's behavior, the loss of Harry's wand at the World Cup, the largely unexplained absences of Crouch, and the strange behavior of Bagman, who persists in trying to assist Harry in the tasks. They depart without any clear ideas, but learn that Bagman was suspected of being a follower of Voldemort and that Crouch's son died in Azkaban after he was convicted by his father for doing the same. Fourth, Harry and Krum encounter Crouch one evening on the Hogwarts grounds; he's deranged but says he must speak to Dumbledore. Before Harry can return with the headmaster, Crouch disappears and Krum is found stunned on the spot. Fifth, one day, Harry has a disturbing dream in which Voldemort is punishing Pettigrew for a serious blunder. Harry leaves for Dumbledore's office for advice. There, he is left alone and begins to investigate a strange, shallow, magical basin filled with a silvery substance. Drawn in, much the same way he had entered Tom Riddle's diary, Harry finds himself witnessing events from many years ago: the trials of Bagman, several followers of Voldemort, and Crouch's son, who had been involved in the torture of Neville's parents. Mentally crippled by the experience, they now reside in an insane asylum, still alive, contrary to what everyone has assumed. In addition, Harry learns that Snape was suspected of supporting Voldemort but had in fact become an informant serving the Ministry of Magic at great risk to himself. Harry had entered Dumbledore's Pensieve, used by the Headmaster to store important memories. Guided out of these thoughts by the headmaster, Harry relates the story of the dream to him, and they discuss it along with other related issues. Dumbledore calmly informs Harry that Voldemort has been growing stronger all year.

Around these distractions, Harry finds time to put in long hours of practice with Hermione and Ron for the third and final task. It arrives at the end of the school year. Harry and the other champions must enter a large maze that has been grown on the Quidditch pitch; they will have to negotiate it, encountering magical obstacles along the way, until they reach the Triwizard Cup. The first champion to claim it will win the tournament. Once begun, things go exceptionally well for Harry until he encounters Krum using the Cruciatus Curse on Cedric. Harry stuns Krum, rescuing Cedric, and the two of them signal the judges to come and get the Durmstrang champion. Deducing that Fleur has already left the competition, they continue on their separate ways. In a short while, Harry catches sight of Cedric racing for the Cup. Harry shouts a warning to him; he is unaware that a large spider will get him before he reaches the Cup. Both he and Harry manage to immobilize it, but Harry injures his leg in the attempt. Victory awaits Cedric, except that he declines to take it. Only Harry's warning and subsequent injury would allow him to win, and he insists that Harry claim the prize. Harry convinces Cedric that they should claim it together, and they both grasp the Cup simultaneously.

They suddenly find themselves in a strange and distant cemetery. The Cup was a Portkey, and Pettigrew awaits them. Without delay, he kills Cedric on the command of Voldemort. Taking a stunned Harry in hand, Pettigrew binds him, and prepares the magic that will restore Voldemort to his body. A bone from the grave of the villain's father, blood from Harry, and Pettigrew's own hand, which must be severed from his arm, go into a steaming cauldron into which he places a small, deformed body, which Harry knows to be his enemy. In moments, Voldemort rises from the brew.

Voldemort summons his followers by touching a mark on Pettigrew's arm. One by one, they magically appear—the Death Eaters, with Malfoy among them. Voldemort turns his attention to Harry, taunting him. He tortures Harry with the Cruciatus Curse but then has Pettigrew release him and return his wand. Voldemort will demonstrate his superiority in front of his supporters. He uses the Imperius Curse, but Harry resists. After further torture, Voldemort shouts "*Avada Kedavra*" to dispatch Harry once and for all, but Harry responds with *"Expelliarmus".* Their wands become bound by a golden beam of light; it lifts them both from the ground and surrounds them within a strange force field. Large beads of light begin to travel toward Harry's wand, as it shakes uncontrollably, but he knows what to do, almost as if a friendly voice were instructing him. Overcoming Voldemort's strength, he keeps the connection and sends the beads back toward the villain's wand. Once they touch it, ghostly figures emerge: Cedric, the old man from the dream, and Harry's parents. His mother tells him to break the connection and grab the Cup; it will return him to Hogwarts. Harry does as instructed, and dodging the attacks of the Death Eaters, he grabs hold of Cedric's body and the Cup.

Transported once again, Harry finds himself—and Cedric's still lifeless body—under the worried gaze of Albus Dumbledore, who tells him to stay put before hurrying off to speak with the Diggorys. Within seconds, Moody appears and takes him back to the castle. Back in his office, Moody pumps Harry for information, pointing a wand at him. Slowly coming to his senses, Harry wonders what is going on. Moody reveals that he had sent Harry to Voldemort, stunning Fleur, causing Krum to attack Cedric, and transforming the Cup into a Portkey. In Moody's Foe-Glass, a mirror that reveals his enemies' approach, Harry sees three shadowy figures emerging. Just as Moody prepares to kill Harry, the door to the room is blasted open. Moody is sent tumbling, unconscious, onto the floor. Dumbledore, McGonagall, and Snape, appearing clearly in the Foe-Glass at last, stand in the doorway.

Dumbledore tells Harry that this cannot be Alastor Moody. He opens the trunk in the office to reveal a secret room in which the sleeping body of the real Mad-Eye lies. Someone had been using Polyjuice Potion to impersonate him all year. Dumbledore sits down to wait. Soon the impostor takes on his real appearance. He is Barty Crouch, the son of the head of the Department of International Magical Cooperation. Dumbledore revives him after administering Veritaserum, a truth-telling potion. Crouch reveals that years ago his mother and father had faked his death at Azkaban, but then he had been kept prisoner at home, under the control of his father's Imperius Curse. This year, he had been at the World Cup, under an invisibility cloak and in the care of Winky, but he had learned to fight the curse. He stole Harry's wand and conjured the Dark Mark. Then Pettigrew and Voldemort had rescued him from his father's home and the tables were turned. The elder Mr. Crouch was under Voldemort's control. Within a week, they attacked Moody, and the younger Crouch was able to assume his identity. Later in the year, Pettigrew let the elder Crouch escape—a mistake for which he was punished. Mr. Crouch had fought off the curse and attempted to confess all to Dumbledore at Hogwarts, but before he could do so, the younger Crouch, disguised as Moody, was able to stun Krum and murder his father.

Additional revelations follow. Harry describes events in detail to Dumbledore and Sirius and learns that his wand and Voldemort's both contain feathers from Dumbledore's phoenix, Fawkes—a fact that was responsible for the rare Reverse Spell effect that connected the wands. Harry is escorted to the infirmary, and he learns that Cornelius Fudge had a dementor administer its kiss to Barty Crouch over the vocal protestations of McGonagall. He cannot now testify about his actions. Dumbledore tries, without luck, to dissuade Fudge from plotting a cover-up and signals without ambiguity that he shall not follow that course. A parting of the ways is in the offing. Dumbledore will rally resistance against Voldemort. If Hagrid and Madam Maxime agree, he will send them as emissaries to the giants. He encourages Snape and Sirius to overcome their mutual animosity. Snape reveals his own Dark Mark, the same as those on Pettigrew and Karkaroff, and is dispatched on an unspecified mission. Sirius leaves to seek out Lupin and others for assistance. Mrs. Weasley promises that Mr. Weasley will work to do the same at the ministry.

Still more revelations follow as the year ends on a somber note because of Cedric's murder by Pettigrew and Voldemort. True to his word, Dumbledore leads the students in a toast to Cedric's example and informs them of what happened. Returning to London aboard the Hogwarts Express, Harry learns a great deal about Rita Skeeter and Ludo

Bagman. Skeeter is an unregistered animagus. She had been spying all year disguised as a beetle; Hermione had put all the pieces of this puzzle together and finally captured Skeeter on the night of Cedric's death. She was now safely, if also furiously, stowed in a glass jar. Fred and George explain Bagman's strange behavior. He owed them quite a bit of money due to a wager he placed with them at the World Cup, but he owed still more to others. He tried to assist Harry all year, because he had bet upon his winning the Triwizard Tournament. Since Harry technically tied with Cedric, Ludo was in hiding from a group of very angry goblins. With the train stopped at the station, Harry insists that Fred and George take his winnings (one thousand galleons) from the tournament as an investment in a joke shop that they want to open after graduation. Circumstances suggest that everyone will need more than a few laughs. Harry leaves the station with Uncle Vernon, resigned to face the future.

THAT'S NOT HOW IT'S SUPPOSED TO WORK

Throughout *The Goblet of Fire*, Harry comes up short when he acts on his own. Without the help of Hagrid, the false Moody, and Hermione, he would fail the first task. Without a hint from Cedric, encouragement and direction from Myrtle, and the Gillyweed given him by Dobby, he would fail the second. Only in the third task, after long hours of practice with Hermione and Ron, does Harry come into his own. But even then, his passage through the maze is made easier by Barty Crouch because of his own evil designs. Heroes aren't supposed to be this way. So, what's going on?

Clearly, Rowling's conception of heroism does not depend upon the magical abilities that she gives her protagonist. It resides in his moral abilities. We can catch a glimpse of them in the exchange between Harry and Cedric in front of the Triwizard Cup:

"Take it, then," Harry panted to Cedric. "Go on, take it. You're there."

But Cedric didn't move. He merely stood there, looking at Harry. Then he turned to stare at the cup. Harry saw the longing expression on his face in its golden light. Cedric looked around at Harry again, who was now holding onto the hedge to support himself. Cedric took a deep breath.

"You take it. You should win. That's twice you've saved my neck in here."

"That's not how it's supposed to work," Harry said.[21]

But that is how it works between two individuals who place a higher value on acting morally than on winning glory.

Both Harry and Cedric prove themselves to be such individuals. Their special abilities serve their moral choices, rather than the reverse. Although Harry's magical gifts are considerable for a wizard his age, they are only incidental to the trials that confront him. The same is true for Cedric. But even acting morally does not provide safeguards against fate. Nothing does, as they both learn all too soon. Neither magical abilities nor ethical heroism guarantee success in life. Despite its great length, the central moral of *The Goblet of Fire* is a rather simple one: special abilities are far less important than the desire to do the right thing.

Harry's confrontation with Voldemort is instructive in this regard. The episode makes plain two related developments: Harry can resist Voldemort's use of the Imperious Curse by refusing to submit, and he can force the beads of light back upon the villain's wand by using his greater powers of concentration. In both instances, Harry's strength of will—his desire to do good—is superior to Voldemort's. Unable to best his enemy with the magical skills of an adolescent wizard, Harry uses the only thing available to him, his uncompromising intention to resist evil.

As we should expect, Dumbledore makes the same point near the end of the book. Speaking of Cedric's memory, he enjoins the students to make the same decision Harry has already made several times:

"Remember, if the time should come when you have to make a choice between what is right and what is easy, remember what happened to a boy who was good, and kind, and brave, because he strayed across the path of Lord Voldemort."[22]

Choices, rather than anything else, best reflect the qualities of the person making them.

Yet, *The Goblet of Fire* offers more as well. Both the frequent assistance Harry receives and his own actions on the behalf of others illustrate the importance of empathy and solidarity. The book suggests that more than self-interest must motivate actions. These themes are further developed in Dumbledore's attempts to unite opposition to Voldemort, to strengthen ties among individuals across generations, families, school houses, and even different nations. As the battle lines are drawn between good and evil in *The Goblet of Fire*, we can sense the likely continuing importance of these themes to Harry's moral development in future books.

And Harry does develop rather than staying in place. This last book in Rowling's series also depicts the consolidation of the lessons Harry learns in earlier books. In the first, his self-scrutiny leads him to a greater degree of comfort with things beyond his control, including the possibility of his own death. Likewise, this unceasing process brings him to the important realization, in the second, that choices make people who they are, rather than their inborn traits. By the third, he becomes more conscious of how moral principles must be applied in context and of how he is free to follow his parents' examples. By the fourth book, Harry gains even more awareness of his own weaknesses and a still better sense of his strengths. Harry is still subject to forces beyond his control but he is far more self-conscious. For Rowling's hero, "what would come, would come . . . and he would have to meet it when it did."[23]

3
Harry Potter's Morality on Display

A Primer on Stoic Virtue

Good men toil, spend and are spent, and willingly; they are not dragged along by Fortune but follow her and keep in step. If they knew how, they would have outstripped her.

—Seneca, in "On Providence"

FRUSTRATION

In an important sense, understanding Harry Potter's moral decisions is dependent upon understanding how he copes with frustration. In other words, we must see how well he balances his own desires against the world's demands. This question of balance is the central challenge posed by Stoic philosophy, and it is one that Harry answers frequently. Alain de Botton explains the problem suc-

cinctly in his book *The Consolations of Philosophy*, when discussing the
Roman Stoic Seneca:

> Though the terrain of frustration may be vast—from a stubbed toe to
> an untimely death—at the heart of every frustration lies a basic struc-
> ture: the collision of a wish with an unyielding reality. The collisions
> begin in earliest infancy, with the discovery that the sources of our
> satisfaction lie beyond our control and that the world does not reli-
> ably conform to our desires.[1]

Of course, how Harry and other characters manage those collisions is
another matter entirely.

Again, de Botton gives us important insights by elaborating upon
the instruction offered by Seneca:

> A single idea recurs throughout his work: that we best endure those
> frustrations which we have prepared ourselves for and understand
> and are hurt most by those we least expected and cannot fathom. Phi-
> losophy must reconcile us to the true dimensions of reality, and so
> spare us, if not frustration itself, then at least its panoply of pernicious
> accompanying emotions.[2]

Frustrations, then, cannot be avoided entirely, because their sources are
beyond an individual's control, but responses to reality's habit of
intruding in undesirable ways can be shaped through acceptance,
readiness, and perception. Only such mental preparedness can keep
adverse circumstances from spinning out of control and drawing the
individual along with them into a debilitating anger, grief, or anxiety,
which have the potential to make matters worse and no ability to
change the circumstances.

Harry, of course, experiences each of these emotions, along with
still others, throughout his adventures. Often enough, in fact, they serve
him in positive ways, contrary to strict Stoic teaching, by persuading
him to see things anew. But he has also displayed an ability to bring
them under control, quickly when events require it or over time when

circumstance allows it. He lets his emotions speak to him and then uses these insights to appraise the causes of his frustration in a rational manner. He assesses what courses of action remain open to him.[3]

This tendency is very much in keeping with Stoic principles maintaining that anger is madness, grief impermanent, and anxiety encumbering. As de Botton makes clear, each feeling arises from failing to reconcile the self with an inherently and inescapably imperfect existence. He observes, following Seneca, "what makes us angry are dangerously optimistic notions about what the world and other people are like." Shocking circumstances are certainly "unusual and terrible," but they are not "abnormal" or outside the realm of human experience. Only optimism and long periods of relative ease lead us to believe otherwise. Yet, fate bestows both bounty and bane, and not always in equal measure. It is difficult but not impossible to adjust to the whims of fortune. Random and contingent events shape human destinies, and there is no guiding principle of justice behind changing circumstances, but undue anxiety over this state of affairs interferes with the enjoyment of life and the proper assessment of right and wrong. The answer to this situation, offered by Seneca, as well as the other Stoics, is an indifference to what fortune provides. Enjoyment of life's bounty is just fine, but when it is denied, that, too, must be accepted. It is not hypocritical to live a life of ease and fulfillment, but no unfairness has been suffered when fate decides otherwise, even if its dictates are delivered by unjust, cruel, and evil agents.[4]

Seneca offered the following parable to explain both the workings of fate and the fruitlessness of overly emotional responses to them:

> An animal, struggling against the noose, tightens it . . . there is no yoke so tight that it will not hurt the animal less if it pulls *with* it than if it fights *against* it. The one alleviation for overwhelming evils is to endure and bow to necessity.

Isn't Seneca implying that it's not even worth trying to fight back? In his commentary on this passage, de Botton notes that one could understand it as a suggestion to live passively and as a victim to circumstance. In answer, he continues:

But Seneca's point is more subtle. It is no less unreasonable to accept something as necessary when it *isn't* as to rebel against something when it *is*. We can as easily go astray by accepting the unnecessary and denying the possible, as by denying the necessary and wishing for the impossible. It is for reason to make the decision.

Reason thus ultimately strikes the balance between individual desire and unrelenting reality. Ambiguities certainly persist, but it is our own "distinctive freedom" to choose our attitudes toward them.[5]

We find a perfect illustration of how the Stoics understand the relationship between desire and reality in *Harry Potter and the Sorcerer's Stone*, when Dumbledore explains the powers of the Mirror of Erised:

> "Now, can you think what the Mirror of Erised shows us all?"
>
> Harry shook his head.
>
> "Let me explain. The happiest man on earth would be able to use the Mirror of Erised like a normal mirror, that is, he would look into it and see himself exactly as he is. Does that help?"
>
> Harry thought. Then he said slowly, "It shows us what we want . . . whatever we want . . ."
>
> "Yes and no," said Dumbledore quietly. "It shows us nothing more or less than the deepest, most desperate desire of our hearts. . . . However, this mirror will give us neither knowledge or [sic] truth. Men have wasted away before it, entranced by what they have seen, or been driven mad, not knowing if what it shows is real or even possible.
>
> "The Mirror will be moved to a new home tomorrow, Harry, and I ask you not to go looking for it again. If you ever *do* run across it, you will now be prepared. It does not do to dwell on dreams and forget to live, remember that."[6]

Later in the book, we also find how striking the balance between desire and reality applies to moral decisions.

It is no mere coincidence that when Harry again sees himself in the Mirror of Erised, he sees himself as he is, in possession of the Sorcerer's Stone. He obtains it (thanks to Dumbledore's magic), not because he intends to use it, but because he intends to protect it from misuse, an intention that has motivated his actions right from the start. For in exercising his distinctive freedom to choose his attitude toward fate, Harry is as unrelenting as the realities beyond his control. He finds the right thing to do when confronted with conditions that he cannot escape. When Dumbledore muses to Harry in the hospital wing, "You *did* do the thing properly, didn't you," he is speaking about more than Harry's investigative powers.[7] Before the Mirror, in Voldemort's malevolent presence, Harry accepts what is necessary without denying what is possible. He strikes the Stoic balance, and not for the last time.

AMBIGUITY

Striking this balance is difficult, because life is so full of uncertainties. But they need not become overwhelming. In fact, the Stoics' basic distinctions between, for example, the internal and the external, reason and emotion, virtue and vice, or the preferred and the rejected, outlined earlier in chapter 1, represent their systematic attempts to make sense of life's numerous ambiguities. They approach the problem as something to overcome for the sake of living well, for the sake of being a successful human being.

The English word *ambiguity* comes to us from the Latin *ambiguitas*, derived from the verb *ambigere*: to wander around. Ambiguous meanings, whether symbolic or circumstantial, thus wander about, rather than remaining stable or fixed. Simply, ambiguity refers to the condition or state of having two or more possible meanings. Using the word to describe something implies an indefinite or imprecise quality about the thing. Stoics disliked such implications. In her book on Stoic responses to ambiguity, Catherine Atherton puts it this way:

> Ambiguity thus reveals itself as a threat to secure happiness, but one disarmed by a dialectic which imparts correctness in the use of language, and in the interpretation of impressions, as well as in reasoning.

The Stoics thus see ambiguity as a potential defect in communication, perception, and sound judgment. Often enough, they argue that language would be better off without it. Nevertheless, the Stoics became, at times, lovers of paradox because of the teaching opportunities it offered.[8]

The best proponent of this view in Rowling's books is Dumbledore, who provides numerous examples of his preference for precise usage, accurate descriptions, and clear courses of action, even if his mentoring of Harry Potter sometimes relies upon leaving things unsaid. The best instance of this approach is Dumbledore's encouraging Harry to use Voldemort's name, rather than the preferred euphemisms employed by most others in the wizarding world: "Call him Voldemort, Harry. Always use the proper name for things. Fear of a name increases fear of the thing itself."[9] His insistence that Harry describe, in detail, the painful events leading to and following upon Cedric's death, before he can hope to recover from them, can be viewed in this light as well. Dumbledore encourages Harry to confront immutable realities rather than ignoring them. The same moral is to be found in his forthright descriptions of Voldemort's evil and the proper response to it, delivered to the assembled student body of Hogwarts. In each case, Dumbledore acts to diminish ambiguity.

But Rowling's stories taken as a whole do not seem to suggest that uncertainty can be eliminated outright. To the contrary, it can only be recognized and assessed. Even Dumbledore concedes as much in telling Harry that it is impossible to foresee all the consequences of his actions. Rowling thus challenges her readers with numerous episodes that rely upon the ambiguous depictions of characters and events. Her portrayal of life in Harry's adventures as something fraught with uncertainty often sends her critics into orbit, but I would argue that it makes her books especially useful for discussing moral issues with children. By developing a view consistent with basic Stoic teaching about the inescapable perils of ambiguity, Rowling's books enable readers to experience ethical difficulties right along with Harry.

What kinds of moral ambiguities do readers encounter? At the risk of oversimplifying, I would contend that Rowling explores ambiguity in her development of plot lines corresponding to four principal categories of uncertainty: (1) rule-following versus rule-breaking; (2) emotion versus reason; (3) inherited predisposition versus acquired adaptability; and (4) fate versus free will. More than a few episodes illustrate the largely unresolved tensions existing between the terms in each pair of linked concepts. In each case, Rowling considers in Stoic fashion the nature of given realities—what is beyond one's control—and the autonomy inherent in choosing responses to them—what is within one's control.

Rule-Following versus Rule-Breaking

Most prominent is Rowling's exploration of the ambiguity surrounding rules and regulations. Breaking the rules is pervasive in Rowling's books, but within the context of the stories, it serves both literary and ethical purposes. Periodic escapes from rules and regulations are essential to the success of fantastical stories. They create both tension and excitement, and they allow characters to exercise freedom away from direct oversight and constraint. Yet, rules are important and provide safety and security. Insofar as they both ensure order and free individuals from being constantly on guard, they must be seen as both repressive and liberating. This is the essence of their ambiguity.

In terms of moral implications, the existence of rules raises important questions about power, particularly about who has it and how it is exercised. Harry's adventures interrogate the legitimacy of various claims to authority in exercising power over others. Sometimes, authority is not challenged, while at other times, it most certainly is—for both good and bad reasons. Often enough, Rowling's characters misbehave simply because they want to do so, but at other times, they violate regulations or the law because teachers are capricious, the Ministry of Magic can't be trusted, or the threat of greater evil is too imminent. They violate rules the ways kids do in asserting their independence, but they also recognize the nature of relations between rules and the principles they are intended to uphold, and they ultimately find guidance in them rather than solutions. As a result, most rule-breaking at Hogwarts serves to uphold, rather than subvert, important moral values.[10]

Harry makes this case for the first time toward the end of *The Sorcerer's Stone*, when he explains how rules don't always serve larger moral principles:

> "Don't you understand? If Snape gets hold of the Stone, Voldemort's coming back! Haven't you heard what it was like when he was trying to take over? There won't be any Hogwarts to get expelled from! He'll flatten it, or turn it into a school for the Dark Arts! Losing points doesn't matter any more, can't you see?"[11]

Essentially the same argument can be advanced to explain major violations of the rules in each subsequent book in the series. It is interesting to note that Dumbledore confirms this approach in *Harry Potter and the Prisoner of Azkaban*, when he conspires to secure Sirius's escape, and in *Harry Potter and the Goblet of Fire*, when he acts to form an alliance against Voldemort outside official channels. Rowling is suggesting that the relationship between following the rules and breaking the rules is not as simple as we might assume.

Emotion versus Reason

A related ambiguity is found in Rowling's depiction of the tensions between emotion and reason. Their relation to each other is complicated and symbolizes to some extent a familiar dynamic between what is not and what is within one's control. Emotional responses signal, to some degree, a loss of control, while rational responses signal, to some degree, its recuperation. But just as rule-following or rule-breaking do not automatically signify right or wrong, reason and emotion do not entirely imply propriety or impropriety.

More than a few episodes throughout the books highlight this ambiguity and seem to imply that both emotional and rational responses to events are perfectly justifiable, at least in some cases. We can see how this works if we briefly consider Harry's justification for rule-breaking that I quoted above, which is more of an angry tirade than my abridgement might imply. In this case, justifiable anger leads to a reasonable moral judgment. In fact, despite his largely Stoic demeanor, Harry is capable of displaying significant emotional responses to events. Nonetheless, in numerous additional episodes, he channels his emotions in productive directions, even if he is not capable of overcoming them completely.

We see the opposite tendency at work in Hagrid's actions. His more extreme descents into depression or ascents into buoyancy are even more interesting than Harry's temporary vacillations between emotion and reason, when it comes to assessing the ambiguous relationship between the two. Within the context of the stories, Hagrid's mood-swings often help other characters comprehend their emotions, particularly Harry, Ron, and Hermione. When they "read" Hagrid's emotions with empathy, they find themselves either prompted into action or soothed into hopefulness. They apply reason to circumstances and plan for the future. As we can see in Hagrid's joy or despondency over events involving Norbert the dragon, Buckbeak the Hippogriff, or his own perceived humiliation by Rita Skeeter, Hagrid lives largely unselfconsciously. Although this way of living is clearly not an option for Harry, Hagrid's demeanor, in fact, makes his cabin a place where other characters can give voice to troubling feelings that haven't yet been sorted by reason or repressed by decorum. Both Hagrid's actions and his presence communicate the propriety and value of emotions, even if they must ultimately be subordinated to reason. In less obvious ways, other places, notably the Hogwarts Express, the Gryffindor common room, and the Three Broomsticks, provide similar opportunities for demonstrative emotional release.[12]

But emotions can be debilitating as well. Rowling provides ample evidence of this view in Hagrid's own drunken and debilitating bouts with depression, but she develops it further in numerous illustrations of ignorance as the all-too-common origin of immoral, emotional behavior. Although readers are quite likely to find Professor Lupin an appealing character, it is worth noting that most members of the wizarding world do not. His status as a werewolf renders him a suspect outsider. In an interview, Rowling makes the case plainly:

> Professor Lupin, who appears in the third book, is one of my favorite characters. He's a damaged person, literally and metaphorically. I think it's important for children to know that adults, too, have their problems, that they struggle. His being a werewolf is really a metaphor for people's reactions to illness and disability.

Emotional reactions to the potential threat that he poses far outweigh the more reasoned responses made possible by his ability to control his condition. Yet, these emotional reactions harm Lupin, as well, causing him to question his own worth, even though reason tells him otherwise.[13]

Inherited Predisposition versus Acquired Adaptability

Ambiguity is emphasized in a third way, as well, whenever Rowling places inherited predisposition and acquired adaptability in juxtaposition with each other. These comparisons echo the moral tensions between regulation and transgression, and between unthinking emotion and careful responses to it. Again, we find Rowling describing the vicissitudes of unyielding realities while highlighting the freedom individuals possess in choosing how to meet them.

Most significant in Rowling's depiction of the tension between predisposition and adaptability are the stereotypes sometimes on display and how they function within Harry's stories. For example, "nationalistic" caricatures of students from Beauxbatons and Durmstrang, as well as Hogwarts, can be found throughout the texts (along with still other examples). Likewise, "ethnic" or "class" attributes are central in depictions of Muggles, the Muggle-born, goblins, centaurs, house-elves, and giants. In addition, quite a few "gender" assumptions seem to explain the behavior of both male and female characters. Finally, "personality" profiling seems to be at work in the assignment of students to one of four school houses at Hogwarts. What's going on here? Are characters the way they are because they were born that way, or because they became that way over time? The answers that Rowling's descriptions suggest are ambiguous: characters often act in stereotypical ways, but they often act according to different routines as well. On the one hand, destiny appears to shape them; on the other, their behavior appears to be independent of fate. Thus, a number of themes in Harry's adventures point to the difficulty inherent in considering the tension between inborn traits and learned behavior.[14]

If we briefly consider the role of the Sorting Hat, we can come to a better understanding of this tension. The hat *peers into* the brains of Hogwarts students. What does it see in them, predisposition or adaptability? The simple (though still ambiguous) answer is both. Members of wizarding families tend to find themselves in the same houses over generations but not always. Members appear to possess the traits associated with each house but not always. Slytherin produces dark wizards but not always. In other words, Rowling uses the Sorting Hat to illustrate individuals' predispositions *and* their adaptability in controlling them. So, for example, Parvati Patil is in Gryffindor, but her identical twin Padma is in Ravenclaw; Neville Longbottom belongs with the brave at heart, even though he doesn't act that way; and Snape might have been drawn toward Voldemort but chose to work with Dumbledore and the ministry instead. We can see clearly how this ambiguity works in *Harry Potter and the Chamber of Secrets*, when, as a result of the Sorting Hat's decision, Harry comes to recognize that he is not inevitably either good or evil; he possesses the potential for both.

In an interesting way, the presence of Slytherin House at Hogwarts provides us with an opportunity to assess this situation in a slightly different way. Why is Slytherin given a home? Wouldn't the school be better off without such students? Answers to these initially puzzling questions might be forthcoming if we consider the house as *emblematic* of the nature of evil. In other words, we should see the house as a constant and consistent reminder that some people are prone to immoral behavior, at least some of the time. When we do, we come close to Rowling's understanding of what it means to live with evil. It cannot be entirely avoided, since it is a permanent part of the human condition. Slytherin has a home at Hogwarts not because it deserves one, but because the evil it represents cannot be entirely eradicated. The school would indeed be better off without the house, but in an important sense, the place cannot exist without it. Like evil, Slytherin must be endured, even if it must be fought as well. The house is emblematic of a particular kind of human predisposition, but its students' potential, like Snape's, is also symbolic of human adaptability in overcoming it.

The same tension between predisposition and adaptability can be seen in plot lines exploring other themes as well. When it comes to assessing the behavior of individuals according to gender, class, ethnic, or nationalistic stereotypes, those stereotypes, it turns out, don't prove to be very useful at all for predicting the actions of particular persons. In some cases, these generalizations appear to be completely groundless. In others, like the case of Slytherin, they may have a basis in the actual behavior of some group members, but those tendencies are contradicted by the actions of other individuals from the group. For example, centaurs tend to be aloof toward the affairs of others, but Firenze is not; house-elves tend to be meek in accepting their lot, but Dobby is not; and giants tend to be violent, but Hagrid is not.

Thus, readers should not easily equate characters' inherited traits with their destiny, even if they or other characters persist in seeing such a relationship. What is most remarkable about Rowling's understanding of the ambiguous tensions between predisposition and adaptability is that likable characters, as well as unlikable ones, frequently misunderstand the nature of the relationship. As numerous passages show, stereotypes abound, and everyone can fall prey to their debilitating effects. Rowling reminds her readers that prejudice is not only for bigots. The ethical implication is that there is a little bit of Slytherin in everyone.

Throughout Harry's adventures, Rowling presents a complex picture of the relationship between predisposition and adaptability. For the most part, they both exist in a kind of dialectic with one another, signaling both unchanging realities and the human potential for addressing them. If we find, at times, a strong case for "nature," we also find, at other times, a strong case for "nurture."

Fate versus Free Will

Rowling depicts the problem of ambiguity in a fourth way by placing Harry between the competing demands of fate and free will. In an important sense, each of the previous three ways that Rowling explores moral ambiguity can be related to this nexus. Harry lives under regulations that others establish, experiences debilitating emotional incidents that scar him both literally and metaphorically, and inherits particular traits that he did not choose. He is the victim of fate. Yet, he works under those regulations to the best of his abilities, brings his emotions under control, and makes use of his talents and skills to serve his understanding of what is right. He exercises his free will. This central tension between fate and free will subsumes all the others, since it encapsulates the inherent problem confronting individuals who experience things beyond their control but who desire to shape their own lives. Because Harry cannot foresee the outcome of events, he can only choose his own course of action.

For this reason, Harry's stories ultimately favor rule-breaking (in limited instances), reason, acquired adaptability, and free will. They emphasize active choice instead of passive acceptance. But, at the same time, they never wholly abandon the experiential certitude of rule-following (in most instances), emotion, inherited predisposition, and fate, since they unceasingly call attention to things that can't be controlled. To put it a bit differently, Rowling's works suggest that individuals make their own ways through the world, but only within inescapable constraints created by regulation, feelings, inborn traits, and contingency.

By placing this view of the world in a radically different context, we can see how it operates a bit more clearly. Assume that I want to be a professional basketball player. I can only play basketball if I understand the game. (I do.) I feel bad that I want to be well over six feet tall and able to dunk the ball, but I am not and can't. (Maybe I should get over it, since I can do nothing about it.) I am, as it turns out, a pretty good hockey player. (I know the game, I enjoy it, and my height isn't a disadvantage.) Despite my desire to be a professional basketball player, I realize how unlikely it is that I will become one and how I might potentially pursue another sport. In this thought experiment, we see how I can make my own way through the world, even though it presents me with many things I cannot change.

Ambiguity in Harry's stories works to convey the same essentially Stoic message. Through her representations of uncertainty and various ways to respond to it, Rowling tells her readers that while the world is imperfect, people need not surrender to its difficulties. After all, when it comes to living in this world, its challenges and opportunities give rise to the only game in town.

HARD QUESTIONS AND ADULT MENTORING

By presenting morality as a matter afflicted by ambiguity, Rowling asks hard questions of her readers. If we accept my claim, made earlier in this chapter, that Harry's *moral code* finds its root in his responses to frustration, we must also be cognizant that his *moral choices* emerge in response to serious problems, rather than mere disappointments. In an exceptionally perceptive review of the Harry Potter books in the *New Yorker*, Joan Acocella considers the nature of Harry's moral dilemmas and how Rowling puts them to use:

> She asks her pre-teen readers to face the hardest questions of life, and does not shy away from the possibility that the answers may be sad: that loss may be permanent, evil ever-present, good exhaustible.[15]

In *J. K. Rowling's Harry Potter Novels*, Philip Nel, an English professor at Kansas State University, likewise sees Rowling asking tough moral questions of her child readers. He also relates this practice to the insights of C. S. Lewis, who felt that stories written down to children were likely bad stories for them, as well as unappealing to adults. That is, such stories are marked by a morally naive refusal to take up big issues, which children do, in fact, find appealing. If Acocella and Nel are right about Harry's problems, and I clearly think they are, then his stories provide opportunities for children to sort through some very significant issues.[16]

This aspect of the stories, of course, raises an important question about *how* children should sort through Harry's problems. The stories themselves ambiguously seem to suggest two avenues, each taken at different times by the child characters depicted: they may choose to do things on their own, or they may seek guidance from adult characters. This state of affairs seems to mirror how most real children go about their lives. It should suggest to adult caretakers that complete control over the children in their lives is an impossibility, and unwise to attempt. This claim, of course, should not imply surrender, especially since Harry's stories do often make a virtue of adult mentoring and informed guidance.[17]

Again, the stories offer insights, if a bit mixed at times, into how children strike a balance between their own independence and their continuing dependence upon adults in so many ways. A number of commentators have sought to assess the role of adult characters and their relation to Harry's difficulties, both as the causes of and as answers to his concerns. They have reached conclusions somewhat at odds with one another. For example, Julia Eccleshare concedes that there is nothing patronizing or condescending in Rowling's stories, since they depict children *as children* working their way through problems; kids do not have to become temporary and miniature grown-ups to solve them. Nonetheless, she contends, the stories do present adults as ultimately wiser and more accomplished, as role-models worthy of emulation. In contrast, Alison Lurie sees things otherwise: "Though Rowling's child heroes are imperfect, they are usually smarter and braver than adults." She does concede that some adult characters play important roles as mentors but insists that their approaches tend to be hands-off, rather than intrusive.

Both Eccleshare and Lurie recognize the divergent avenues available to Rowling's child characters in meeting serious demands, but each chooses to place the emphasis on a different one—submitting to authority versus going it alone. Rowling's own stated intentions don't really clear things up, though they *seem* to support Lurie's views at first glance: "I was thinking of a place of great order, but immense danger, with children who had skills with which they could overwhelm their teachers." What, I think Eccleshare might respond, is the source of that "great order"? Perhaps we can square this circle by concluding that both Eccleshare and Lurie are right, as Rowling's own remarks, upon reflection, seem to suggest. Children are, after all, both dependent upon adults and increasingly independent of them as they find their own way in the world. The Harry Potter stories reflect this.[18]

We might be able to move a bit further out of this quandary if we take seriously Deborah De Rosa's understanding of Harry's independence. An English professor at Northern Illinois University, De Rosa notes that Harry's stories illustrate both the need for parental nurture and its fulfillment through adult surrogates. In De Rosa's reading, Rowling skews the traditional rite of initiation (leading from safety through danger to awareness), in order to emphasize the importance of psychological nurture to Harry's growth into an adult. Unlike the typical hero, he is nurtured *while simultaneously being tested*. Child readers, De Rosa continues, can thus follow obvious parallels with their own development into adolescents and young adults. Harry's need to be nurtured and its fulfillment do little to diminish his independence; rather they engender it.[19]

If we look to children's comments about Harry's stories, we can see this important dynamic between independence and nurture playing itself out in their reactions. In Sharon Moore's *We Love Harry Potter! We'll Tell You Why*, most of the children quoted can't get enough of Harry's adventures. They are mostly interested in his independence, imagining themselves in similar exciting circumstances, free to exercise their own choices and abilities. But a few voices speak to the longing that is in Harry's own heart: "I hope Harry's parents come back in the next book." In discussions of the books with librarians, the children of Appleton, Wisconsin, likewise emphasize the freedom of adventure, before circling back to the desire for security.[20]

Rowling's secret is to satisfy both types of children's cravings. They aspire to an unbridled independence, but they justifiably rely upon the comforts of a sheltered dependence. In the stories, we can be sure, Harry will find a way to triumph over adversity on his own, but he will do so in a context distinguished by his relationships to others. In this way, Rowling has found a way to express the apparently contradictory Stoic themes of self-reliance and empathy. Solutions to the serious problems confronting Harry require equal measures of both. He learns this lesson at Hogwarts, and so do children reading his adventures.

Although the ancient Stoics gave little thought to childhood development, they did pay a great deal of attention to the importance of education in their works. This emphasis stems from their cosmopolitanism, their egalitarian ethic, which insisted upon the dignity of reason in all people. Through education, they sought to foster the good in others. But teaching for the Stoics was a matter of inspiring independence, rather than a means of instilling doctrinaire prescriptions. As Martha Nussbaum tells us in *The Therapy of Desire*:

> Because *practical reason has intrinsic value*, Stoicism constructs a model of the teacher-pupil relationship that is strongly *symmetrical and anti-authoritarian* (italics in original).

Stoic teaching offered guidance but repudiated subservience. Seneca, for example, repeatedly cautioned those seeking his help that he was imperfect and toiling; others had to take charge of their own educations. Stoics did not promise perfection, but they did promise progress if their pupils were willing to work. Their pedagogy offered students a freedom commensurate with their abilities, rather than an image of self-worth dependent upon status, reputation, or fortune.[21]

In keeping with their emphasis upon individual freedom, the earliest Stoics often invoked a perfect (if also hypothetical) sage who was the model of wise behavior. Although, in time, they abandoned their pursuit of such perfection, preferring to speak instead of an "apprenticeship to wisdom" or "degrees of wisdom," *self-conscious* imitation of the sage remained an important aspect of their message. In the Harry

Potter books, we can see an *imperfect sage* (like Seneca) at work in the character of Albus Dumbledore. He guides Harry without forcing an orthodoxy upon him. Adult readers can find in Dumbledore a model for their own behavior as they lead the children in their lives toward higher degrees of wisdom and independence. Harry certainly sees him that way.[22]

CONSTANCY IN THE FACE OF EVIL, AND OTHER VIRTUES

Harry's own apprenticeship to wisdom begins when he sees through the illusions of reputation following his first encounter with other wizards and witches:

> "Everyone thinks I'm special," he said at last. "All those people in the Leaky Cauldron, Professor Quirrell, Mr. Ollivander . . . but I don't know anything about magic at all. How can they expect great things? I'm famous and I can't even remember what I'm famous for. . . ."
>
> "Don't you worry, Harry. You'll learn fast enough. Everyone starts at the beginning at Hogwarts, you'll be just fine. Just be yourself."[23]

Of course, he must learn other lessons as well, but already in this simple interchange, while Harry ruminates over things beyond his control, Hagrid reminds him to focus upon those things within his power. The outlandish, wild, hirsute, gentle giant speaks what could be a Stoic aphorism: "Just be yourself."

In her *Guide to the Harry Potter Novels*, Julia Eccleshare briefly calls attention to Harry's "fortitude and stoicism" but leaves the theme largely undeveloped. A few other reviewers call attention to Harry's stoical deportment, even if they do not use that precise term to describe it. For them, Harry's demeanor is simply a response to the perpetual problems that he must face. It's just one aspect of the stories that contributes to his heroism and his triumph over evil. In contrast, as I first stated in chapter 1, I see Harry's Stoicism in the face of adversity as the key to his morality.[24]

Throughout his adventures, Harry takes Hagrid's simple advice to heart and cultivates the virtues necessary to realizing it self-consciously. He accomplishes this feat in the face of extreme evil by remaining constant. He is persistently resolute in his affections, loyalties, and faithfulness to what is right and good. In his moral resolve, he is not simply "stoical"—placid and indifferent to danger and suffering; he is "Stoic"—active and committed to the genuine good, even if its attainment leads through peril. We can see why if we pay closer attention to several Stoic themes running throughout Rowling's series. Although I shall paint with very broad brushstrokes, I hope to give readers a good sense of Stoic views and how they are manifest in Harry's adventures.

Constancy and Fatalism

As we saw in my analysis of *The Sorcerer's Stone* and *The Chamber of Secrets* in chapter 2, a certain view of fatalism runs throughout Rowling's series. It is not wholly out of character with the ancient Stoics' understanding of the problem, derived from their conception of "nature." For them, nature is the unfolding of a providential design (fate or fortune) that shapes both events and human norms. The essence of this design is reason, which, according to the Stoics, is precisely what humans find within themselves through therapeutic self-examination. Nature thus places within humans the ability to live according to its plan, and thereby find fulfillment, through the exercise of reason. Seneca's depiction of human life as a combination of both fate and free will might clarify this view: "Good men toil, spend and are spent, and willingly; they are not dragged along by Fortune but follow her and keep in step. If they knew how, they would have outstripped her." Seneca's point is that even the best of us cannot hope to do better than understanding the nature of the realities confronting us and making our own desires conform to them. Epictetus suggests likewise when he states, "demand not that events should happen as you wish; but wish them to happen as they do happen, and you will go on well."

It is worth remembering that the Stoics are not counseling passivity. Rather, they recommend a particular kind of engagement with the world, an active and rational constancy through the cultivation of virtue that renders them indifferent to external concerns. Such concerns are the source of neither harm nor greatness. We can see this idea at work in a passage from Seneca's essay *On Constancy*:

> The wise man can lose nothing. He has everything invested in himself, he trusts nothing to fortune, and his own goods are secure, since he is content with virtue, which needs no gift from chance, and which, therefore, can neither be increased nor diminished. . . . Fortune can snatch away only what she herself has given.

Again, Epictetus makes a similar point in a somewhat skeptical description of the uses of divination to foretell the future (which is particularly appropriate to an examination of Harry Potter):

> First clearly understand that every event is indifferent and nothing to you, of whatever sort it may be; for it will be in your power to make a right use of it, and this no one can hinder. . . . Come to divination [when] no opportunities are afforded by reason or any other art to discover the matter in view.

Epictetus is suggesting that divination is simply one tool among many for assessing the future—and clearly the least important among them. More significant, however, is the implication that whatever the future may have in store, the individual who remains constant will meet it with confidence. Both Seneca and Epictetus counsel contentment with virtue and the need to adapt to maintain it. Boldness and audacity play no role in this scheme, because they have little relation to inner contentment.[25]

In the Harry Potter books, we see this theme in persistent reminders that Harry deals successfully with things beyond his power. Other than Voldemort's threat upon Harry's life, the most obvious example is Harry's acceptance of the Dursleys' cruelties. But he also learns, for example, that wands choose their wizards, that the Sorting

Hat will decide his fate at Hogwarts, that death cannot be denied, and that, as Hagrid points out, everything seems to happen *to* him regardless of his own actions. Of course, as a Stoic counterpoint, Hagrid, Dumbledore, and Sirius—his most important mentors—counsel Harry to remain constant and to have little concern for glory (which he sometimes entertains but always represses). They encourage him not to worry about things beyond his control, to accept adverse circumstances while adapting to them, and to realize that choices make people who they are.

Two particularly good examples of the tensions between fatalism and moral constancy can be seen in episodes involving Firenze the centaur and Professor Trelawney, the divination teacher. Centaurs, as a group, read the stars to see what is "foretold," and then meekly accept it, choosing not to get involved in others' affairs. But Firenze sets himself against evil "because the planets have been read wrongly before." Trelawney, in contrast, always misreads the signs in her efforts to foretell the future but does nothing about it. Both she and her subject are revealed as fraudulent, and the wisest characters ignore her predictions. She does manage to get it right once, but, tellingly, she does so unconsciously in a trance-state that she cannot later recall. (My own theory is that Trelawney is periodically "possessed," a circumstance that could serve as further warning of the dangers of divination.) These episodes pit active engagement against passivity and clearly suggest that the former is the best course of action—within reason. If one follows fate, one must not tempt it.

Harry, of course, consciously acts out his fate, like Seneca's "good men," in each of the central challenges put to him. He also prefers reason, like Epictetus, to "any other art" when assessing the nature of realities confronting him. In contrast, Harry's nemesis, Voldemort, tries to deny fate to his own loss and humiliation. His first words to Harry, "see what I have become," reveal the extreme depths of his folly. Harry's constancy, in contrast, is emblematic of his Stoic wisdom. Harry's heroism, thus inflected, is neither bold nor audacious.[26]

Endurance and Perseverance

To this point, my portrayals of the many disappointments and pitfalls confronting Harry should suggest to readers that his constancy coexists with at least two additional Stoic virtues. For if fate bestows both generosity and calamity, endurance and perseverance are necessary tonics for warding off the effects of adversity. Epictetus writes the prescription against disappointments in this manner:

> Remind yourself of what nature they are. . . . If you have a favorite cup, that it is but a cup . . . if it is broken, you can bear it; if you embrace your child or your wife, that you embrace a mortal—and, thus, if either of them dies, you can bear it.

This easy juxtaposition of cups and family members is pretty rough medicine, but it is intended to suggest that bearing loss is necessary rather than easy. Unfortunately, life provides many additional opportunities for disappointment, because vice is so pervasive in human affairs.

Stoics concede that there is enough evil in the world to justify a perpetual anger, but for this very reason, they will not allow vice in others to affect their own inner tranquility. Marcus Aurelius reminds us why when he writes, "it is madness to expect inferior men to do no wrong, for this is to desire the impossible." But he goes in a different direction in another passage, noting, "men are born for each other's sake. So either teach people or endure them." The Stoics thus counsel a kind of detachment from the world as a means of surviving its many disappointments, but they do so within the context of a cosmopolitan and egalitarian ethic. Anger will mislead, but endurance and perseverance will bring good counsel: patience in the fight against evil. For this reason, it is worth calling attention to Chrysippus's definitions of courage, which he relates to endurance and perseverance, rather than daring or bravado: it is "scientific knowledge of matters requiring persistence" or "a tenor of the soul fearlessly obedient to the supreme law [reason] in enduring and persisting."[27]

If we keep these ideas in mind, we can thus see the source of Harry's own courage in his acceptance of circumstances he did not choose. Among still other misfortunes, Harry survives life with the Dursleys, the loss of his parents, the animosity of Snape, serious injuries, the depravity of the dementors, competition in the Triwizard Tournament, Cedric's death, and Voldemort's promised threats upon his life. Most telling, Harry manages to thrive as an increasingly self-possessed individual despite such profound adversity. He endures and perseveres. Harry's particular form of heroism, as Chrysippus would see it, results from his conscious willingness to do so.

Self-Discipline and Reason

If we recall Harry's moral growth in *The Prisoner of Azkaban* and its consolidation in *The Goblet of Fire*, outlined in chapter 2, we can see how both are dependent upon Harry's increased self-awareness. This consciousness emerges, I would argue, because of the self-discipline and capacity for reason that comes with age, two virtues highly valued by the Stoics. Epictetus makes the point by way of analogy:

> Do not, like children, be now a philosopher, then a publican, then an orator, and then one of Caesar's officers. These things are not consistent. You must be one man, either good or bad. You must cultivate either your own reason or else externals; apply yourself to things within or without you—that is, be either a philosopher or one of the mob.

Stoics thus place a high value upon reason and a concomitant self-discipline, seeing them as essential to a successful life, and as essential to happiness.

In fact, as I argued earlier, the Stoics claim that nature gives humans the capacity to live according to its design through reason. As the great Roman orator Cicero reports, Chrysippus saw reason as godly: "For he says that divine power resides in reason and in the mind and intellect of universal nature." In order to be happy, it is incumbent upon humans to use reason to bring themselves into accord with nature's design. We can see this clearly in an outline of Stoic definitions of the purpose, or "end" of life provided by the fifth-century Greek anthologist, Stobaeus:

> Zeno represented the end as: "living in agreement." This is living in accordance with one concordant reason, since those who live in conflict are unhappy. . . . Cleanthes, his first successor, added "with nature," and represented it as follows: "the end is living in agreement with nature." Chrysippus wanted to make this clearer and expressed it thus: "living in accordance with experience of what happens by nature."

In other words, the Stoics see a universal reason at work in nature, the comprehension of which the exercise of practical reason makes possible. The result, they claim, is happiness.

Reason thus leads to knowledge of the most important things in life. Epictetus provides a concise explanation of the workings and benefits of practical reason in discussing the value of particular pleasures:

> If you are dazzled by the semblance of any promised pleasure, guard yourself against being bewildered by it; but let the affair wait your leisure, and procure yourself some delay. Then bring to your mind both points of time . . . [when you enjoy it and when you later reproach yourself] . . . and set before you, in opposition to these, how you will rejoice and applaud yourself if you abstain.

Epictetus is not implying pleasures are not worth pursuing; he is instead suggesting they be in accord with true happiness—with nature, with reason. In a moral treatise, Plutarch brings up the Stoics and makes the same point, by way of negative example:

> It is called irrational whenever an excessive impulse which has become strong and dominant carries it [the soul] off towards something wrong and contrary to the dictates of reason. For passion is vicious and uncontrolled reason which acquires vehemence and strength from bad and erroneous judgment.

When Seneca asks, "What is best in man?" he answers without hesitation, "Reason: with this he precedes the animals and follows the gods. . . . Perfect reason is called virtue and it is identical to rectitude."

Reason thus leads to true nobility. Directed outward, its exercise makes humans vigilant, discerning, and committed to the truth. Cultivated internally, it liberates the self and leads to a better understanding of personal capacities. This rational self-discipline makes philosophy a way of life.[28]

Harry embodies a true nobility because of his indifference to "externals" and through his "living in accordance with experience of what happens by nature." Both are made possible by higher levels of reason and self-discipline. Harry consistently maintains an active agency in the face of constraining circumstance, and he persistently chooses what is right over what is easy.

Rowling communicates the importance of reason and self-discipline in a number of ways throughout her series. The earliest palpable examples include sharp juxtapositions between Harry and Dudley Dursley. The latter's books go untouched and he is in possession of too many video games. Harry, in contrast, reads diligently each summer and engages in more worthwhile activities. Hermione's intellect and her willingness to use it also serve to emphasize the significance of rational engagement with the world. Throughout Harry's stories, in fact, central characters seek information, discuss their options, and assess the decisions they reach. They may not be philosophers, as Epictetus would have it, but they are not members of the unthinking mob either.

Numerous examples of this theme can be found throughout Rowling's books. Harry and Hermione, in particular, have a knack for seeing things that others can't. Lupin and Sirius consistently pursue the truth, even if they sometimes falter or arrive at insights late in the process. McGonagall teaches prudence and precision. And, as I pointed out earlier, Dumbledore embodies a life of learning, intellect, and discipline.

Much of Harry's growth consists of learning to avoid extremes. When he enters into a reckless rage, as he does several times in *The Prisoner of Azkaban*, he soon overcomes it. Free to wander Diagon Alley, in the same book, he exercises a lot of self-control. Feeling sorry for himself, he considers the plight of others. Made aware of his weaknesses, he cultivates—with the assistance of others—his prowess, daring, deduction, and ability to cope with danger to compete in the Triwizard Tournament. Most important, again and again, Harry sees himself as personally diminished when he realizes that he has done something wrong. A number of characters counsel him in the ways of prudence. Lupin calls attention, for Harry's benefit, to his own reckless and thoughtless actions as a youth. Cautioning awareness, Sirius encourages the careful accumulation and analysis of information. Even the false Moody teaches vigilance through harsh lessons to foster knowledge of what is at stake.

Of course, Dumbledore models reason and self-discipline most consistently of all. He counsels Harry to be prepared before the Mirror of Erised, reminds him to keep busy rather than brooding in times of uncertainty, and encourages not only curiosity but caution. At the end of *The Sorcerer's Stone*, Dumbledore speaks oracularly of truth as a beautiful but terrible thing, something that might be withheld but should not occasion lies. It is significant that Harry finds guidance in the headmaster's reactions to events. He soars upon being complimented for doing things properly and reflects upon his actions at the merest note of disappointment in the sage's voice. Before the final task in the Triwizard Tournament, Harry learns that Dumbledore has spent all year piecing together information related to Voldemort's return, even reading Muggle newspapers to correct a curious blindness among most in the wizarding community.

Harry learns the lessons of rationality and self-control. This ability is signaled subtly near the end of *The Goblet of Fire*, when Harry considers the aftermath of the previous evening's horrible events along with Ron and Hermione:

> He felt as though all three of them had reached an understanding they didn't need to put into words; that each was waiting for some sign, some word, of what was going on outside Hogwarts—and that it was useless to speculate about what might be coming until they knew anything for certain.[29]

The moral is clearly that any action taken out of ignorance is unwise. Sensing future dangers, in good Stoic fashion, Harry, Ron, and Hermione take stock of themselves and the situation confronting them.

Empathy, Solidarity, and Sacrifice

One of the chief hallmarks of the Harry Potter books is Harry's activity on behalf of others. This may seem strange given the Stoics' emphasis upon indifference to events in the world, but their conception of individual autonomy never implies surrendering to evil. It implies exactly the opposite. In light of this fact, self-sufficiency is always balanced by a strong commitment to others through the virtues of empathy, solidarity, and sacrifice. Stoic ethics, as I pointed out earlier, are cosmopolitan and egalitarian.

Stoic treatments of empathy take many forms, but we can quickly assess their implications in the writings of Hierocles, a Stoic philosopher active around the year 100 C.E. For this reason, his views are worth quoting at length:

> Each one of us is as it were entirely encompassed by many circles, some smaller others larger, the latter enclosing the former on the basis of their different and unequal dispositions relative to each other. The first and closest circle is the one which a person has drawn as though around a center, his own mind. For it is virtually the smallest circle, and almost touches the center itself. Next [extending outward, come circles including] . . . parents, siblings, wife, and children . . . uncles and aunts, grandparents, nephews, nieces, and cousins . . . other relatives . . . local residents . . . fellow-tribesmen . . . fellow-citizens . . . people from neighboring towns . . . fellow-countrymen. The outermost and largest circle, which encompasses all the rest, is that of the whole human race. . . . It is incumbent upon us to respect people from the third circle as if they were those from the second, and again to respect our other relatives as if they were from the third circle. . . . The right point will be reached if, through our own initiative, we reduce the distance of the relationship with each person.

Hierocles, thus, gives much fuller form to Marcus Aurelius's claim that "we were born for each other's sake."

In practice, such Stoic empathy seeks to recognize the human dignity in every person. The implication is that, if individuals are responsible for and to themselves in their cultivation of virtue, they must also recognize this potential in others. Reason demands, therefore, that their own safety is of no greater value than the safety of others. We thus find at least some Stoics espousing a politics of mercy and gradualism. It is appropriate to judge the actions of others when human dignity is threatened, but mercy ought to be shown in the administration of punishments. Stoics thus recognize the virtuous potential in reacting to tyranny, but their goals are always limited to the cultivation of human potential. Their politics are thus built, like their educational ideals, upon the universal value of human dignity and a belief in its preservation through self-government. Indifferent, as individuals, to worldly distinctions, Stoics espouse a similar politics that is antisectarian and antinationalist. It implies universal citizenship.

As I described in chapter 1, this view of human solidarity is dependent upon an empathetic imagination that replaces the emotional intensity of compassion—which can lead to cruelty as well as kindness—with a more powerful (at least according to the Stoics) rational recognition of radical human equality. Thus, pity and sympathy, as forms of compassion, become suspect, but empathy and mercy—arrived at through reason—can lead to a similar imaginative extension of the self, while skirting the inherent dangers associated with impulsive, emotional responses.

This empathetic imagination, therefore, can lead to an incredible willingness among some Stoics to sacrifice themselves in the name of reason. (Lest anyone believe that these are mere words, we must remember that Seneca followed the example of his hero Socrates in state-prompted suicide, when his former pupil, the Roman Emperor Nero, demanded his death.) Note how Epictetus formulates the problem:

When, therefore, it is our duty to share the danger of a friend or of our country, we ought not to consult the oracle as to whether we shall share it with them or not. For though the diviner should forewarn you that the auspices are unfavorable, this means no more than that either death or mutilation or exile is portended. But we have reason with us; and it directs us, even with these hazards, to stand by our friend and our country.

Only death or mutilation or exile? Since within the Stoic scheme of things, life is ultimately less important than virtue, in some instances, self-destruction becomes the necessary means of self-preservation. Remember, however, Stoics never encourage rash behavior of any sort, let alone the taking of one's own life. Only a proper assessment of circumstance occasions self-sacrifice.[30]

It is difficult to read the Harry Potter books without noticing the emphasis they place upon the virtues of empathy, solidarity, and sacrifice. Although Harry often enough finds himself in danger without pursuing it on his own, in both *The Sorcerer's Stone* and *The Chamber of Secrets*, he consciously chooses to put his own life at risk on behalf of others. In *The Prisoner of Azkaban* and *The Goblet of Fire*, Harry finds himself in difficult circumstances and, yet, willingly assumes greater risks in order to correct an injustice and to show mercy on the survivors of a murder victim. Harry's empathy, the imaginative extension of himself, provides the justification.

A particularly good illustration of the importance of empathy, solidarity, and sacrifice is found in *The Prisoner of Azkaban*, because, within it, we find the motivation that implicitly underlies so much selfless behavior in Harry's stories: the protection of innocent life. I have in mind an exchange between Sirius Black and Peter Pettigrew:

"Sirius, Sirius, what could I have done? The Dark Lord . . . you have no idea . . . he has weapons you can't imagine. . . . I was scared, Sirius, I was never brave like you and Remus and James. I never meant it to happen. . . . He-Who-Must-Not-Be-Named forced me—"

. . . "He—he was taking over everywhere!" gasped Pettigrew. Wh— what was there to be gained by refusing him?"

> "What was there to be gained by fighting the most evil wizard who has ever existed?" said Black, with a terrible fury in his face. "Only innocent lives, Peter!"
>
> "You don't understand!" whined Pettigrew. "He would have killed me, Sirius."
>
> "THEN YOU SHOULD HAVE DIED!" roared Black. "DIED RATHER THAN BETRAY YOUR FRIENDS, AS WE WOULD HAVE DONE FOR YOU!"[31]

In this short, yet poignant, passage we encounter the empathy so necessary to acting on behalf of others. Despite his less-than-Stoic rage, Sirius imagines the effects of evil and subordinates his own sense of self to them. Perceiving a larger threat, he determines that his own safety is irrelevant. In contrast, Pettigrew displays his incapacity to imagine the suffering of others. Fearing for his life, Pettigrew expressly indicates that he is incapable of extending himself beyond his own skin. From this illustration emerges a number of themes: circumstances beyond an individual's control must be met with resolve; they provide no justification for acting immorally; evil must be resisted regardless of cost; and death is preferable to treachery or submission.

Needless to say, many additional episodes illustrate self-denial. Whether we consider Ron's sacrifice in defense of the Sorcerer's Stone, Sirius's continuing loyalty to Harry, or Cedric's sense of fairness, we see that an empathetic connection to others motivates moral behavior. What makes such episodes in Harry Potter so striking is that they seldom result from emotional sentimentality. Reasoned assessments of what is right usually prompt them, even if sympathy or compassion sometimes plays a role. Harry always acts out of solidarity rather than a sense of obligation; other characters do as well. This is important because obligation can imply a relationship between persons who are unequal in status. Solidarity, in contrast, carries no such connotation. It is therefore important to note that Harry never condescends even when he works on Dobby's behalf, regrets the relative poverty of the Weasleys, consoles Hagrid, or rescues Fleur's sister from the merpeople during the second task of the Triwizard Tournament. Even if we do not consider the overt attention paid to prejudice and bigotry in Harry's stories, we can see that their hero always displays an egalitarian ethic. Given Dumbledore's antisectarian challenge to the assembled students of Hogwarts at the end of *The Goblet of Fire*, it seems a safe bet to assume we'll see more of the same in the future.

To conclude my discussion of Stoic virtues, I want to emphasize a point that I made right at the start of this work: J. K. Rowling develops an *updated* Stoic moral system. If readers turn to some of the Stoic texts mentioned in my analysis, they will encounter some things that won't easily find a home in Harry's adventures. In fact, what Martha Nussbaum has labeled "normative" Stoicism is quite at odds, at times, with much of Rowling's imaginative world. Some problems may already have occurred to readers on the basis of my own descriptions of Stoic virtues. In Harry Potter, we do not explicitly find nature unfolding its providential design in accordance with natural law. We also do not find reason overtly identified as nature's essence. Likewise, we do not encounter characters seeking to extirpate their emotions completely. And we do not encounter the view that any virtue encompasses all virtues or that any vice encompasses all vices. So what's up? In brief, I have attempted in this chapter to illustrate Stoic tendencies in Rowling's fiction, rather than arguing in favor of her works' absolute conformity to normative Stoicism. In point of fact, Rowling offers her young readers something much better. She offers them access to important Stoic ideas in an easily comprehensible format.

GROWING UP, GROWING PAINS

In *Cultivating Humanity: A Classical Defense of Reform in Liberal Education*, Martha Nussbaum puts the Stoics to use as part of a larger argument about the direction of college education in the United States. She briefly outlines some of their ideas about fostering autonomy and links their cosmopolitanism to an increasingly global world. In *Upheavals of Thought*, she focuses upon their ideas as they relate to emotions, developing a "contemporary neo-Stoic view," which might help us come to a better understanding of how to apply "the intelligence of emotions" within political communities. In these works, as well as still others, Nussbaum makes clear that the Stoics have plenty to teach us some twenty-three hundred years after Zeno began to lecture from the painted porch of the Athenian Agora.[32]

If only coincidentally, Harry Potter tells us the same thing. If we could extract a central moral from Rowling's series it might be that life presents us with both opportunities and disappointments and that it is up to each of us as individuals to make of them what we will. As I hope I have made clear, this moral is not so divorced from the ideas of the Stoics. It is also one that children might do well to learn. For growing up does entail growing pains, especially for children in their teens. At no other stage in life are individuals presented with both possibilities and discontents in such large measure. And, yet, it is at precisely this stage of life that society begins to demand higher degrees of moral responsibility from them. Harry learns lessons about ethical accountability, and so, too, can the children reading his adventures.

In general terms, fantasy literature offers children some important opportunities to sort through difficult moral questions in a relatively safe and secure context. Although fantasy has received relatively little attention in the field of developmental psychology, in their review of the topic, Deborah J. Taub and Heather L. Servaty, both professors of education at Purdue University, suggest that some findings to date are encouraging. By age three, most children can distinguish clearly between fantasy and reality. Things become a bit more ambiguous when it comes to "magical thinking" in three-, four-, and five-year-olds, who still often persist in believing that imagining something can make it happen. Nonetheless, this type of thinking tends to shift with context, so that some situations are more likely to produce it than others. Regardless, Taub and Servaty tell us, no evidence suggests that reading the Harry Potter series interferes with older children's abilities to distinguish fantasy from reality, even though the settings of the books encourage play with the boundary between the two. In fact, some researchers suggest, fantastical thinking has many beneficial effects. Real issues can be addressed in the context of play, which offers opportunities for the exploration of serious questions. It has even been argued that "scary" books can help children control irrational fears, and that realistic portrayals of death and grieving can help them understand death prior to any real-life experiences of it. In light of these findings, it seems likely that older children's exposure to Harry's adventures, especially when accompanied by adult guidance, can help foster intelligent responses to real-life moral questions.[33]

We might get a better sense of what children take from their encounters with Harry Potter if we take some time to assess how they think about moral problems. In publications dating from the 1970s and early 1980s, Lawrence Kohlberg presented a developmental model of moral progress during childhood. Even though his model has been criticized in recent years as too rigid and too indifferent to the contexts of moral reasoning, it still serves as a useful outline of the different types of moral reasoning available to children. It offers a scheme of moral maturation occurring through three levels of progress, each consisting of two stages displaying slightly different types of moral reasoning:

I.   Preconventional Morality
    1.   Punishment and Obedience
    2.   Instrumental Exchange

II.   Conventional Morality
    3.   Interpersonal Conformity
    4.   Social System and Conscience Maintenance

III.   Postconventinal Morality
    5.   Prior Rights and Social Contract
    6.   Universal Ethical Principles

Kohlberg saw each level as relatively discrete. With the exception of level one, which he saw as largely instinctual, each subsequent level followed upon the previous one with growing intellectual capacity. He found little evidence of backtracking or inconsistency (a view that critics have attacked), linked moral progress to an increased emphasis upon abstract principles (a notion also questioned by others), and concluded that most children reach the conventional level by age nine; some adults remain at this level.[34]

What kinds of reasoning take place at each level? The preconventional level involves moral reasoning among the youngest children and focuses upon the avoidance of negative consequences and the pursuit of rewards. Reasoning at stage one (Punishment and Obedience) amounts to a "might makes right" approach to the world, but since children have little might with which to enforce their wills, they behave out of the fear of punishment. Stage two (Instrumental Exchange), in contrast, is a bit more advanced, since it involves reasoning dependent upon expectations of cooperative engagement. It can easily be equated with the adage, "you scratch my back; I'll scratch yours." By age nine or ten moral reasoning at the conventional level goes further still and results in actions corresponding to the expectations of others. It leads to the internalization of societal expectations. Stage three (Interpersonal Conformity) amounts in essence to the "golden rule"—the idea that one should act toward others as one would hope others would behave toward oneself. The internalization of expectations at stage four (Social System and Conscience Maintenance) corresponds roughly to the formation of the "superego" as described in the work of Sigmund Freud, a conscious check upon individual appetites and desires. For some older children and adolescents between the ages of thirteen and sixteen reasoning at level three involves both a better sense of moral ambiguity and a greater desire to appeal to universal ethical principles. At stage five (Prior Rights and Social Contract), rules may be broken if higher moral principles are at stake. It represents morality not as it is taught, but as it is discovered and crafted by individuals who recognize competing claims to what is right. It acknowledges the utilitarian dimension of regulations, which exist for mutual benefit and by common agreement. Moral reasoning at stage six (Universal Ethical Principles) usually invokes the principle of a still higher, absolute law completely beyond human convention. Unfortunately, Kohlberg provided few useful examples of stage-six reasoning (leaving his critics somewhat befuddled) and stated that few individuals other than charismatic leaders are capable of justifying rule-breaking in observance of universal and inviolable ethical principles. Stage six strikes me as simply a more strident, but less convincing, version of stage five. Like most developmental psychologists, we can safely ignore it since it is never found in children.[35]

Another key component of Kohlberg's developmental model of moral progress is his understanding of how moral improvement is generated in children and adolescents. He outlined three basic forms, with each method positioned along a spectrum extending from engagement to observation. First, children must experience directly the cognitive friction of moral conflict, what psychologists have called "cognitive disequilibrium." In other words, they must be able to assess competing claims to moral solutions in light of the real-world problems confronting them and others in their lives, such as the conflicting demands of loyalty to friends or family and following the rules. Further, they need to discuss proposed solutions to such problems. Second, imaginative role-playing can produce the same results, since it provides children with opportunities to adopt different perspectives and to try out different solutions within the secure context of play. Third, experience within a community that actively pursues just solutions to problems can lead to more rapid moral development. In this case, members of the community model acceptable moral behavior and communicate ethical values to children in the process. It is, of course, not surprising to learn that "because I said so," doesn't prompt moral improvement.[36]

Both Lana A. Whited and M. Katherine Grimes, English professors at Ferrum College, have related Kohlberg's model to moral decision-making in the Harry Potter books. They establish the significance of his ideas by linking them to the moral ambiguity most children experience as they move toward adulthood:

Kohlberg believed that children between the ages of ten and eighteen progress through more moral stages than people at any other age because they are beginning to test their independence and have developed more formal reasoning abilities. For them, a black-and-white world is replaced by varying shades of gray.[37]

In applying Kohlberg's model, Whited and Grimes do find moral progress on display and conclude that young readers can take much of value from Harry Potter. They will come to recognize the workings of bullying, power, and oppression, along with the "moral retardation" of certain unlikable characters—all indicative of preconventional moral reasoning. In a more positive vein, they will see important friendships being formed and kindnesses being displayed. Within Kohlberg's model, such actions represent attempts to make society function smoothly through loyalty, sensitivity, and respect—all virtues pointing toward the conventional level of moral reasoning. But Harry's adventures offer more to children, as well, through depictions of postconventional decision-making. The stories feature both ethical reversals (when bad becomes good and vice versa) and positive portrayals of moral education and improvement. Most important, they provide numerous opportunities to provoke children's moral development in all three ways described by Kohlberg.[38]

Despite the real strengths of Kohlberg's model, we should hesitate before accepting it in its entirety. A number of developmental psychologists question its formal and highly abstract character. In particular, the model offers too little opportunity for the consideration of context in understanding how children make moral decisions. Children do not move through moral development as they would an assembly line; they pick and they choose in ways that reflect not only particular situations, but their own cultural experiences as well.

This problem is made clear in psychologist Robert E. Grinder's early critique of the model. He questions just how discrete and incremental each stage of development actually is. His own studies show that regression is common and that individuals are quite capable of reasoning in multiple ways, particularly in certain contexts. Periods of transition, stress, and peer pressure may all play roles in moral decision-making.[39]

A much broader but related critique is offered by the eminent Harvard University psychologist Carol Gilligan, who questions the wisdom of granting too much weight to an abstract "ethic of justice" at the expense of a more concrete "ethic of care." (Kohlberg coined these phrases in sorting through his differences with Gilligan, a former student.) She suggests that two different moral orientations are possible, one that emphasizes justice and rights and another that emphasizes care and response. Granting priority to the former, as Kohlberg does in stages three and four, diminishes the importance of gender distinctions in moral reasoning, since boys are more likely to associate their views with justice, while girls are more likely to speak in terms of care. Likewise, Kohlberg's model emphasizes independence and downplays cooperation as a moral value. Gilligan suggests that understandings of adolescent development should take into account "interdependence" and not just "individuation"—that is, independence.[40]

Gilligan's insights have been applied with an eye on other variables as well. Dartmouth education professor Andrew Garrod and University of Massachusetts psychologist Carole R. Beal show that, although a number of studies challenge the gender implications of Gilligan's argument, numerous studies support her contention regarding an ethic of care and the importance it places upon cooperation. In their own analyses, they find that different class or cultural contexts could affect children's responses to moral problems posed to them in fables. In other words, children will offer solutions consistent with their real-life experiences. The Brandeis University expert in education, Joseph Reimer, likewise questions Kohlberg's model from class and cultural perspectives, suggesting that context is far more important to moral reasoning than he allows.[41]

Kohlberg's critics add an interpretive richness to a developmental theory whose origins date back some forty years or so. As Harry's adventures themselves illustrate, individual characters are quite capable of different kinds of decision-making at different points in the stories. As in real life, context does matter. If we spot some inconsistencies in their actions, we should not be surprised. The same, of course, holds true for the real children in our lives. Still, Kohlberg's critics do not really challenge the kinds of moral reasoning that he describes (except for level three, stage six "Universal ethical principles"); rather, they rightly question, to some degree, the values he attaches to abstract moral principles at the conventional level. Following Whited and Grimes, I still believe that Kohlberg's model offers adults important information about the types of moral reasoning children adopt and adapt in making sense of the world. I'm also convinced that Harry's stories will help them with that task.

Most significant to my analysis of the Stoic moral system on display in the Harry Potter books is the tension between rule-following and rule-breaking typical of level-three, stage-five moral reasoning. We see plenty of examples of level-one reasoning, which usually results in behavior the Stoics would find unappealing, regardless of whether it produces moral or immoral actions. They would not, however, be surprised by it and would find it typical of children's inconstancy in response to the world. Level-two reasoning, in contrast, would appeal to them because of its dependence upon an egalitarian ethic and the imaginative extension of the self that grants dignity to the reason inherent (though often unrealized) in all people. They would encourage bright children to reason in this fashion. Ultimately, however, they would seek most to encourage stage-five reasoning. Here, we must recall the Stoics' gradual shift away from the pursuit of perfection in human affairs to their more practical emphasis upon progressing through various degrees of wisdom. Later Stoics, while still speaking perhaps in terms of universal reason, would see within stage-five reasoning the practical limits of the more idealized, but ultimately impossible, stage-six invocation of universal and inviolable ethical principles.

For these reasons, the Stoics (who were often lovers of paradox) would applaud Rowling's portrayal of the necessity of prioritizing rules and ethical principles in particular contexts. They would recognize a kindred spirit in Professor Dumbledore, who, like themselves, is always more interested in the "why" of ethical decisions than in the mere application of rules. They would also be content with Rowling's depictions of multiple and competing forms of moral reasoning in Harry's adventures and the opportunities they provide for genuine moral engagement and autonomous learning. These complexities ensure that her fiction resembles the "real world" of uncertainties, ambiguities, and disappointments. Finally, they would certainly find value in Rowling's depictions of a community characterized by the pursuit of justice, however imperfect it is.

In conclusion, I want to make one final observation about the Stoics. Although they have some very clear ideals, they make no secret of the fact that living up to them is extremely difficult. With that thought in mind, I'm going to give J. K. Rowling the last word in this chapter on Harry's morality and Stoic virtue:

> What's very important to me is when Dumbledore says that you have to choose between what is right and what is easy. This is the setup for the next three books. All of them are going to have to choose, because what is easy is often not right.[42]

4

Greed, Conventionality, Demonic Threat

You should trust the children; they can stand more than we can.
—P. L. Travers, author of *Mary Poppins*

KIDS AMONG THE CRITICS

The Harry Potter books please children. In chapter 1, I addressed some of the reasons why kids find the books so engaging and worthwhile. The question is now why some adults harbor reservations or fears regarding children's interest in the stories. Although criticisms of the books take many forms, they do tend to share a view of children as largely passive recipients of meaning and tend, more or less, to ignore evidence that suggests otherwise. Despite many claims that the books are immoral or present questionable values, chil-

dren themselves rarely take this view upon reading the stories and often emphasize the goodness of likable characters. Adults are in a good position to help them better understand why.

Let me begin with a brief history of critical reaction to the books. In the United Kingdom in 1997, early reviews of *Harry Potter and the Philosopher's Stone* were overwhelmingly positive. The same was true of the book's reception in the United States, where it was published as *Harry Potter and the Sorcerer's Stone* in 1998. It was only later that doubts began to creep into some otherwise positive reviews, when the arrival of the second book in the series, *Harry Potter and the Chamber of Secrets*, turned into a genuine cultural sensation. Due probably to suspicions of the books' growing popularity or their own heightened expectations, some critics began to suggest that the books were too formulaic or lacked the artistic or philosophical depth of other well-known (and well-loved) children's books. With the publication of *Harry Potter and the Prisoner of Azkaban*, debate about all three reached a more fevered pitch, as both social critics and religious critics found much to distrust in the series.

In *J. K. Rowling's Harry Potter Novels*, Philip Nel provides an assessment of the situation and that time. He notes that most reviewers still found much to praise and heralded the continuing series as a major contribution to children's literature. But, in contrast, a pulsing few gave voice to a suspicious distrust of popular culture and its sustaining ideology, the conviction that any story about witches is dangerous to Christian values, or an elite literary snobbery that finds little of value in anything written primarily for children, excepting a few "classics." This outline pretty much reflects, as well, the critical reception of Rowling's fourth book, *Harry Potter and the Goblet of Fire*.[1]

Shortly after the publication of this fourth book in the series, however, analysis by academic experts began to appear, and several authors writing from a variety of perspectives brought out book-length studies. While many critics readily concede that the books are imaginative, clever, and exciting, many also conclude, if only implicitly, that kids are being drawn to some things that are not right or proper. I'm largely uninterested in literary snobbery, given my concern with the moral system of Rowling's series, and I'll not pay much attention to critics guilty of it. Instead, throughout most of this chapter, I'll focus my attention on the social and religious critics, explaining their views and offering my own reactions. Although their complaints take many different forms, they tend to fall within three loose categories, which will shape my own analysis below. In brief, social critics ruminate over children's exposure to the books' (1) apparent contributions to commodity consumption within a capitalist framework or (2) ostensibly positive portrayals of conservative political values and oppressive cultural conventions, while religious critics, in contrast, worry about (3) depictions of an allegedly demonic witchcraft and relativistic morality.

In general terms, the social and religious critics of Harry Potter see children as mostly passive. Accordingly, kids absorb values through their contact with images and narratives that give shape to the author's version of how it is and how the world ought to be. They fall victim to the "allure" of what the stories put on display. These stories tempt, entice, glamorize, and fascinate, according to the critics, in much the same way magicians and witches were believed to do in earlier centuries. For secular-minded critics, this magical allure is, of course, metaphorical, but for fundamentalist religious critics, it is something quite real—no less than the seductions of the devil. And, yet, the stories, for all their attractive powers, ultimately provide little that is worthwhile and obscure a deficiency or deformity at their core, just like the works of magicians and witches of old. Or so the critics would have us believe.

I have good reason to doubt this is the case. In early December 2002, I had the opportunity to participate in a forum on morality in the Harry Potter books that took place at the Parkside campus of the University of Wisconsin. Speakers included a selection of adults offering different perspectives and Zach Tutlewski, a regular kid who had begun reading the books a few years ago when he was a second-grader. He certainly loved Harry's adventures, and admitted that they had influenced him, but he was especially thoughtful when he began to explain why. He noted how the books had become a family affair, as first his mother then his father joined him in reading and discussing them. He outlined further how the stories had encouraged him to read more books, including more demanding ones, to join a book club at his local public library, and to begin writing books of his own.

I'm more than willing to concede that Zach probably would have become an avid and thoughtful reader had J. K. Rowling never imagined Harry Potter. He's clearly a bright kid with supportive parents. But none of this changes how he chose to engage the books themselves through his own active imagination. In other words, Harry had worked no magic upon Zach beyond the ordinary kind that creates opportunities for a loving family to come together and for a thoughtful kid to exercise his own creativity. Maybe there is one other kind of magic in the books, as Zach himself suggested, the kind that encourages kids to become "good, brave, loyal, moral, loving, kind, smart, hard-working, creative, nice, and patient." If this is the allure of Harry Potter, so much the better.[2]

Again, I'll concede that not all children have as fulfilling an encounter with Harry, but I would hazard to guess that many (and probably most) of them do. If children reading the books grow up to become greedy consumers, intolerant chauvinists, or dabblers in malevolent witchcraft, they will not do so because of what they read in Harry's adventures. Sure enough, in those stories, they encounter realistic depictions of materialism and social inequities, along with an attractive portrayal of witchcraft, but they also come upon numerous episodes that question excessive consumerism and inequality or make vibrantly clear the fanciful nature of the magic on display. Rowling's literary creation asks children to assess, rather than accept, what they see on display, even if it usually does so in a gentle, fun-loving fashion.

Too many critics of her work seem to undervalue children's abilities to make these assessments—to choose right from wrong, to balance competing desires, to recognize the moral dimension of the tales. As one adolescent has noted, "I think the books are good. They make me think about people and what makes them act the way they do." If children's comments on Harry's stories serve as a guide to their reactions, we can readily see in them evidence of genuine thought rather than mere submission.[3]

A recent surge of scholarly analysis has emphasized this point in relation to the Harry Potter phenomenon. Rowling has sparked not only an imaginative engagement with her hero, but his stories are leading to ever larger creative efforts on the part of many readers regardless of age. According to Rebecca Sutherland Borah:

> From Internet web pages to classrooms to reading circles to corporate-sponsored chat sessions, her readers share their experiences by discussing plots, writing fan fiction, throwing theme parties, devising games, asking and answering questions, passing rumors, and creating artwork.

While I have little doubt that most of these activities are celebratory, rather than focused upon moral issues, they nonetheless sustain the notion that Rowling's readers actively engage her art and are anything but passive recipients.[4]

Certainly it is right to see readers as influenced by what they read, but it is a serious mistake to view them as having no or little control over the nature of that influence. Readers always bring to what they read particular sets of assumptions, values, and experiences, which shape the ways they engage the texts before them. They enter into a kind of dialogue with what is being said, and they respond to it in very real ways, even if they cannot change the words written on the page. In a sense, a multitude and variety of readers make impossible any single "correct" way to read a story. Despite the reality of shared values and shared ways of viewing the world within a given work's audience, there will always be readers whose own particular views have the potential to interrupt not only common understandings of the work, but the author's intentions as well. The fancy term for what I am describing is "reader response theory" but its central idea is a simple one: stories cannot be read in "the right way," because individual responses to them come from a variety of perspectives. No work, in light of this realization, can remain "stable," a single thing conveying a single meaning.[5]

I raise these issues to emphasize three important points, which I hope readers will keep in mind. (Note, however, that I cannot force this ability upon them.) First, as I hope I have shown, child readers of the Harry Potter books are able to shape what influences they take from their reading. They may not be as discerning as adult readers but they are not as passive as is often presumed. Second, as we shall see in the rest of this chapter, adult critics of the books are no less the product of their own assumptions, values, and experiences than are all readers, children or adults. And this situation is as it should be. Their concerns rightly shape their understandings of the stories in question and prompt them to offer their views to others. Third and finally, we should *expect* to see disagreement among the readers of Harry Potter, even if we see large areas of agreement among them much of the time. Differences of opinion not only make our lives more interesting, even if they make living more difficult, they also constitute a permanent part of our cultural landscape. They will not go away any time soon. What a dreary world we would inhabit if everyone thought the same.

None of this is intended to imply a loose relativism, be it moral or otherwise, or that we must give all opinions an equal hearing. Some opinions are better than others because they are more thoughtful (or more humane), but ultimately different opinions are significant because they reflect dissimilar values. It is for this reason that people bother to express their ideas and to defend them. That these ideas might be contingent upon a set of beliefs that others might not share is the most significant point of all.

The most vociferous critics of Harry Potter mount their attacks because of such foundational beliefs, whether political or religious in nature. In other words, they question the propriety of Harry's adventures according to their own assumptions about how the world is and how it ought to be. We can see most clearly how this process works when we look at various critical assessments of J. K. Rowling's imagination. As I pointed out in chapter 1, the complaints made against Harry's world stem from seeing it as either not imaginative enough or as too imaginative. These incompatible understandings arise from highly divergent assumptions.

How then do these assumptions translate into critical commentary that finds fault with Rowling's imagination? Let me show you. Those critics who fault her for not making Harry a social revolutionary *do not find enough* in the works to challenge contemporary standards and institutions. Accordingly, life is too ordinary: characters shop too much, live within nuclear families, expect boys to be one way and girls another, find no fault with the elitist culture of boarding school, and are too accepting of class and racial disparities. They are too "suburban." The world they inhabit offers no glimpse of an alternative, and more progressive, future. What's the use of fantasy, I can hear the social critics saying, if it simply recreates what needs fixing in the real world? In contrast, those critics who fault Rowling for not making Harry a model of religious piety *find far too much* in the works to challenge contemporary standards and institutions. Accordingly, life is too extraordinary: characters recite spells, invoke invisible powers, bend the rules or lie, ignore authority figures, and rely upon their own notions of good and evil. They are too "enchanting." The world they inhabit offers no glimpse of God or a divinely sanctioned moral order. What's the use of storytelling, I can hear the religious critics saying, if it fails to teach enduring, universal truths about the nature of God and religious faith?

In answer to these questions, J. K. Rowling offers a vision of personal morality that is not dependent upon either political or religious commitments. In Harry's world, morality stands apart as a constant obligation toward others to be worked on and maintained, rather than as a fixed orthodoxy (secular or religious) to be accepted and followed. Nevertheless, this morality can easily translate into political action, on the one hand, and it can easily open itself to the spiritual values of a profound faith, on the other. A number of critics fault Rowling for deciding to present morality in this fashion, seeing it as mere relativism. And given their ideological commitments, this fact should not surprise us.

It is my contention that the nature of the morality on display in Rowling's books is ultimately *personal* rather than *political* or *religious*. That is, the moral system is directed toward the cultivation of the individual instead of sweeping political change or charismatic religious affirmation. It is hardly relativistic but it is not doctrinaire either. Rowling (and her characters) recognize that these two options present us with a false choice. Persons following either path too strictly ("anything goes" versus "obey the rules") will soon find themselves in circumstances far worse than those who recognize the wisdom behind both flexibility and rule-following—the wisdom of understanding how to apply principles in particular contexts.

If readers assess Rowling's works with an eye on political values, they will certainly find social problems addressed, but not in ways overtly related to liberal or conservative ideologies. Her own politics might fairly be described as left-liberal, given her comments on single-motherhood or the welfare state, and in light of her activities on behalf of Comic Relief (a British charity devoted to fostering the welfare of children around the world), but there is nothing inherently leftist about the way social problems are raised in her Harry Potter series. Many conservatives, too, object strongly to problems such as inequality, prejudice, and bigotry, even if the means they envision for eliminating them are not the same means found within a progressive liberalism.

This general assessment largely holds true for Rowling's treatment of religion, as well, even if it is on display less often than social issues, or not at all. She has identified herself as a Christian and a member of the Church of Scotland, but readers will look in vain for doctrinaire pronouncements or a missionary sentiment. Still, as many commentators have pointed out, the morality she displays in the books is consistent with Christianity, as well as other creeds, even if it is not represented as expressly so. Again, her morality focuses upon the cultivation of virtue within the individual, the simple things that can coexist quite easily with a variety of political commitments or religious beliefs.[6]

Rowling's decision to focus on personal morality thus provides adult readers opportunities to shape their children's development as politically and religiously sensitive people. Parents can discuss how personal morality should inform political action and how it coexists with religious values. And the openness of Harry Potter on these topics allows parents even greater control over these potentially controversial spheres of life. For this reason, critical opinions can have significant value for adults hoping to educate their children and to instill certain kinds of values in them.

Worries over the negative influences of greed, conventionality, and demonic threat are certainly not characteristic of most readers' responses to Harry Potter, but being able to understand why some people harbor them is important. Neither adults nor children can really avoid hearing charges like this directed against the books and toward their young audience. It is likely that your children have already been confronted at school or at play with the kinds of charges that I've described. But with the right kinds of encouragement, in the future, they can respond with their own assessments of Harry's personal ethic and explanations of how it both does and does not correspond to their own political or religious beliefs.

Critics believe that their opinions are worth expressing and defending, precisely because they reflect dearly held values. The same should hold true for adults who approve of Harry but, nonetheless, hope to shape what their children take from their encounters with him. Kids already find themselves confronting the critics. It is incumbent upon adults to help them understand why.

In *Boys and Girls Forever: Children's Classics from Cinderella to Harry Potter*, the Pulitzer Prize–winning author, Alison Lurie, observes that nowadays "what many authorities in the field seem to prefer are stories in which children are helped by and learn from grown-ups." If this is true, we seem to have returned, in some respects, to the attitudes of the mid-nineteenth century, when a rough consensus existed around instructional literature that taught children a doctrinaire morality based upon unchallenged social assumptions. Yet, during the twentieth century, little consensus has emerged regarding precisely what children should be taught. Adults across the political spectrum seem to want to maintain control over children, but they can't decide what form that control should take. For this reason, debates persist about what is appropriate, what will corrupt, and what will foster virtue. Some authorities value realistic portrayals of society, while others value more idealistic ones. Others hope to encourage diversity, while still others would emphasize conformity. Some critics want children to respect authority, and some would have them question it. But regardless of all the talk about introducing children to appropriate values, as Lurie notes, children themselves aren't expressly interested in becoming responsible adults. They tend to favor adventure, comradery, rule-breaking, a good scare, and subverting adult authority. In fact, despite the desires of well-intentioned adult critics, children's literature since the nineteenth century has tended to avoid overt moralizing in favor of portraying individual discovery. We can, perhaps, take heart in what P. L. Travers, the creator of Mary Poppins, told us many years ago, "You should trust the children; they can stand more than we can."[7]

Many of the critics whose views I shall discuss below offer doctrinaire prescriptions, from the left and the right, unappealing to many readers of the Harry Potter series. (The imaginative openness of the books is, after all, one of the chief reasons they are so popular.) But no books—and especially ones so popular—are impermeable to criticism for the reasons outlined above. Careful readers with a mind to bring their own understandings to what they read should be aware of what others have to say. Readers who value a plurality of approaches to life and how to live well can learn from ideologically driven critiques, even if they question the basic assumptions of those offering them. Critiques—even the most outrageous—can offer valuable food for thought and provide fuller understandings of what is at stake in all the hoopla surrounding Harry. And what hoopla it is!

A CULTURE OF CONSUMERISM

Writing for Toronto's newspaper the *Globe and Mail*, Rex Murphy harrumphs, "Potter is one with the weekend mega-movies, pop stars, sitcoms and reality TV, and belongs to the same machine that feeds their crass, short, forgettable lives." Summing up the situation in the more staid tones appropriate to the *Horn Book* magazine, a journal devoted to the study of literature for children, Roger Sutton muses:

> So I'm feeling suckered—neither by the book nor by the publisher, but by the cosmic forces that have ordained that this likable but critically insignificant series become wildly popular and therefore news, and therefore something I'm supposed to have an opinion about.

Even fans of Harry worry about his success. In Michael Gerber's humorous (but loyal and admiring) take-off, *Barry Trotter and the Unauthorized Parody*, "Barry" finds himself up against "evil Lord Valumart and his legion of Marketors." Harry Potter it seems is a bona fide capitalist.[8]

As it turns out, most social critics of the Harry Potter books have a hard time disentangling them from all the surrounding hype and commercialism. In some cases, they choose not even to try, emphasizing instead the stories' connections to the politics and economics of consumer culture. Harry Potter as a "cultural phenomenon," according to this view, is a manifestation of corporate greed, the never-ending capitalist pursuit of profit. Though most critics are careful not to attribute such motives to J. K. Rowling directly, they nonetheless fault her imagination and depict her creation as serving nefarious interests.

Critics focusing their attention on the economic aspects of Pottermania contend that Harry is so popular because he is so good at meeting the demands of consumer desires. Further, they contend, corporate interests are more than willing to shape those desires in order to capitalize upon them. These interests create the "corporate sponsored" Harry that kids find so appealing. He offers "manufactured" images of socially normative messages, not the "genuine" pleasures of childhood. As a desirable commodity, he communicates to children the notion that they must "buy" their childhood, purchase it along with their identities, values, and beliefs.

The critics who argue this case offer a paradox that is worth considering: in order for something to become extraordinary and phenomenal (that is, extremely desirable), it must simultaneously be ordinary and conventional (that is, more of the same). In other words, in order to delight, a product must gratify its audience's expectations. This paradox is the secret of Harry's magic.

As someone who is skeptical of just how "free" the global market economy is, I'm *somewhat* persuaded by this line of inquiry. After all, Harry Potter is bigger than most pop-cultural phenomena, and he certainly generates more money. Clearly, interests are being served beyond those of kids caught up in adventure stories, and it is worth considering how. Ultimately, however, I remain unconvinced by arguments of this type, because they tend, as philosophers would say, to "beg the question." Popularity cannot be the explanation for popularity. Corporate interests are always pushing products they hope to sell at maximum profit. Yet, not all of those products sell so well. In the case of Harry Potter, the publishing history of the books seems to suggest that the stories themselves created reader interest, rather than corporate-generated hype. I'll leave it to my readers to decide whether the stories offer something that is especially in tune with the global market economy.

One of the earliest and more thoughtful assessments of the works from this perspective comes from Jack Zipes, a folklorist and expert in children's literature at the University of Minnesota. While leaving little doubt that he finds nothing new or particularly worthwhile in the novels, he nonetheless avoids some of the more outrageous language frequently employed by their critics:

> I believe that it is exactly because the success of the Harry Potter novels is so great and reflects certain troubling sociocultural trends that we must try to evaluate the phenomenon. In fact, I would claim that the only way to do Rowling and her Harry Potter books justice is to try and pierce the phenomenon and to examine her works as critically as possible, not with the intention of degrading them or her efforts, but with the intention of exploring why such a conventional work of fantasy has been fetishized, so that all sorts of magical powers are attributed to the very act of reading these works.[9]

His diagnosis of the phenomenon suggests that it is indicative of a condition well beyond the control of the individual reader.

In a concluding essay to *Sticks and Stones: The Troublesome Success of Children's Literature from Slovenly Peter to Harry Potter*, Zipes tries to show how Harry Potter is particularly well suited for sale to an unsuspecting public driven by the desire for "commodity consumption," like so many other books written for children. Throughout the book, he details how particular cultural conditions have shaped the production and reception of "literature for the young." Institutional arrangements dependent upon educational systems, family relations, corporate control of the mass media, and the capitalist market contribute to setting the limits of what might be considered appropriate reading materials and proper aesthetic tastes. Our friend Harry, accordingly, is only the most recent commodity decked out for popular consumption.[10]

Media coverage and marketing campaigns are mostly responsible for these circumstances, according to Zipes, because they wheedle an audience into having a certain kind of experience. Carefully crafted entertainments are just that—packaged commodities offering amusement and distraction. They rely upon giving the public what it wants while presenting it as unique: a homogenized sameness masquerading as something special. Zipes recognizes the inherent contradiction, or paradox, of this dynamic, yet he persists in seeing it behind Potter-mania:

> In the case of the Harry Potter books, their phenomenality detracts from their conventionality, and yet their absolute conformance to popular audience expectations is what makes for their phenomenality.[11]

They seem to offer something different but only in order to satisfy a craving for the conventional.

How then does this play itself out? In Zipes's analysis, Harry Potter is a conventional phenomenon in two different but related ways: his reception in the media and the attributes of his stories. In each case, behind the phenomenon, we find what we would expect.

If we look to the media for the "story" of Harry's stories, we find a number of themes displaying the paradox laid out by Zipes. The myth of J. K. Rowling's rags-to-riches life—her rise from single mother on welfare to best-selling author—corresponds nicely with what audiences expect when it comes to princesses living happily ever after. In addition, her work's rejection by a number of publishers before its acceptance likewise illustrates a fairy-tale transformation, wherein the dark horse beats out the competition. Furthermore, the controversy surrounding the books' depiction of witchcraft serves only to emphasize their straight-laced (and conventional) morality. In all these ways, conforming to expected convention secures Harry Potter's status as a genuine cultural phenomenon.

We find this same dynamic at work, according to Zipes, if we turn to Harry's stories themselves. Harry is an ordinary—even nerd-like—boy in possession of extraordinary powers. How easy it is to desire the same for ourselves. But the attraction is enhanced by the formula at work in each of the books, which consists of four basic elements. First, Harry is imprisoned; the hero, the anointed one, is confined and denied his true identity. Second, he is summoned and informed of his calling; he can grow and take on his special responsibilities. Third, he embarks upon adventures in a magical realm, extraordinary in its features; he is tested but prevails. Fourth, he returns reluctantly to his place of origin; though exhausted, he has learned from his travails, a better person for all his troubles. Though Zipes concedes that Rowling's stories display far greater complexity and inventiveness, he emphasizes that their plots overtly adhere to the basic structure of the conventional fairy tale, while borrowing liberally from other popular genres such as mystery novels, adventure films, and sitcoms. He locates her stories' popularity in their blending of these popular entertainments.

The upshot of the analysis offered by Zipes is that the packagers of homogeneity have duped enchanted readers into opening their wallets and parting with their hard-earned cash. Perhaps I overstate the point, since he does concede that readers experience the stories passionately and find them personally significant. But how else should we read his views, given his emphasis upon the mediating system of "commodity consumption" that he finds so prominent in the production and reception of children's literature? In a brief passage, he notes that Rowling describes the Dursleys as "coarse, pragmatic materialists," and then asks, "But is Harry really different?"[12] I find the question telling. I also think most readers would respond, "Uh, yes, he *is* different," without much hesitation, after they got over their initial confusion at the question.

The Harry Potter books, like so many others, Zipes ultimately concludes, contribute to the "process by which we homogenize our children. Making children all alike is, sadly, a phenomenon of our time."[13] The larger implication is, of course, that we are all victims of the same process. Despite my ability to see, at times, the insights this line of inquiry offers, I can't help but note that depicting Harry's fans as suckers tends to homogenize them in a no-less-egregious fashion.

In "Pottermania: Good, Clean Fun or Cultural Hegemony?" Tammy Turner-Vorbeck, a specialist in curriculum studies, pursues the same line of inquiry but elaborates upon the connections between consumer culture and conservative values (touched on by Zipes as well). She outlines what children are "buying" in their encounters with Harry Potter. She sees little "good, clean fun" and quite a bit of "cultural hegemony," that is, only values consistent with the political, social, and economic mainstream, especially in regard to limited representations of the family, gender relations, and cultural diversity.[14]

Once again, we see corporate interests manipulating children and childhood experiences through images and products. Through various media, Turner-Vorbeck claims, the commercialization of childhood through Harry Potter reproduces only "social normative messages and middle-class cultural hierarchies." It constructs and presents images that legitimate current understandings of proper social order. These images appear "normal and natural" to children and do not invite any critical scrutiny. She continues:

> The trespassing of manufactured images into the landscape of the imagination of children is limiting children's capacities to freely imagine; yet, these manufactured images also come with both overt and covert embedded messages.[15]

What, precisely, are these messages?

Turner-Vorbeck groups them loosely into three categories. First, representations of intact nuclear families predominate within the stories; fathers serve as heads-of-household and mothers fulfill the role of primary caretakers. No attention is paid to alternative models of the family experienced by many members of the books' audience. Divorced, step, single, gay, adoptive, or foster parents are simply invisible. Second, gender stereotypes abound, with male characters taking active roles and females, more passive ones. Third, the stories display only token cultural (racial and ethnic) diversity, and social hierarchies prevail among magical people and creatures.

Each of these forms of representation serves to maintain conservative values, Turner-Vorbeck suggests, because they communicate to readers the appropriateness of processes of exclusion. The absence of other more diverse representations signals implicitly who can and who cannot be part of the conversation about values. The stories portray who may legitimately speak and be heard. But there is a more insidious tendency at work here, as well, dependent upon representations of exclusivity as normal or natural. By maintaining the *appearance* of inclusiveness, through portrayals of free will and individual responsibility, the Harry Potter stories perpetuate the idea that social problems are, in fact, individual problems. Society is not to blame for inequities; the inadequacies and failures of particular persons are. In other words, those who are outsiders or nonparticipants choose their own subordinate status.

In a larger sense, Turner-Vorbeck would have us believe, this process of exclusion is at work on the readers of Harry Potter. Forces beyond their control shape their consumption, but these same forces encourage them to believe the opposite. In particular, the rhetoric and culture of free market capitalism encourages children to become consumers because, within a capitalist context, consumption is accepted without question as normal—just the way things are and should be. Viewed in this light, Harry Potter's conservative values do little to convince children otherwise.

If the stories really were this reactionary, and if child readers really were this gullible, we would indeed be facing serious problems in Harry Potter. I'll grant that Turner-Vorbeck makes several points worth considering, but ultimately her analysis fails for two reasons. On the one hand, it overstates how narrowly the stories represent family, gender, and diversity. On the other, it undervalues readers' abilities to comprehend their own consumer habits. I do not doubt that readers, both children and adults, feel the pressure of the hype surrounding Harry, but I also doubt that they bend under its weight as unknowingly as this argument suggests.

Like Zipes and Turner-Vorbeck, Andrew Blake takes on consumerism in his book, *The Irresistible Rise of Harry Potter*, but he does so in an unexpected way. As head of Cultural Studies at King Alfred's College in Winchester, England, he is certainly no friend to homogenization or cultural hegemony (and sees both at work in the series' appeal to some degree). But he is ultimately more aware of the books' ambivalence in relation to diversity and more interested in deducing why readers choose to read them. He finds an answer in the books' reinvention of the past—and a particularly *British* past at that.

According to Blake, Harry Potter imaginatively situates the new within the old. The books offer a "retrolutionary" vision that sets forth "aspects of the future through terms set by the past, in order to make it seem palatable." Note how this argument both highlights the books' ambivalent treatment of contemporary society and sees in this ambivalence one of the chief reasons for their appeal to consumers:

The Harry Potter phenomenon has indeed rebranded, and reglobalized, Britain, presenting to the world a country confident in its past but trying harder than usual to work out the possibilities for the future. . . . Hogwarts School is no utopia; it's a parallel world, not a better one. Through the clever past-and-present reinvention of the school story—set simultaneously in an imagined 1950s of steam trains, boiled sweets, and teachers wearing gowns, and in the present of jeans, trainers [gym shoes] and badly behaved sports crowds—contemporary ethnic, gender, and class differences are explored, clashing

values are (so far) left ambivalent rather than resolved, and the fundamental questions of good and evil are explored in a magical but secular setting. Coincidentally "the reader" is at the same time preserved
and modernized into the new—functionally literate—consumer.
Harry Potter is a retrolutionary figure; he is also a contemporary boy.
He has some way to rise yet.[16]

Blake does not pull any punches in asserting that the reinvention
of the past, the retrolutionary turn, both consciously and unconsciously serves contemporary consumer culture. Harry Potter is only
the best example of it and contributes greatly to "literary fast-food consumerism." Though the stories themselves warn, at times, against mate-
rialist consumption (think of the Dursleys on one extreme and the
Weasleys on the other), their phenomenal success—not to mention
movie spin-offs and various products for sale—ensures that children
are being groomed in its ways. Yet, Blake reminds us, so, too, are adults:
"the generations are joined through the act of consumption." As Harry
yearns for the pleasures of possessing the world's best racing broom, we
must note that our hero is not immune to consumerism's temptations.[17]

Blake's critique of the Harry Potter phenomenon is bracing. As a
professional historian, I find much to admire in its portrayal of the
books' contributions to "retrolutionary" culture. Still, I would argue,
we ultimately learn more from Blake about Bloomsbury Publishing's
marketing campaign, Tony Blair's England, and cafés in bookstores,
than we do about the values communicated by Harry's adventures and
kids' reactions to them.

Though the arguments of Zipes, Turner-Vorbeck, and Blake will
clearly strike many readers as a bit strange and extreme, it's important to
avoid overreacting. (Eli Lehrer, senior editor of the *American Enterprise*
magazine, has chosen to tell us "Why the Left Hates Harry Potter," but
ignores much favorable commentary from liberal-minded critics.[18]) If we
label, denounce, and dismiss these ideas as leftist propaganda unworthy
of consideration, we have stopped thinking ourselves. Thoughtful readers
can learn from these arguments, even if they ultimately reject them. We
must keep in mind that social critics offer their views of the Harry Potter

phenomenon because of deep-felt commitments to political and social egalitarianism. Harry Potter might be "good, clean fun" after all. But, by asserting as much, we really haven't stamped out poverty, disease, discrimination, and environmental degradation, which are real social ills condoned if not exactly created by the global market economy. Criticizing children's literature might not be the best way to correct these problems, but we should at least entertain the notion that the values we instill in our children will contribute to either the decline or growth of these evils in the future. Concern over how children are educated has led to debate about Harry's values well beyond condemnations of consumerism. It is to other facets of this debate that we now turn.

FAMILIAR (AND UNEXAMINED) ASSUMPTIONS

Writing in London's *Independent* newspaper, Terence Blacker informs us that Harry Potter sustains a "Blairite social conservatism with a smiling liberal face." Pico Iyer expresses a similar sentiment in otherwise favorable commentary in the *New York Times Book Review*. He likens Hogwarts to an English public school (that is, an elite private school, in the American sense) "designed to train the elite in a system that other mortals cannot follow." In "Harry Potter and the Closet Conservative," posted on Britain's *The Voice of the Turtle*, Richard Adams goes a step further and simply labels Harry a "Tory." So, it seems, Harry is not merely a capitalist; his credentials as a conservative seem to be in good order as well.[19]

As we can see, a number of social critics of Harry Potter worry about values without directly associating them with consumerism. The capitalist "hype" surrounding Harry may still be a concern, but it is less important than certain values conveyed by the books themselves. These critics fault Rowling for failing to imagine her way out of gender stereotypes, traditional family dynamics, social and economic inequalities, forms of political domination, and an authoritarian ethic.

What makes some of this commentary particularly interesting is that it is often delivered by critics who still find reasons to celebrate the books. For the most part, they encourage careful reading and thoughtful discussion of them. They accept that kids are reading the adventures, and they hope to enrich these encounters by raising significant questions for consideration. Although I often agree with these critics' political causes, I take them to task for simplifying, overstating, or misrepresenting aspects of Rowling's stories, which are not nearly as contrary to those causes as they imply.

A particularly good example of this kind of criticism is offered by Christine Schoefer, writing for the Internet publication Salon.com in January of 2000 (before the appearance of *The Goblet of Fire*). She hailed the books as imaginative, exciting, and compelling, but then offered a confession: "Believe me, I tried as hard as I could to ignore the sexism. I really wanted to love Harry Potter. But how could I?" Her enjoyment was ultimately marred by what she saw as the books' conventional treatment of gender relations. Stereotypes abound.[20]

In Schoefer's reading, Harry Potter represents the world as a place properly run by men. Female characters are either "silly or unlikable" or depicted in supporting roles as "helpers, enablers, and instruments." Even female characters who may, at first glance, strike readers differently, such as Hermione or Professor McGonagall, display the attributes of common gender stereotypes upon closer examination. Hermione is irritating, too emotional (despite her brainpower), more easily frightened than the boys, and mostly dependent upon them. She wins their respect eventually, but it is a grudging respect, due ultimately to her complicity in their schemes. Following her use of Polyjuice Potion to unravel the mystery of *The Chamber of Secrets*, she must cower, covered in cat fur, while the boys go about their business. McGonagall displays similar traits, adapted to her role as an adult character. Although she's respected, she is a clear second to Dumbledore, deferential and rule-bound. Where Dumbledore represents wisdom, McGonagall represents conformity. While the headmaster remains in control and shows knowing pride in the aftermath of Harry's exploits in the Chamber of Secrets, McGonagall melts in a puddle of barely restrained emotions, still fearful of the now-dissipated dangers he confronted there.[21]

Even if patriarchal conventions are ultimately to blame, unlike many critics, Schoefer holds Rowling personally accountable:

> I remain perplexed that a woman (the mother of a daughter, no less) would, at the turn of the twentieth century, write a book so full of stereotypes. Is it more difficult to imagine a headmistress sparkling with wit, intelligence, and passion than to conjure up a unicorn shedding silver blood? More farfetched to create a brilliant, bold, and lovable heroine than a marauder's map?[22]

Clearly, Rowling has not been imaginative enough.

But Schoefer's catalog of stereotypically feminine traits tells only half the story. Males act in stereotypically masculine ways as well, and not always to good effect; plenty of negative, typically masculine behavior is on display. What are we to make of Draco and Lucius Malfoy's conceit and cruelty? Of Lockhart's egotistical incompetence? Of Pettigrew's easy treason? Or of Ludo Bagman's doltish school-boy behavior? Certainly, the "silliness" of Lavender and Parvati mirrors the juvenile antics of Dean and Seamus (let alone Ron and Harry). If we are to make a lot of Hermione's disgrace in using Polyjuice Potion, we must certainly make as much of Ron barfing up slugs following his unthinking attempt to be chivalrous when Malfoy calls Hermione a "Mudblood."

In addition, we can find plenty of behavior that disrupts expected gender norms. McGonagall is not as priggish as she often appears and quite a sports fan to boot. (After all, Harry is rewarded with a place on the Quidditch team following a particularly serious breach of the rules.) And in Dumbledore's absence, she fills in as headmistress of Hogwarts, which has a long history of female leadership, on display in paintings of (mostly) sleeping figures in Dumbledore's office. (It is worth noting that McGonagall is also a classic stereotype of the assistant principal or executive officer. They play the enforcer for the more benevolent caretaker played by the principal or commanding officer.) Likewise, Hagrid's gentleness and sensitivity balance his hyper-masculinity, just as Harry's deeply felt personal insecurities balance his prowess in sport. Both male and female characters (even likable ones) display both positive and negative attributes, because, despite the simplicity of Rowling's prose, her characters are complex. It might even be the case that Rowling is satirizing and lampooning such stereotypical gender associations, as I believe she does particularly well in several scenes in *The Goblet of Fire* (which was unavailable to Schoefer at the time of her writing).

Nevertheless, even though Schoefer doesn't call our attention to negative masculine stereotypes or the transgression of expected norms, her larger point about gender relations is valid in several ways. There are, in fact, fewer central (let alone secondary) female characters than male ones. Our hero is a boy, rather than a girl. And the two most powerful characters, Dumbledore and Voldemort, are both men. Schoefer suggests that there is something troubling about our easy acceptance of this state of affairs. And I think she is right, even if I believe she has overstated her case and I would not label the books "sexist." In concluding her essay, Schoefer calls attention to an important question: Why is it that girls are able (or expected) to identify with male characters but boys are unable (or not expected) to do the opposite? I am left with the uneasy feeling that the adventures of "Harriet Potter" would not be as popular—even if they included her sidekicks, faithful "Rona Weasley" and brainy "Hermes Granger." I hope my daughter Rowan, too young now to read Harry's adventures, grows up to encounter a heroine of Rowling's invention, loved by boys as well as girls.

The conventional aspects of the Harry Potter series are critiqued by a number of scholars in *Harry Potter's World: Multidisciplinary Critical Perspectives*, edited by Elizabeth E. Heilman, a professor of education at Michigan State University. In "Blue Wizards and Pink Witches," we find Heilman herself developing in greater detail Schoefer's basic ideas, but in other essays, we find attention to different unexamined assumptions about conventional morality as well. Elaborating upon some of the problems that Tammy Turner-Vorbeck (writing in the same volume) related to capitalist consumerism, various authors take up conservative family dynamics, unfair social and cultural hierarchies, and hegemonic political institutions.

Each of the authors addressing these issues is neither terribly hide-bound nor blind to many of the ambiguities and countervailing tendencies on display in the Harry Potter series in relation to conventional norms. Nevertheless, while they find much to value in the series, they end up reaching rather critical conclusions. Children's literature experts John Kornfeld (Sonoma State University) and Laurie Prothro (Sonoma County, California) elaborate upon stereotypical family roles and relationships. Despite the books' vision of home and family as vital and necessary, their "comical, conventional, superficial, [and] predictable" depictions of the Dursleys and Weasleys ultimately offer harmful misrepresentations of family life. In another essay, Heilman and Anne E. Gregory, an education professor at Boise State University, reach similar conclusions about representations of "privileged insiders and outcast outsiders." Again, according to the authors, although some criticism of privilege is offered by the Potter books, their treatment of social class, peer group affiliations, race, and nationality ends up legitimating various forms of inequality, along with the norms, rituals, and traditions that sustain them. Likewise, Rebecca Skulnick and Jesse Goodman of Indiana University note, even though Harry acts admirably as a leader within his community, he unwittingly fails to challenge the many basic injustices on display in his world. "For all of his compassion and identification with those characters from the lower rungs, he never questions the gender, class, or European hegemony of his world," they argue. To the credit of each of these authors, they encourage more contact with the Harry Potter stories, through critical engagement, rather than less of it. While they do not share my more positive understanding of the moral system on display in the books, they do share my opinion that both children and adults can learn from them.[23]

Inquiry into conventional and largely unexamined assumptions in the Harry Potter series is taken a step further by Farah Mendlesohn, a literary scholar at Middlesex University in Great Britain, in her essay, "Crowning the King: Harry Potter and the Construction of Authority" in Lana A. Whited's collection of essays titled *The Ivory Tower and Harry*

Potter. Mendlesohn's critique encapsulates many others and makes the most cogent critical response to my claim (made earlier in this chapter) that Rowling presents a moral system relatively free of political or religious commitments. It is worth the time to quote her at length:

> There is no obvious political or evangelical intent other than relaying an oft-told tale about the battle of good against evil. She is not an authoritarian writer with a message to be propounded via the morality tale, nor is she seeking to create a society or world that can, through its mere depiction, inspire us to change. To demand that she do any of these would clearly be an unacceptable imposition from critic upon author. However, while Rowling clearly does not intend to engage with ideology, its role in her work is inescapable. Rowling's Harry Potter books are rooted in a distinctively English liberalism that is marked as much by its inconsistencies and contradictions as by its insistence that it is not ideological but only "fair." Its ideology is its very claim to a nebulous and nonexistent impartiality.[24]

Accordingly, the fairness on display in Rowling's imaginative world is anything but.

Mendlesohn takes this argument further, contending that an invisible ideology of fairness serves (1) to interrupt critical inquiry, (2) to promote a particular conception of authority, and (3) to invert the subversive potential of fantasy. It is the second point in which she is most interested, because she sees within Rowling's conception of authority an ultimately disturbing message: "Leadership is intrinsic, heroism born in the blood, and self-interest simply the manifestation of those powers that ensure a return to order."[25] She thus recasts Harry's story in light of these claims.

Underlying Mendlesohn's retelling is the fact that Harry's power is inherited—a right of birth—even if the narrative veils this fact at times. He is the returning prince, claiming his birthright, and yet simultaneously an incomprehensibly nice child, acting with magnanimity toward all. The moral of this combination must therefore be that virtue is inborn. At no time, according to this understanding of Harry, are his actions the result of hard work or, by extension, hard choice. Harry's self-development is, in this sense, magical, not something achieved through striving. Readers know the hero is good, because they are told that he is, not because they see him acting that way.

Mendlesohn also informs us that Harry relies ultimately upon the support of his companions when his own innate power cannot guarantee success. His friends make it possible while Harry receives the credit. He also seems oblivious to their assistance and learns little from their service. They are presented in the stories as extensions of Harry and make of him a peculiarly passive hero—one who does little to secure his own fame.

But there are additional factors at work in Mendlesohn's vision of how authority is constructed in Harry's adventures. Secondary characters, particularly those who are socially inferior, like Hagrid, are constructed merely to show us how wonderful Harry can be when he deigns to be nice to them. Moral conflicts are really about alternative forms of *conservative* ideological solutions—arguments, really, about the bigotry of the Malfoys versus the materialism of the Dursleys versus the moderation of the Weasleys. Liberal-minded characters provide the appearance of egalitarianism but work ultimately to maintain the status quo—there never is a real possibility of radical change. Harry's adventures are more about his inherent talents than about active learning. "Hereditary assumptions" become most manifest in the "ever-present destinarianism of Hogwarts"—the fact that only a chosen few are entitled to the privilege of attending school. While some characters speak of moral freedom, the examples of the Sorting Hat and house-elves prove otherwise; each illustrates that character is inborn and social mobility an illusion. In the final analysis, through all the window-dressing of Harry's goodness and fairness, readers may at last glimpse his "natural immunity" to evil: "He was not asked to hold out against temptation because he was asked to give up nothing." In Rowling's imaginative world, justice is bestowed from above rather than taken from below. Hierarchy in all its guises—social, cultural, economic, political—is never challenged.[26]

For this reason, Mendlesohn's critique, more than most, ends pes-
simistically:

> The result is a muddled morality that cheats the reader: while the
> books argue superficially for fairness, they actually portray privilege
> and exceptionalism, not in the sense of "elitism" but in a specifically
> hereditarian context that protects some while exposing others; they
> argue for social mobility while making such mobility contingent on
> social connections, and they argue for tolerance and kindness toward
> the inferior while denying the oppressed the agency to change their
> own lives.[27]

In her recasting of the Harry Potter stories, Mendlesohn sees goodness
transformed into its opposite, and what child readers recognize as
virtue becomes a recipe for moral inertia.

What, then, should readers make of all this? Well, as it turns out,
these pessimistic claims do create a terrible "imposition from critic
upon author," especially one whom Mendlesohn herself describes as
"not an authoritarian writer." I just can't shake the feeling that this
reading of Harry turns Rowling into precisely that.

Nevertheless, maybe there is something behind the notion that
Harry's virtue is "born in the blood." After all, there are hints in *Harry
Potter and the Sorcerer's Stone* that there might be something "special"
about Harry beyond his survival of Voldemort's attack:

> "But why would he want to kill me in the first place?"
>   Dumbledore sighed very deeply this time.
>   "Alas, the first thing you ask me, I cannot tell you. Not today. Not
> Now. You will know one day . . . put it from your mind for now,
> Harry. When you are older . . . I know you hate to hear this . . . when
> you are ready, you will know."[28]

If the reason turns out to be akin to what Mendlesohn sees as the
"hereditary assumptions" at work in the books, I shall return to her
analysis with a newfound eagerness for insight. But I doubt that I will

have to. For Rowling has already gone to great lengths to develop her hero's morality as something that must be cultivated, rather than something that is simply given, even though she has hinted that Harry, at some point in his adventures, might be revealed to be Gryffindor's heir (an idea I'll expand upon in the next chapter).

Until that time, however, in the absence of such a plot turn, I must argue that Mendlesohn's analysis is dependent upon a selective reading of the books published to date. Only by repressing or ignoring countervailing tendencies in the Harry Potter texts can she sustain her conclusions. She consistently undervalues how Rowling depicts (1) Harry's own agency, (2) his admiration for and cognizant reliance upon friends, (3) his identification with the weak, (4) his conflicted attitudes toward wealth and status, (5) his basic assumption of egalitarianism, and ultimately (6) his own moral development. Rowling creates a world of deceptive ambiguity and striking complexity, which Mendlesohn cannot entirely explain away. Social, cultural, economic, and political relations are presented as "realistic" in the ambiguous and ambivalent ways that many children currently experience them.

Contrary to Mendlesohn's description of Harry's goodness, Rowling has chosen to represent Harry's own moral agency as he strives to develop and maintain his virtue. Birthright and success have little to do with his "goodness" and "fairness." He manages to hone his moral instincts and actions not only in the face of his misery, anger, doubt, and failure, but because of them as well. Mendlesohn's misrepresentation of Harry is particularly egregious when it comes to his attitude toward his friends. She uses several episodes to make her points and implies a thoughtlessness I simply do not find in them: Is Harry really oblivious to Ron and Hermione's roles in securing the Sorcerer's Stone? Does he really undervalue Hermione's unraveling of the mystery of the basilisk? Does he really believe he would have won the Triwizard Tournament without assistance from Hagrid, Dobby, and Cedric in each of the tasks? Hardly.

Unfortunately, we find similar misrepresentations of Harry's empathy for oppressed characters, his internal debate about his own wealth, and his understanding of what motivates his actions on behalf of others. In each case, Mendlesohn must repress or ignore important aspects of the texts. Her Harry would not bother to help Dobby or work to prove Hagrid's innocence. He would not feel for Ron and the Weasleys, as he does, when confronted with their relative poverty. (This feeling goes well beyond mere embarrassment at his own riches.) And he would not worry—seriously worry—that he belonged in Slytherin House, because of his own moral doubts. To read each of these plot developments as reflecting just the self-interested acts of privilege and entitlement misses important aspects of Rowling's portrayal of Harry's growth. He worries that he should be in Slytherin because he shares certain traits with Voldemort, but comes to see, with Dumbledore's encouragement, that his choices and actions make him a Gryffindor.

The best evidence of Mendlesohn's misreading can be seen in her use of several plot developments to make her case:

> In the first book his popularity is assured by his inheritance of sport-ing ability *and* the gift of a new, supercharged broom by a wealthy well-wisher. . . . In the second book, *Chamber of Secrets*, his success depends on a magical cloak inherited from his father; in the third, *Harry Potter and the Prisoner of Azkaban*, on the gift of a magical map. In the fourth book, he has "inherited" the ability to withstand a curse, and the best touch of all, he has "inherited" part of Voldemort, which is crucial in the wand selection that helps him withstand the villain.[29]

While these points are all true to some extent, they are also given far greater significance than is merited.

An alternative reading can be presented, more in line with how most readers understand Harry's "goodness," I would argue. This reading downplays Harry's inborn powers and magical gifts (which are present in the texts) and highlights instead what prove to be keys to Harry's success, his strength of character and moral acumen (which are emphasized in the texts). In each case, powers and gifts serve moral choices; they do not generate them. In the first book, Harry withstands Voldemort's temptation and Quirrell's assault because of his *intellect and moral resolution*, not because of his immunity to Voldemort's touch. He sees through the false promises and chooses to withstand the extreme pain of contact—his immunity does nothing to change the debilitating effects of that contact. Likewise, in the second book, his *faithfulness* (to Dumbledore, to Hogwarts, to Ginny) provides him with the tools necessary to confront Tom Riddle and the monstrous snake identified as a basilisk in the Chamber of Secrets. Note again how magical powers or gifts—Fawkes, the Sword of Gryffindor—only help Harry in service of a moral decision he has already made. We see the same basic theme at work in book three, where Harry's *wisdom and empathy* prove far more significant than the magic that allows him to undertake his quest. Rescuing Ron, sparing Pettigrew, and saving the innocent Black and Buckbeak result from assessing right and wrong. The Time-Turner and *Patronus* Charm are merely the means used in service of what is right. The clearest example of this dynamic emerges in the climax to the fourth book. Harry is overwhelmed by powers vastly superior to his own, both in the form of the assembled Death Eaters and a reincarnate Voldemort. He has only one weapon in his arsenal, his *strength of will*. A quirk of fate, in the form of the Reverse Spell effect of *Priori Incantatem*, gives him the opportunity to use it. This quirk—an inheritance, I'll concede—does not guarantee Harry's victory. Quite the opposite, it puts his will directly against Voldemort's in mental rather than magical combat. We again find magical powers and gifts far less significant than Harry's strength of character, his *decisions* to do the right thing.

Mendlesohn may ultimately be right that there is an ideology at work in the Harry Potter books. It might even be a familiar liberal ideology rooting itself in the legacies of Western European political philosophy. But it is most certainly not the "liberalism" her analysis elaborates and denigrates. It is, on the one hand, much simpler and, on the other, more inviting of multiple interpretations and applications. Rowling asks her readers to assess the nature of fairness and justice by portraying a world in which there are competing claims to what is right. She does so within the framework of a personal moral system whose extent—in terms of both limits and possibilities—children can comprehend and apply. This moral system will not change the world, but it might encourage some readers to think more carefully about their places within it.

Social critics of the Potter books are doing their best to raise concerns worth thinking about. I believe they often do so in unconvincing ways. As Karin E. Westman of Kansas State University has recently shown in her essay, "Specters of Thatcherism," each of the critiques can be turned upside down, their evidence seen as part of Rowling's clever use of satire and parody. In other words, a serious playfulness is present in the Harry Potter volumes, which some critics on the left have missed. I can think of no better way to describe Rowling's keen ability to delight and instruct her readers. We shall now turn to how some critics on the right also miss this aspect of Harry's adventures.[30]

THE BIG DEAL ABOUT WITCHCRAFT

Judging by the sheer amount of media coverage, we might deem religious critiques of the Harry Potter books more significant than commentary focusing on social problems. I have chosen not to take this view, and, consequently, my coverage of religious issues will be somewhat less detailed than my preceding accounts of social issues. Ultimately, I just don't think that (to date) Harry Potter has much to do with religion. As a professional historian and a specialist in religious culture, I do not hear Harry speaking to me in spiritual ways—either positively or negatively. I see him as a largely secular phenomenon. My central reason for reaching this conclusion is that while Harry's adventures advance a coherent ethical system, and address some interesting social and political issues at times, they really do not take up religious faith in any expressly meaningful ways.

In saying this, I do not intend to be dismissive of readers who find in Harry Potter either an ethical system consistent with their creeds or parables giving shape to spiritual messages. I agree, to greater or lesser extents, with both of these observations, and I think thoughtful readers (both children and adults) can, and should, assess the books in light of their faith and spirituality. Martin Luther suggested as much about 450 years ago, when he described Aesop as a fine teacher of morals and took up the question of non-Christian literature:

> So far as moral precepts are concerned, one cannot find fault with the industry and earnestness of the heathen. Nevertheless, they are all inferior to Moses, who gives instruction not only in morals but also in worship of God.[31]

In this respect, despite vast and significant areas of firm disagreement about the morality of the books, I find myself in agreement—in one (and only one) sense—with the most strident religious critics of Harry Potter: his stories do not offer a message of transcendence through religious faith.

This view can be expressed in a number of different ways. It can be presented ignorantly and deliriously, as it is in Stephen Dollins's *Under the Spell of Harry Potter*; it can be argued thoroughly but naively, as it is in Richard Abanes's two books, *Harry Potter and the Bible* and *Fantasy and Your Family*; or it can be stated succinctly and without hyperbole, as in Gene Edward Veith's "Good Fantasy and Bad Fantasy."[32] Regardless of how these authors make their points, I am in agreement with them that Harry Potter just does not offer a religious message.

Of course, critics who worry that Harry's adventures do not offer an expressly religious message usually put their claims a lot more forcefully, choosing to see the stories as a direct threat to faith and morality. In addition, however, they almost always write from a Christian perspective and share the presumption that the only legitimate faith is one that embraces Christ. And here, with all the respect I can accord their views, I must part company with them (and Luther). What each of these authors assumes is an audience whose beliefs more or less match their own. Readers who do not share their particular understandings of Christianity will not be convinced by their arguments, regardless of how wildly, extensively, or thoughtfully they are presented.

Furthermore, the harshest criticism of Harry Potter usually (but not always) reflects a particular, *evangelical* Christian view, quite out of step not only with defenders of the books writing from different Christian perspectives but with some other evangelical perspectives as well. We can see this playing itself out in some of the earliest debates on the religious meanings of the Rowling books. In a radio interview for *Breakpoint Commentary* in November 1999, the born-again evangelical minister (and former Watergate conspirator) Chuck Colson spoke in defense of the Potter books. He praised their inventiveness and assured concerned readers that the magic depicted was "mechanical," rather than "occultic" (sic), and that the basic ethic of self-sacrifice offered in the books encouraged opposition to evil as a real presence. Ted Olsen sounded similar themes a month later in a piece for the evangelical magazine *Christianity Today*, which outlined the variety of opinions offered by religious periodicals such as *Focus on the Family, World Magazine, World, Christianity*, and the *Christian Century*. Olsen sought to emphasize the presence of favorable opinion coming from Christians and that most critical assessments were, in fact, mixed, hardly able to avoid noting Harry's many positive attributes. *Christianity Today* has continued to run positive commentary on Rowling's series, and its editors explained why in a brief commentary from January of 2000 that casts the books as a fun-loving "Book of Virtues."[33]

Why was it necessary for these evangelical Christians to defend Harry Potter? In short, some Christians had taken it upon themselves to denounce the books, and these actions were getting considerable coverage in the media. The books were challenged in schools and libraries, and a host of Web sites had begun to suggest that the books would encourage children to turn to the occult—oftentimes through very extreme language, questionable logic, and convoluted interpretations of scripture. As a result, the popular media began to depict Christianity, particularly in its fundamentalist forms, in less-than-attractive ways.

Kimbra Wilder Gish took a different approach to this problem later in 2000. She offered a thoughtful assessment of fundamentalist objections to the Harry Potter books in the *Horn Book* magazine. Although she ultimately cautions parents against forbidding them and suggests constructive engagement instead, she leaves little doubt about her own fundamentalist leanings. As Debra J. Taub and Heather L. Servaty note in an essay on the perceived threats of Harry Potter, Gish offered a particularly useful commentary on a passage from Deuteronomy 18:9–12, which often serves as the starting point for religious criticism of the books:

> When you come into the land that the Lord your God is giving you, you must not learn to imitate the abhorrent practices of those nations. No one shall be found among you who makes a son or daughter pass through fire, or who practices divination, or is a soothsayer, or an auger, or a sorcerer, or one who casts spells, or who consults ghosts or spirits, or who seeks oracles from the dead. For whoever does these things is abhorrent to the Lord; it is because of such abhorrent practices that the Lord your God is driving them out before you.

Gish notes that, in her view, witchcraft is as real as any other religion and that it is fundamentally evil in nature. Further, she reports, Christians who share her beliefs worry that children reading the books will be drawn to witchcraft, become desensitized to it, or, at least, come to see its practices as acceptable, rather than as occult or satanic. The books are a threat because they present witchcraft in a favorable light, not because Rowling intends to corrupt children. If magic is understood to be real, then the various activities of Harry and company can only be seen as contrary to faith.[34]

Ultimately, conflicting understandings of the "reality" of witchcraft center the debate among Christians about Harry. Three different positions emerge from religious commentary on the books: (1) Magic is not real; (2) magic is real, but not the magic in Harry Potter; and (3) magic is real, and therefore the books' fanciful depictions of magic may lead readers to real occult or satanic beliefs and practices. Christians taking the first and second positions choose to emphasize magic's depiction as fantasy in the books, while those taking the third position choose to highlight its resemblances to the practices listed in Deuteronomy. We thus come, once again, to a fundamental disagreement over the nature of Rowling's imagination.

Although I shall comment briefly on Christian defenders of the books a bit later in this chapter, I'd like to explore in some detail the critiques of authors who associate their ideas with the third position. In particular, I'll take up the opinions of Stephen Dollins, Richard Abanes, and Gene Edward Veith, which I find to be emblematic of three different approaches to the question of how magic in Harry Potter translates into a demonic threat. I'll begin with the most extreme version, take you through a thorough presentation of the case, and conclude with the most concise, an approach not entirely unlike that presented by Gish.

The self-proclaimed "former Satanic High Priest" Stephen Dollins assures us in his introduction that he has seen "witchcraft packaged in many clever forms, but never as clever as [this] one. To be blunt, this is witchcraft in the form of a child's book." His rhetoric becomes even more extreme as the book progresses. He begins with a primer on occult symbols (triangle, lightning-bolt S, crest of Diana, pentagram, and ankh), and implies that they abound in the books (through questionable interpretations of the artwork on the covers of the American editions). In the next chapter, he briefly reports on each story, commenting upon the dangerous morality communicated by them. In chapter three, he tells us he has little to say about J. K. Rowling, but then condemns her for any number of things: playing witches and wizards as a child; implying there is good magic; using Latin; receiving the idea for Harry Potter all at once, when (as she claims) it "popped" into her head; using the phrase "mind's eye"; understanding "MUCH more about witchcraft and wizardry than she is letting on"; and appearing in a photograph ("sent to me by an anonymous source") dressed in a witch's robe and giving the "coven greeting," an arm gesture ostensibly used by some modern witches.

More of the same follows, as Dollins returns to the stories before looking at the broader cultural phenomenon of Harry Potter. Chapter 4 outlines how Harry's stories contain elements resembling historical occult practices, convey immoral messages, and, in fact, glorify the occult. Chapters 5, 6, and 7, in turn, castigate Christian defenders of

Harry, take on first the movie, and denounce the sale of merchandise aimed at children. In chapter 8, he outlines "Satan's Plan":

> You whet the appetites of children who are confused and not quite grounded in family morals, values, and standards (especially those young enough not fully grounded [sic] in their faith in Jesus) and introduce them to Harry Potter. . . . You then bolster their interests in these [magical] practices and instill in them the idea that there is no good or evil, only magic, and that it's okay to practice Witchcraft, because it is a moral, wholesome thing to do. . . . Finally, when their interest in these practices is at its highest peak, offer the use of the Internet, which is exploding with information that is theirs for the taking, and teaches them how they too can be just like Harry Potter!

Dollins's final chapter asks the question "What can be done about Harry Potter?" The answer turns out to be turning away from the books and actively campaigning against them.[35]

Dollins's account is such a jumble of breathless claims that it's difficult to assess in a systematic fashion. But it is not meant to appeal to systematic thinkers, as I think his remarks on "Satan's Plan" above make clear enough. To whom does the "you" in the passage refer? Well, it strikes me as peculiar to address the devil as "you" in this context, so Dollins must be up to something else. But it makes even less sense to attribute these motives to parents of children reading the books, although that is clearly what Dollins hopes to imply. Unfortunately, *Under the Spell of Harry Potter* commits far worse transgressions. Often enough, the book presents readers with half-truths, erroneous factual claims, and photographs and quotations both ripped from context and presented without specific attribution. In this regard, however, the book is not unlike many of the Web sites devoted to denouncing Harry Potter.[36]

With Richard Abanes's two books, *Harry Potter and the Bible* and *Fantasy and Your Family*, we enter into an entirely different world in terms of presentation. The books are fairly well organized, lengthy, and copiously documented, as one would expect from a journalist. Factual claims and direct quotations are mostly accurate and backed up by

citations to the appropriate sources. Despite these admirable qualities
in the books, Abanes still manages to argue in ways that lead him to
conclusions strikingly similar to those reached by Dollins.

Harry Potter and the Bible presents its conclusions in two parts. The
first takes up the stories themselves. In a series of short chapters,
Abanes provides synopses of the four books in the series available to
him and then takes "a closer look" at each one. He thus elaborates upon
what he sees as the "real-world occultism" present in them, their
morally confusing "Potterethics", and the age-inappropriateness of
some episodes. The second part of the book takes a look at related
issues: evil and the occult, the occult's attraction to the young, the
spread of new-age spirituality, Christian fantasy in the works of J. R. R.
Tolkien and C. S. Lewis, and the controversy over the Harry Potter
books in public schools and the media. "Most importantly," Abanes
sums up in his introduction, "Part 2 clearly explains why God is so
against occultism and where it is condemned in scripture."

The synopsis of each book describes Harry's adventures in a
straightforward fashion and seeks to avoid editorializing. The commentaries that follow, however, make clear that the books convey messages contrary to scripture, display a relativist morality, and contain
accounts of events too disturbing for children. We can see the crystal-
lized form of these complaints in the book's final chapter, where
Abanes outlines the (bad) morals the books communicate:

(1) Lying, stealing, and cheating are not only acceptable, but can
     also be fun.

(2) Astrology, numerology, casting spells, and performing
     "magick" [sic] can be exciting.

(3) Disobedience is not very serious, unless you get [sic] caught.

(4) Being "special" means you deserve to escape punishment for
     behaving badly.

(5) Adults just get in the way most of the time.

(6)   Rules are made to be broken.

(7)   Revenge is an acceptable course of action.

According to Abanes, good characters and good literature do not depict any of these things if they hope to communicate appropriate, moral messages.

Part 2 takes things in a different direction, elaborating at length on how Harry Potter has found a place in the modern world. In chapter 9, Abanes presents a Christian understanding of evil, locating its origin in humanity's disobedience of God's commands, before linking it to Rowling's use of the occult, contemporary paganism, and the temptations of the devil: "Ultimately, only a short distance needs to be covered in order to cross over from Harry Potter's world into the realm of occultism." In chapter 10, he outlines in detail the effects of the occult in the early 1980s upon a seventeen-year-old boy who was drawn to satanic practices. In order to link this unrelated case to Harry Potter, he next establishes that "occultism often accompanies violent, criminal behavior in young people," and then turns to biblical denunciations of occult practices. In chapter 11, the spiritual values of a "Post-Christian America" are questioned, in light of a young "Spellbound" generation, rampant popular "Media Magick" (sic), and "New Age" spirituality.

In a surprising turn, in chapter 12, Abanes negatively contrasts Harry Potter to the wholesome "mythopoetic" fantasies of J. R. R. Tolkien and C. S. Lewis, set in worlds that are not our own:

> Unlike Lewis's and Tolkien's creations, Rowling's fantasy is set in our twenty-first-century world, complete with contemporary forms of occultism . . . and references to persons and events from our own human history. . . . Rowling's novels also use a vastly different definition of "magic" than the one used by Lewis and Tolkien. Furthermore, the Harry Potter series promotes a concept of right and wrong that is radically altered from the one presented by Lewis and Tolkien.

In brief, the works of Tolkien and Lewis present moral systems consistent with and inspired by Christianity, while Rowling's do not.

Abanes closes his book with two concluding chapters. Chapter 13 calls for an end to the "bitter war of words" waged over Harry Potter by both Christian and secular extremists, before taking on the claims made by supporters of Harry Potter. Chapter 14 briefly takes up the question of childhood development, outlines Harry Potter's immorality, and criticizes the way it is being taught, particularly in relation to the theories of Joseph Campbell's *The Power of Myth*. Abanes ends by encouraging Christian parents to guide their children and to share Christian perspectives with others.[37]

Fantasy and Your Family repeats the basic arguments of *Harry Potter and the Bible*, but develops several themes in a bit more detail. In particular, it presents a defense of fantasy as a genre and pays a bit more attention to its relation to childhood development. We find abbreviated condemnations of contemporary paganism and the Harry Potter books and a radically expanded defense of Tolkien's. Likewise, the book's last section critiques supporters of Harry in greater detail than the earlier book.

If readers are willing to grant Abanes's two basic assumptions, that magic is real and its fanciful depiction leads to occult or satanic practices, they will accept his arguments, which are consistent with these premises. If they do not, his conclusions about the supposed immorality of the Potter books fall like so many houses of cards. All of the voluminous evidence he presents—in terms of both textual criticism and cultural analysis—is skewed by his *particular* understanding of what it means to be a Christian.

We can see how Abanes often skews his evidence in the early pages of chapter 2 in *Harry Potter and the Bible*, "Sorcery in Stone: A Closer Look":

> J. K. Rowling came up with the idea for her books in 1990 while traveling on a train. Without any warning, she suddenly just saw Harry "very, very clearly" in her mind. His visible image actually popped into her thoughts from out of nowhere as a "fully formed individual." During one interview, Rowling stated: "The character of Harry just strolled into my head. . . . I really did feel he was someone who walked up and introduced himself in my mind's eye."

Most readers understand Rowling's description as an account of her moment of *poetic* inspiration. (In fact, the word "popped" is her own, which Abanes fails to indicate.) Abanes, in contrast, carefully codes his description so readers who share his suspicions of Harry Potter will read the passage as an account of *demonic* inspiration, which is really the whole point of his second chapter.[38]

Before I continue my brief explication of Abanes's claims, I must admit that he has given me cause to take issue with him personally. He quotes my own work in a similarly questionable manner. I have the honor of providing an epigraph for a chapter titled "Just the Facts: Bypassing the Propaganda" in *Fantasy and Your Family*. Unfortunately, Abanes presents the passage entirely out of context, without engaging my argument, in order to create a half-truth at best. He blithely ignores the fact that my argument is quite counter to his own. It is ironic that such questionable use of my claims is made in a chapter ostensibly devoted to correcting "factual errors" in the work of Harry's supporters, but which really takes up questions of interpretation. But his use of the quotation—without due attention to its contextual implications—is also indicative of how his arguments frequently proceed. Again, it is a tendency his books share with the more extreme book, *Under the Spell of Harry Potter*.[39]

We can see this tendency toward taking things out of context at work early in Abanes's synopses of Harry's adventures in *Harry Potter and the Bible*. They try to avoid editorializing, but they fail to do so in two important ways. First, they systematically downplay what Harry and his friends learn from their experiences, preferring instead to dwell on morally questionable behavior. Second, they consistently understate the degree to which Rowling puts moral ambiguity to work in order to instruct child readers. What Abanes tries to present as "objective" fact usually turns out, upon closer examination, to be anything but.

The same complaint may be made about the way Abanes reports what others have said about Rowling and what she has said about herself. Note this example, which is meant to imply sinister intent, where none is to be found:

> Her ex-husband, Jorge Arantes, confirmed this in London's *Daily Express*, saying that Rowling "had planned the full series of seven books because she believed the number seven has magical associations."

I have been unable to locate other reports confirming this claim, but even if it accurately reflects what Arantes said, it fails to prove that Rowling believes in the reality of magic. Historically, the number seven is believed to have magical associations, and Rowling has put this fact to use in developing a series of books that explicitly portray fanciful magic. For example, during a 1999 interview on the Barnes and Noble Web site, Rowling said of magic, "I have always been interested in it, although I don't really believe in magic. I find it a picturesque world." Likewise, in another interview for the same site later in the year, she admitted, "Yes, I have done research on witchcraft and wizardry, but I tend only to use things when they fit my plot, and most of the magic in the books is invented by me." Abanes usually works his way around these and many similar statements by Rowling, casting her sincerity into doubt, even as he quotes or cites her. Again and again, he employs the same tactic both to besmirch Rowling's claims that she does not believe in the reality of witchcraft and to underplay her identity as a Christian. This habit reaches truly reprehensible forms in an endnote to *Fantasy and Your Family*. It begins:

> It should be noted that despite her interests in occultism, Rowling is a member of the Church of Scotland . . . [source citation]. Church membership, of course, does not always reflect one's innermost religious convictions.

The fact of her church membership, I must emphasize, is conspicuously absent from the main body of Abanes's text, which reads: "Rowling maintains she is not a witch. Yet questions remain because of her unwillingness to discuss at length her spiritual beliefs (see endnote for a discussion of Rowling's faith)." Surely, someone who is genuinely interested in Rowling's faith would not relegate her Christianity to an endnote? But Abanes is clearly more interested in implying that Rowling's reticence betrays something ominous about her beliefs.[40]

Another questionable aspect of Abanes's style of argumentation is his tendency to denounce as "factual errors" what are really differences in interpretation. While not absent from *Harry Potter and the Bible*, this feature emerges most clearly in the ninth chapter of his *Fantasy and Your Family*, which purports to be concerned with "Just the Facts: Bypassing the Propaganda." Here, in assessing "nothing that might be considered subjective," Abanes answers "Argument #1" through "Argument #33" presented by Harry's supporters. (I should note that "arguments," by definition, cannot be equated with "factual errors" at all, though the premises of the arguments could contain such errors.) Note just a few of these "errors":

(#1) Harry Potter's world is an alternate universe; a realm separate from our own; a parallel universe; a sub-creation.

(#2) Harry Potter is a classic good vs. evil story with clearly defined good characters.

(#5) Harry Potter contains examples of *agape* love, a foundational practice of Christians.

(#8) Whether or not Harry Potter is child-appropriate is an issue of Christian freedoms.

(#11) The magic in Harry Potter is not real, just mechanical—i.e., pretend magic, similar to high-tech devices used in science fiction.

(#24) Harry Potter critics are just a bunch of idiotic, book-burning fools.

Surely, while these matters involve questions of fact, they are definitely open to interpretation. Unless, of course, you subscribe to the assumptions made by Abanes.[41]

This tendency toward denunciation of alternative interpretations as contrary to fact is really rather rich coming from someone who commits a few "factual errors" of his own. One egregious example of this can clearly be seen in the claim that there is no moral ambiguity in the works of J. R. R. Tolkien. According to Abanes, in *The Lord of the Rings* and *The Hobbit*, good characters are good, and evil characters are evil, with no shades of gray in between; likewise bad behavior is always punished or is an occasion for atonement. Note the following "factual" claim:

> Tolkien's stories also do not include episodes of good characters doing bad things (e.g., lying to friends or stealing from authority figures) in order to accomplish good tasks.[42]

In considering *The Hobbit*, a story that follows the adventures of Bilbo Baggins, we can see that Abanes is incorrect. The hero departs with the wizard Gandalf and thirteen dwarves to reclaim the lost kingdom of the Lonely Mountain from Smaug, a marauding dragon that had destroyed the realm many years earlier. Central plot developments, in fact, turn on acts of theft or deceit. To begin, Bilbo's friend, the wizard Gandalf, tricks the hobbit into accompanying the dwarves. Later, Bilbo steals a magic ring from Gollum, an evil creature that threatens the hobbit's life, and then lies to the dwarves about the precise nature of his escape with the ring, which makes him invisible. Gandalf then uses deception to obtain food and lodging for his fellow travelers. Later still, during the climax of his adventures, Bilbo steals the Arkenstone—a precious gem without peer—from Smaug's hoard, which rightfully belongs to Thorin Oakenshield, the leader of the dwarves, and turns the stone over to Thorin's enemies. Although readers will rightly see Gandalf and Bilbo's actions as justified, they really can't deny that they involve "lying to friends and stealing from authority figures."

The same is true of *The Lord of the Rings*, Tolkien's sweeping fantasy of battle between good and evil in Middle Earth. It follows Frodo Baggins's attempt to destroy the magic ring left to him by Bilbo. The ring, Frodo discovers from Gandalf, was crafted by Sauron, an evil being bent upon the destruction of all that is good and on establishing complete dominion over the lands of Middle Earth. With the ring, which is far more powerful than the hobbits realize, Sauron could not be withstood. Frodo, along with companions appointed to the task, must therefore destroy the ring in the fires of Mount Doom, where Sauron had forged it long ago. Early on, Frodo deceives his good friends, Merry, Pippin, and Fatty Bolger, when he does not tell them he will leave the Shire. Frodo's manservant, Sam, likewise deceives Frodo when he acts as a "spy" for Frodo's friends, telling them of his master's intentions, until their "conspiracy" is "unmasked" and they reveal that they knew of his plans all along. In fact, similar "white lies" abound in the story, with characters withholding the truth from one another. The story also contains theft from authority figures, as is the case when Pippin takes a palantir (a stone that allows communication with those who possess similar ones) from Gandalf. Instead of being punished for this misdeed, Pippin is rewarded by being allowed to travel with Gandalf, who satisfies the hobbit's curiosity about the stone. There remains one additional event of exceptional importance: the "fact" that Frodo fails—utterly fails—in his quest *when he claims the ring for his own* by the fires of Mount Doom. Only through the malicious act of Gollum, who had pursued and then accompanied Frodo, does evil undo itself.

Plenty of readers miss the significance of this "fact," and Abanes is one of them. Tolkien's extremely sophisticated understanding of the nature of evil is completely absent from Abanes's naive reading, which suggests that good is good and evil is evil. He makes the same "factual" mistake in reading Rowling's portrayal of good and evil, which, as I shall argue in the next chapter, is much closer to Tolkien's than Abanes can see.[43]

For this reason, Abanes makes much of the occasional misbehavior of Harry, Ron, and Hermione. For him, any depictions of rule violation, unless they lead directly to punishment and atonement, are inappropriate for children. This naive understanding of how the actions of literary characters translate into the moral messages of literary texts perfectly mirrors his equally naive understanding of how real children's behavior translates into more mature moral sensibilities. Kids lie, cheat, and steal, and they commit still other infractions. Sometimes they're caught and other times they're not. Eventually, they come

to a keener appreciation of right and wrong. They are not nearly as passive or as easily influenced as Abanes implies.

More serious than Abanes's naive interpretations of literature and the
opinions of others are his claims about modern witches, neopagans, and
Wiccans. The same is true about his attempts to associate their beliefs and
practices with sin and satanism. His arguments about the Harry Potter
books' portrayal of "real-world occultism" rely exclusively upon
asserting that certain activities *resemble* other activities drawn from history or contemporary pagan practice. As I showed earlier, Rowling has
admitted as much, but she has also emphasized that these activities are
put to use in fantasy. Magic is not real. Likewise, his evidence about the
lure of Harry Potter and the evils of contemporary paganism is anecdotal
at best, and his arguments about both pretty much ignore what modern
witches, neopagans, and Wiccans say about themselves and what reputable scholars have reported after extensive study.

Abanes and others are obviously free to disapprove on the basis of
their own religious creeds, but misrepresentation based upon spurious
evidence is something else entirely. Contemporary pagans do not wor-
ship Satan, nor do they see themselves as duped by him. Taken as a
group, they do not proselytize—that is, they do not seek to convert
others to their beliefs, even if they are willing to provide information
about themselves. Adherents to paganism and New Age spirituality
have been growing in number, but not nearly to the extent that Abanes
implies. I encourage interested readers to look to the works of T. M.
Luhrmann, Loretta Orion, and Ronald Hutton for informed studies
that present images of paganism quite at odds with those found in
Harry Potter and the Bible and *Fantasy and Your Family*. Likewise, readers
can find spurious claims of satanic ritual abuse debunked in studies by
Kenneth V. Lanning of the FBI, Gail Goodman of the National Center
on Child-Abuse and Neglect at the University of California-Davis, and
Malcolm McGrath, a doctoral candidate at Oxford University.[44]

In the work of Gene Edward Veith, a professor of English at concordia University, we find conclusions similar to those offered by
Abanes, but none of the misdirection or hyperbole. (In fact, Veith wrote

a favorable forward for *Fantasy and Your Family*, which shares the book's worries, but with less anxious indignation.) "Good Fantasy and Bad Fantasy," as the title suggests, focuses the debate on what is really at issue: the values expressed in fantasy literature. Good fantasy stimulates "the imagination in a constructive way." Bad fantasy stimulates "the imagination in a destructive way." Veith makes no secret of what is needed: good fantasy "takes us out of ourselves, countering our darkness with at least a glimpse of the external light." For his Christian audience, the source of this external light is obvious. For Veith, the Harry Potter books, despite some admirable qualities, do not ultimately communicate what he describes in a different context as "the truths of God's commandments from a Christian perspective." Veith shares much with Abanes, including a dislike for paganism, fear of its spread, and the assumption that real magic exists (along with boundless respect for Tolkien and Lewis). But while he clearly believes in the reality of witchcraft, he doubts that Harry will lead many readers to it: "So, yes, Harry Potter falls short, though it is not nearly so bad as some." Veith manages to make his point without misrepresenting Harry's stories and without smearing J. K. Rowling. I have to respect his honesty and moderation, even if I do not share his conclusions or the faith that makes them possible.[45]

I can appreciate the logic of such conclusions, even if I must reject it. As someone who has studied the witchcraft trials in Europe between roughly 1435 and 1760, I am exceptionally familiar with this view. As I have shown, denunciations of magic are to be found in the Bible, and they were put to use executing presumed witches in earlier centuries. This view was the dominant view toward witchcraft for several centuries, before both secular and religious elites subverted it in the eighteenth century by mounting an attack on superstition. But there had always been contrary (if subordinate) opinions toward magic and witchcraft within the Christian community.

This fact is true in a larger sense as well, and it can be seen in relation to both (1) the age-old tensions between biblical literalism and allegorical interpretation and (2) the appropriate meanings and uses of pagan values and literature. There had always been both hardliners and the more accommodating with regard to these matters, and we can see two separate traditions within Christianity. These tensions were familiar to Tolkien, who devoted his whole life to the study of non- and quasi-Christian cultures, and to Lewis as well, who delighted in a medieval cosmology that deviated from his own Christian understandings. They didn't hate pagan religions (as genuine scholars with deep knowledge of the subject, how could they?), though as Christians, they did not accept the claims of these religions to possess spiritual truth.[46]

Although I shall take up this issue again in my next chapter, I wish to note that the more accommodating tradition is alive and well in a growing number of works defending the Harry Potter books and which were written from different Christian perspectives. They are the best rebuttals to religious critiques of Harry and his morality. Connie Neal was the first to respond to religious attacks on the books in *What's a Christian to Do with Harry Potter?* She has since followed up her defense, written from a fundamentalist perspective, with her even more favorable account, *The Gospel According to Harry Potter*, which outlines in detail how Harry's adventures serve as parables communicating central Christian virtues. A similar case is made by John Killinger, a theologian and ordained minister who has served both Presbyterian and Congregational parishes, in *God, the Devil, and Harry Potter*. The Anglican theologian, Francis Bridger, advances a strident vindication in *A Charmed Life: The Spirituality of Potterworld*. And from an Orthodox Christian perspective, John Granger's *The Hidden Key to Harry Potter* argues that the Potter books are essentially Christian allegory. Although no book-length defense of Harry Potter has yet appeared from a Catholic perspective, we may already have witnessed a sign of things to come. In the Catholic journal *Logos*, Catherine Jack Deavel and David Paul Deavel's "Character, Choice, and Harry Potter" argues that the Harry Potter books present a morality consistent with Christianity.[47]

I found each of these works informative and enriching, and reading them was a far less dreary task than engaging the religious critics. Each author makes a compelling case that spiritual experiences are neither unlikely nor inconsistent with J. K. Rowling's literary creation. Still, as I made clear earlier, I do not think that Harry Potter offers a message of transcendence through religious faith. Ultimately, it strikes me as unlikely that, as a result of reading the Harry Potter books, many readers will be drawn either away from their religious beliefs, as Harry's religious critics would have it, or to new spiritual insights, as his defenders seem, at times, to imply. Harry offers something else.

PLURALISM

I began this chapter with the observation that kids like Harry Potter. I'll conclude it by affirming that grownups can feel pretty good about this. The reasons for my delight should be quite plain by now. Harry has prompted such contrary and contradictory understandings of what he's about that there's plenty of work for kids to do in making sense of him. These circumstances also imply that there's plenty of work, as well, for adult readers who want to offer guidance to the children in their lives. Harry can't stand still or become a single thing either to accept or to reject if we don't let him.

In his adventures, Harry must search for the right answers; he must look to many places, because there are no ready-made solutions to his problems. Kids find themselves in similar circumstances, even if adults like to pretend otherwise. And kids aren't passive; they're active learners engaging in the serious play so necessary to becoming adults. Harry's adventures require them to do this. They might at times find themselves swept up by the excitement, but they end up worrying about Harry's predicament. What should he do? Rowling's stories ask children to assess what is on display, rather than encouraging them to remain still.

Many critics undervalue the stories' ability to do this. Kids will learn greed. They'll fall prey to conventionality. They won't recognize the demonic threat. In some sense, the critics of Harry Potter are more in thrall to their own assumptions than the kids reading the books are in thrall to excitement and adventure.

Perhaps I've overstated the case. We've encountered a number of criticisms of Harry's adventures, and I hope I've shown how each is dependent upon particular assumptions about how the world is and how it should be. I've also suggested that these assumptions and the criticisms dependent upon them can help readers understand what is at stake in the debates about Harry. They can also help readers understand something important about the number and nature of opinions out there. Too many of the critics neither recognize nor encourage openness to this variety of opinions—to the competing views that shape our understandings of the world. Still, the critics have something to teach us if only through their negative example. We should expect disagreement over important issues.

What Rowling's religious critics seem not to recognize is how dependent their arguments are upon their own variant of Christianity. Perhaps they do recognize it but just don't care. As I read their works, I can't help but notice how they repeatedly speak only to the converted—to those who share their particular form of religious and moral certainty. I sense minds at rest with that certainty, rather than minds at work with uncertainty. It is to readers' great benefit that not all religious commentators have this trait.

Yet, some of Rowling's social critics are hardly better at moving beyond their own secular orthodoxies. They cling to their own certainties, secure in their dismissive claims. They see in Harry's stories only support and sustenance for inequities rather than seeing the potential for undermining them. Again, it is to the benefit of readers that not all social critics take this view.

Ultimately, Rowling's vision of a personal morality, relatively free of political and religious commitments, makes possible the realization that readers—both children and adults—bear the responsibility for acting morally in the world. The relative openness of this vision provides adults with ample opportunities to help shape what morals children take from the books. Kids can work through the difficulties that the stories raise with *guidance* and by *discussing* them, just as Harry and his friends seek *advice* and always *talk* their way through moral conflict.

Do Harry's stories contribute too much to the global market

economy? Do they convey conventional morality and acceptance of gender, class, and ethnic disparities? Can they be a threat to religious faith? The simple answer to each question is, only if we let them. They will not work these effects on their own.

When we are presented with a variety of opinions, we come to have a better sense of our own. We need not surrender to competing claims, but we need not label, denounce, and dismiss them instead. We can recognize them for what they are, reflections of the intellectual pluralism in whose midst we find ourselves.

In commenting upon medieval cosmology in his book *The Discarded Image*, C. S. Lewis often revealed his delight in things contrary to Christianity and modern scientific theory:

> I have made no serious effort to hide the fact that the old Model delights me as I believe it delighted our ancestors. Few constructions of the imagination seem to me to have combined splendor, sobriety, and coherence in the same degree. It is possible that some readers have long been itching to remind me that it had a serious defect; it was not true.

I can already hear the most strident social critics discrediting me for quoting an old curmudgeon and the most strident among the religious critics assailing me for revealing one of their darlings as a bit of a libertine. But I'm using Lewis to make a point about the value of pluralism—not as a goal in itself, but as a source of learning. In the same work, he continues:

> I hope no one will think that I am recommending a return to the Medieval Model. I am only suggesting considerations that may induce us to regard all Models in the right way, respecting each and idolizing none.[48]

I believe the same holds true for the models of Harry Potter offered by his social and religious critics, despite my own responses to them. We can appreciate both their strengths and recognize their weaknesses without either glorifying or demonizing them.

5

Imagination, History, Legend, and Myth

Stories never live alone: they are the branches of a family that we have to trace back, and forward.
—Roberto Calasso, in *The Marriage of Cadmus and Harmony*

THE FAMILIAR AND THE FANTASTIC

In November of 2001, I had the opportunity to present my views about the morality of Harry Potter on Wisconsin Public Radio. Before taking questions from callers, the show's host Kathleen Dunn and I discussed just how *ordinary* Harry is. He's a regular kid, despite his heroism and unusual adventures. Even his name speaks of his plainness. As Alison Lurie points out, "Harry" recalls, among other

 179

things, two unrefined yet steadfast characters of Shakespeare's Henry IV plays, Prince Hal (later King Henry V) and Harry Hotspur; "Potter" hardly brings to mind images of grandeur, suggesting instead earth and clay, handicraft, and practical endeavor. Although Dunn and I, along with callers to the show, talked about the extraordinary features of Harry's stories, we usually circled back to issues of a simpler or more fundamental nature. I think that there's something to be learned from this unassuming portrayal of Harry and similar commonplaces in his tales.[1]

For, in exercising her vibrant imagination, J. K. Rowling paints not only fantastic images but familiar ones as well. She expertly blends the two in order to create something new: a world not our own yet very much like our own. As Philip Nel tells us, making a similar point, "Rowling offers matter-of-fact fantasy, in which magic is so thoroughly part of the landscape that it's taken for granted." Yet, it is worth noting, Rowling constructs her imaginative world in a particular way, employing both fantastic and familiar elements drawn from history, legend, and myth and situating them in a near-contemporary present. Thus, both the familiar and the fantastic define Harry's world. It would clearly not be the same if one or the other were eliminated.[2]

If we take up the many fantastic aspects of Rowling's tales before turning to the more familiar ones, we quickly notice how multiple magical qualities obscure numerous similarities between Harry's world and our own. Given her flights of fancy, I'd like to suggest that we can read Harry's adventures as a distinct example of *historical fantasy*. Her characters inhabit a universe situated within our own, in which superstitious—but still historically accurate—beliefs, practices, and creatures continue to flourish. Children collect famous wizard cards and learn about the history of magic at school. More striking still, both children and adults actually practice magic as part of their daily lives. They wear hats and robes, carry magic wands, recite charms, brew potions, and know more than a bit about magical plants. Going about their business, they're likely to encounter magical peoples including goblins, gnomes, elves, and pixies. Furthermore, they come into contact with other magical creatures such as fabulous dragons, unicorns, and hippogriffs, or even mundane varieties like toads, cats, and owls, all endowed with special powers. When we take into account that each of these fantastic elements derives directly from historical, legendary, or mythical legacies, we can see Harry's stories as historical fantasy—in other words, they make extensive use of recognizable, though fabulous, features of the human past.

Examples of each of these legacies can be seen early in *Harry Potter and the Sorcerer's Stone*, when Ron and Harry view and discuss the trading cards depicting famous witches and wizards, contained in packages of Chocolate Frogs. Historical figures include the ancient astrologer Ptolemy, the early medieval Saxon King of Britain Hengist, the late-medieval alchemist Nicolas Flamel, and the early modern natural philosophers Paracelsus and Heinrich Cornelius Agrippa of Nettesheim. Legendary figures, drawn from medieval literature, include King Arthur's half-sister Morgana and his advisor Merlin. In addition, Alberic Grunnion (the "grunter") might be an oblique allusion to Alberich, a powerful dwarf who possesses an invisibility cloak in the medieval Austrian *Song of the Nibelungen* (made famous in Richard Wagner's operatic Ring Cycle). The cards also depict figures drawn from mythology: the ancient Greek sorceress Circe and the ancient Celtic Druidess Cliodna. Obviously, with the exception of Flamel, these figures play little direct role in Harry's adventures. Nonetheless, they do sustain the idea that Rowling has constructed a historical fantasy, insofar as she uses them to imply that her alternative version of the present is the product of an alternative version of the past—one in which the superstitious is assumed to be quite real.[3]

Other aspects of the stories work to create the same impression. Rowling makes extensive use of the seventeenth-century guide to medicinal plants, *Culpeper's Complete Herbal*, in giving names to magical plants, ingredients, and even characters. In fact, Rowling's attention to names and word play is rich in historical and literary allusions. McGonagall's namesake Minerva is the Roman goddess of wisdom. (For this reason we should not be surprised when she forecasts Harry's fame at the beginning of *The Sorcerer's Stone*.) Trelawney's first name, Sybill, alludes to any number of prophetesses known as Sibyls in the ancient world. (It is a term often applied to fortunetellers.) Lupin likewise carries a name with historical significance. Remus and his brother Romulus founded Rome after being suckled as infants by a she-wolf. Lupin is derived from the Latin *lupus* meaning wolf. (Since Romulus murdered Remus, we might expect more difficulties for Rowling's tragic character.) In addition, readers might wish to consider Hermione's similarities to Shakespeare's character of the same name in *A Winter's Tale*, Mrs. Norris's relation to one of Jane Austen's invention in *Mansfield Park*, or why Harry's owl Hedwig is named after a medieval saint. Ron, I might point out, is also the name of King Arthur's spear.[4]

Even more significant are Rowling's depictions of magical activities that bear a striking resemblance to beliefs and practices described in European historical sources. In *Magic in the Middle Ages*, Northwestern University historian Richard Kieckhefer provides concise explanations of the principle forms. Popular among the common people, he notes, were various healing arts, the recitation of charms or spells, the use of protective amulets or talismans, and astrological predictions or other forms of divination. (Charms are spoken incantations, rather than objects; amulets and talismans are both objects, but the latter have words or symbols inscribed upon them.) Fears of sorcery, or harmful magic, were also widespread; clearly, it was believed, if magic could be used for good purposes, it could also be used to harm.

But in addition to describing ordinary, everyday magical practices, Kieckhefer outlines learned forms as well. Elite magic resembled its more common variants, but it differed substantially in terms of complexity. In addition, practitioners tended to organize the magical arts according to three basic varieties, which Kieckhefer identifies as astrology, astral magic, and alchemy, along with numerous subcategories. The first proceeded either through the casting of horoscopes or through interrogations and inceptions. Horoscopes represented attempts to ascertain a person's general destiny, interrogations were conducted to foresee the outcomes of endeavors undertaken upon certain dates, and inceptions were completed to choose the most auspicious dates for various activities or tasks. Astral magic, in contrast, represented attempts to change one's destiny rather than predict it; practices could take numerous forms not unlike those within the common tradition: medicines, charms, amulets and talismans, the manipulation of symbols or numbers, and so on. Finally, alchemy represented learned attempts to transmute base metals into gold and to make use of the elixir of life. Like the common tradition, learned approaches to magic distinguished between good and bad magic. According to practitioners, it could be used for both beneficial and malevolent purposes. Nonetheless, a further distinction should be described in relation to how learned magicians understood the sources of magic. Some simply saw magic as "natural," the result of the successful manipulation of invisible forces inherent in the universe. Others saw it as either implicitly or explicitly "demonic," the result of invoking the superior intellect and powers of spiritual beings, or devils. There is little doubt that some learned magicians tried to invoke demons for various ends.[5]

The magic of Harry Potter corresponds to both the popular and elite varieties of magic described by Kieckhefer, although it is never presented as demonic—even when practiced by evil characters. Charms are the most common form, but readers need not look very hard to find potions, amulets, and talismans used for various purposes. Likewise, magical apparatus and ingredients in the stories closely resemble the crystal balls, cauldrons, mirrors, magic wands, and plant or animal products described in historical sources. We also find a similar way of comprehending the basic distinction between good and bad magic: for the most part, the difference depends more upon the intent of the practitioner than the form of the magic. Curses, hexes, and poisons are simply malevolent versions of charms and medicinal potions. If we turn our attention to learned varieties of magic on display in Harry's stories, we see many of the subcategories associated with astrological, astral, and alchemical practices: horoscopes, divination, palmistry, dream-interpretation, numerology (arithmancy), transfiguration, herb-lore (herbology), and potions.[6]

So far I have left largely unexamined demonic understandings of magic, but given the various criticisms directed against Rowling by fundamentalist Christians, I should now address it at greater length. Following Kieckhefer, I have already drawn attention to a distinction between the common tradition of magic and its more learned variants. Historians are almost unanimous in thinking that demonic or diabolical understandings of magic were almost entirely absent from the popular tradition until well into the early modern period. Certainly, many medieval people believed in the existence of supernatural beings such as fairies, pixies, elves, and the like, but these "little people" were rarely associated with notions of the devil or demons, even though some of them could be quite malevolent. By the seventeenth century, however, the situation among the common people changed, as learned ideas about the devil and magic were communicated to them during the course of thousands of public witchcraft trials. Among learned practitioners and their religious critics, in contrast, we find early and significant debates over the nature and sources of magic. While many philosophers contended that magic was natural, numerous Christian theologians insisted upon seeing it as inherently demonic and contrary to doctrine. We witness many strongly worded condemnations of magic, for example, coming from the earliest Christian apologists during the first centuries of their religion's spread. These were given fuller shape by St. Augustine in the fifth century and by St. Thomas Aquinas in the thirteenth. And both Catholic and Protestant scholars in the sixteenth and seventeenth centuries advanced similar views in attempting to rid Europe of what they perceived to be a demonic pestilence.

Basing their views on several rather unambiguous biblical condemnations of magic, Christian demonologists saw the devil behind every magical deed, regardless of its practitioner's intentions. Early on, they soundly condemned any pagan belief or practice as demonic in inspiration and viewed pagan gods and goddesses as demons snaring the ignorant. In subsequent centuries, heretics were likewise condemned as dupes of the devil, and steps to locate, isolate, and eradicate them were proposed and supported. Over the course of the thirteenth and fourteenth centuries, magical practices came to be seen as heretical. By the early fifteenth century, a consensus had formed around the issue, and "demonic witchcraft" became the source of so many ills within Christian society. In effect, the common tradition of magic had been demonized. According to learned demonologists, its practitioners entered into pacts with the devil who "marked" them as his own, invoked demonic spirits, flew through the night, kidnapped and consumed babies and small children, damaged crops and buildings, caused death and disease. Most heinously, they attended "witches' sabbaths," where they engaged in gluttonous feasts, frenzied dancing, and sexual intercourse with the devil and each other.

The late medieval trend toward demonizing the common tradition of magic led ultimately to a very sad chapter in European history. Although there had been a small number of trials directed against those accused of sorcery in earlier centuries, the prosecution of presumed witches reached a new intensity and fervor by the fifteenth. And by the final decades of the sixteenth, thousands of people were being interrogated, tortured, and tried in courts of law, as the result of accusations directed against them by their neighbors. All told, scholars estimate, between 1435 and 1760, approximately one hundred thousand people became suspects in witchcraft trials, 75 to 80 percent of whom were women. Roughly forty to fifty thousand suspects were put to death for their alleged crimes. Trials for witchcraft grew less frequent after 1640, when many judges began to apply stricter rules of evidence. Cases pretty much ceased altogether by 1760, as religious and political elites came to see witchcraft, during the course of the Enlightenment, as superstition based upon ignorance and sought to eliminate that rather than witchcraft.[7]

The Harry Potter series includes several references to the period of the witch-hunts, but it is usually identified as medieval rather than early modern. It is one of history's great ironies that thousands of presumed witches were hanged, strangled, beheaded, or burned at the stake in Europe while the region was also experiencing sweeping trends that historians identify as the Renaissance, Reformation, and

Scientific Revolution. Although the intellectual foundations of the witch-hunts were laid in earlier centuries, the worst of the prosecutions took place between 1580 and 1640, well after the close of the Middle Ages. It's a common mistake to think of trials for witchcraft as medieval, and it is one of the few made by Rowling.

More important to this discussion, Rowling's depictions of magic carefully avoid representing Harry's (or even Voldemort's) as demonic in nature. Unless we accept the idea that all magic is implicitly demonic, like the demonologists of history or some contemporary fundamentalists, it is impossible to see the magic in the Harry Potter books as even remotely related to the devil. When assessing Rowling's images of magic against historical accounts of diabolical forms, *we find within them neither the formulas that learned magicians used to summon demons nor practices associated with the witches' sabbath.*

Rowling may offer some *literary* allusions to the demonic, but there are no *literal* invocations of it. Therefore, while it is true that Voldemort "marks" his Death Eaters and assembles them in a circle, and that these actions may cast him as a diabolical figure, there is nothing to suggest that he is acting on behalf of the devil or some similar power. His evil is all his own. The same is true of the Death Eaters or the dementors, the only other vaguely demonic figures in the books. At most, Voldemort, the Death Eaters, and the dementors are emblematic of radical evil; they do not derive their powers from the devil, the personification of evil within the Christian tradition.

In contrast, when we compare Rowling's magic to modern forms of witchcraft or paganism, we do find some similarities. These observations should neither surprise nor worry us. Both Rowling and modern witches are drawing from the same set of historical precedents; both are likewise generally uninterested in demonic ideas or practices. But there, I would argue, the similarities end, because Rowling puts history to work in fantasy literature, while neopagans use it to give shape to their own modern spirituality. Rowling's fiction is attractive to some pagans, but this hardly proves that she shares their religious views, as some of her critics suggest. Again, we cannot conclude that something diabolical is afoot at Hogwarts, *unless* we choose to see all magic (whether historical or neopagan) as inherently and implicitly demonic. It is not saying too much to note that most reputable scholars do not.[8]

The same fundamentalist complaints are often directed against references made in the Harry Potter books to fantastic legends and myths, but they, too, fall well short of their mark. Rowling asks readers to suspend their disbelief so that they might enjoy a "what if" version of the world. Banishing the imaginative use of supernatural or superstitious tales from literature would deny all of us important elements of our cultural inheritance. Although I began this chapter by noting how ordinary Harry is, I hope I've made clear that his adventures contain a smorgasbord of magical delights.

In order to bring my discussion of the fantastic in Rowling's books to a close, I want to call attention to the sheer number of legendary and mythical references that give her alternative world even greater depth and more vivid texture. Even though the terms *legend* and *myth* are often used interchangeably, *legend* usually refers to stories believed to have some historical basis, while *myth* usually refers to stories about the gods or superhuman heroes. Although I shall describe a bit later how Rowling puts a few legendary or mythical creatures to work in her stories, for the moment, I'd like simply to list the ones we encounter within them. If we look for legendary creatures, we find "little people" such as dwarfs, elves, fairies, gnomes, leprechauns, and pixies; "spirits" such as boggarts, grindylows, hinkypunks, kappas, and red caps; "monsters" such as banshees, basilisks, dragons, giants, goblins, grims, hippogriffs, ogres, trolls, veelas, werewolves, and yetis; and "revenants" (which return from the dead) such as ghosts and ghouls, mummies, poltergeists, vampires, and zombies. If we look for mythical creatures, we find: centaurs, dragons, griffons, manticores, mermaids and mermen, phoenixes, sphinxes, three-headed dogs, and unicorns. (Whew! I'll bet most readers believe that Rowling made a few of these up.) In addition, we find cats, owls, rats, snakes, salamanders, spiders, and toads, all possessing powers or attractions few of us would suspect they have.[9]

If we return now (at last) to the ordinary or familiar aspects of Rowling's tales, we notice that despite its many fantastic qualities, Harry's world is not so different from our own. Because of the near-contemporary setting of Rowling's series, we can read Harry's adventures as an example of *historical fiction*. I don't want to press this point too hard, but let's consider, for the moment, that Harry lives in what is clearly the United Kingdom in the late twentieth century. His surroundings in Little Whinging are not unlike what millions of other people encounter in similar places on a daily basis. If we note that Nearly Headless Nick was executed in 1492, we can determine that he celebrated the five hundredth anniversary of his death in 1992, when Harry was twelve years old. (I should note that in the first book Nick hasn't eaten in close to *four* hundred years, a claim clearly at odds with his Deathday celebrations in the second book.) Through simple mathematics, we can conclude that most events in Rowling's series take place between 1991 and 1998. Since this timeframe implies that Harry is born in 1980, we can surmise that he would be twenty-three years old in 2003—the year that the fifth book in the series, *Harry Potter and the Order of the Phoenix*, was published. I hardly think that we should attach too much significance to these dates, but they do tell us something about Harry's stories as historical fiction— they take place in a recognizably historical social context.

If we consider the 1990s in the United Kingdom as a historical period, we witness several themes playing themselves out. The decade was a period of both economic growth and greater disparities between the richest and poorest members of society. It was also a time of social tensions and dislocations related to each development. The United Kingdom experienced increasing globalization (economic and cultural), increasing multiculturalism (racial, ethnic, religious), increasing consumerism (in communications, entertainment, education, and leisure), and increasing political alienation (on the right and the left). To greater or lesser extents, other parts of the world likewise experienced these same social trends. Harry and his friends do as well, and we can see recent history informing Rowling's portrayals of the international Triwizard Tournament, the ethnically diverse student body at

Hogwarts, shopping trips to Diagon Alley and Hogsmeade (or at Quidditch World Cup), and characters' encounters with an increasingly out-of-touch Ministry of Magic. Precisely when Rowling's stories take place may be somewhat incidental to readers' enjoyment of them, but a heightened awareness of their timing can lead readers to a better understanding of why Harry's world so resembles our own.[10]

Rowling's blend of the familiar and the fantastic is one of the keys to her novels' success. In the *Irresistible Rise of Harry Potter*, Andrew Blake argues that Harry is a "contemporary boy." I clearly think that's true, but he's something else as well. As Philip Nel makes clear, Harry is a "classic fantasy hero" endowed with magical powers. On his heroic quest, he travels an ancient road through initiations and trials, successes and failures, before it will bring him to his ultimate confrontation with evil. Mary Pharr makes a similar point, observing, "although only a boy, Harry walks a line that extends for thousands of years and through numerous narrative structures." In this respect, Harry is also a "historical boy"—a fictional character who reflects the numerous historical, legendary, and mythical legacies that shape him.[11]

To conclude my discussion of how the Harry Potter books blend the familiar and the fantastic, I would like to suggest that Rowling takes up big issues rooted in the past and explores them in the present. As I hope to show in the rest of this chapter, although she doesn't treat history, legend, and myth as a historian would, she does use them in imaginative ways that are available to the novelist. She takes elements from very old tales, which have never really gone away, and reshapes them for a present-day audience that is eager (if only unconsciously) to encounter them in new and contemporary contexts. In her expert hands, an archetypal hero comes to life in the late twentieth century. Readers should, therefore, not be surprised when her fantasy depicts social problems in today's world, confronts age-old conundrums about the nature of evil, and ultimately advances an ancient, but updated, view of morality that is not dependent upon religious faith but still largely consistent with it. Rowling enchants her audience by blending the familiar and the fantastic into a carefully constructed literary myth.

THE USES OF HISTORY, LEGEND, AND MYTH

Needless to say at this point, not all readers find Rowling's stories so enchanting. Her choice to write a work of fantasy in a near-contemporary and familiar setting inspires not only tremendous interest among a highly diverse audience but also quite a bit of hostile criticism. As I suggested in the previous chapter, some readers do not like her vision, seeing it as either not imaginative enough or too imaginative, depending upon their ideological commitments. In assessing Rowling's novels, the social critics respond to what I have termed the familiar, while the religious critics react to what I have called the fantastic.

If we keep in mind the complaints of the social critics, we can see how they distrust Rowling's depictions of existing familiar institutions, practices, and assumptions, which are all the result of historical processes unfolding over the course of centuries. These features of Harry's stories are, in other words, the product of history. They make each novel an example of the particular type of historical fiction whose aspects I described earlier. Because Rowling presents Harry himself as a product of historical trends, some critics have come to see her as too accepting of the status quo.

If we consider the complaints of the religious critics, we can observe how they have misgivings about Rowling's use of bygone fantastic configurations, customs, and beliefs, which she reintroduces to a realistic contemporary environment. These legendary or mythical elements presented in Harry's stories are perceived as inappropriate or perilous. The same is true of historical practices and beliefs now deemed by many to be superstitious. The religious critics, of course, see them all as implicitly demonic. They make each of Harry's adventures into the kind of historical fantasy that I outlined above at some length. Because their author presents them in matter-of-fact (and, indeed, captivating) fashion, some critics have come to see her as too hostile to the status quo.

What most frustrates the critics, therefore, is the fact that Rowling so violates their expectations of what fantasy fiction should be. She does not offer a safely alternative world but a dangerously coextensive one. Consequently, readers of her fiction encounter neither a consciously idealistic utopia effectively challenging contemporary inequalities, which would please the social critics, nor a purely imaginary utopia avoiding any mention of contemporary reality, which would please the religious critics. The Harry Potter books explode the fantasy genre by clinging too close to "reality." This tendency also bothers English professor John Pennington at St. Norbert College, who makes this point in a lengthy review of Rowling's books, even though he really isn't interested in the complaints of either the social or religious critics. Assessing the stories as literature, he asserts, "on aesthetic grounds the series is fundamentally failed fantasy." In other words, he contends, the books simply do not conform to "the fundamental ground rules that define the fantasy tradition."[12]

In my opinion, so much the better. Why? Because there are few apparent costs, aesthetic or otherwise, resulting from Rowling's failure to comply with predetermined notions of what fantasy literature should be. Quite to the contrary, as millions of readers already implicitly agree, that "failure" is one of the things that make Harry's adventures so appealing.

In portraying both the familiar and the fantastic, Rowling draws extensively upon history, legend, and myth—in both prosaic and preposterous ways—to establish the features of her imagined world. In her highly imaginative uses of the past, Rowling is playing a double game. On the one hand, through her realistic presentation of *fantastic elements* taken from the past, she provides an *alternative version* of the world. On the other, through her realistic presentation of *familiar elements* taken from the past, she provides an *ordinary version* of the world. In an important sense, all writers of fiction who make use of the past play this same double game. They draw upon human history to comment upon the human condition. In doing so, they elaborate upon age-old themes and illustrate how they still inform today's world.

This insight is just one of many offered by A. S. Byatt, the famed author of *Possession* and other works of fiction. In a collection of essays titled *On Histories and Stories*, she reviews the "uneasy and unsettled" boundaries between fiction and history and notes that both historians and writers of fiction construct the pasts they portray. Yet, in fiction, encounters with the past become opportunities not only for listening to "the voices of persistent ghosts or spirits" but also for situating them within an imagined present. For, as she asserts, "the writer of fiction is at liberty to invent—as the historian and the biographer are not." In her essay titled "True Stories and the Facts of Fiction," she takes up this issue at some length and addresses the relation between present-day concerns and aspects of the past: "This is a kind of rewriting, or writing between the lines which fiction does with more tact, less whimsy, and infinitely more power" than history or literary criticism. But it is not an uninformed rewriting, and Byatt makes the effort to acknowledge the process of research the writer of fiction follows. The process excavates "recurring themes and patterns" for applications within new fictional contexts. For Byatt, old stories continue to inform the new. In describing her own research leading to the writing of *Angels and Insects*, she reflects upon her pleasure in discovering how myths persist in their effects despite the desire for historical specificity and the closure that it promises.

Byatt continues to develop this theme in another essay, "Old Tales, New Forms," in which she considers how authors use "tales, old, invented and reinvented, to charm, to entice, and to galvanize their readers in turn" and how "old tales and forms have had a continued, metaphoric life." Her assessments of Roberto Calasso's views are particularly insightful. Applying his ideas, she tells us that primal themes are organic and metaphoric in their ability to take on new forms. Why? As Calasso states in *The Marriage of Cadmus and Harmony*, "Stories never live alone: they are the branches of a family that we have to trace back, and forward." What's more, according to Byatt, these old stories, endlessly recounted in newer forms, possess a kind of truth in their basic simplicity. They challenge succeeding generations to consider "the fate of beauty and ugliness, fear and hope, chance and disaster." Returning once again to her own work on old stories, she reflects:

I understood that the tales had power because they were alive every-where. A myth derives force from its endless repeatability. "Origi-nality" and "individuality," those novelistic aesthetic necessities, were neither here nor there.[13]

Byatt's explorations of the relationship between history and fiction strike me as particularly significant for an analysis of the Harry Potter books, even if they do contain a good bit of "whimsy." Rowling listens to the past in order to comment upon the present. She rewrites the past but in a well-informed fashion—in a way dependent upon considerable research. She charms, entices, and galvanizes her readers through the metaphoric power of the past, and she gives new life to historical, leg-endary, and mythical themes. Most important, her updated, fictional considerations of "beauty and ugliness, fear and hope, chance and dis-aster," among still other tensions, rewrite the simple historical parables that Byatt and Calasso (and millions of readers) find so appealing.

I can only conclude, with some irony, that what makes Rowling's works problematic in the eyes of so many critics are precisely those things that Byatt and Calasso value so highly. The critics interpret the attractions and benefits of "old tales" in "new forms," "recurring themes and patterns," and "endless repeatability" as only so many dangers. The critics see them as support for conventional morality or as an invitation to false belief. From their perspectives, Rowling's various uses of the past, in both familiar and fantastic ways, conspire to render her work either too conservative or too radical.

Let's abandon Rowling's critics for a while in order to examine how the past serves her. In her fiction, she explicitly uses the past in roughly three different ways, which, I believe, make her stories all the more appealing. By this point, they should sound familiar to readers. First, she employs simple and exotic elements of history, legend, and myth to give her magical world its form. In addition, she places each of her characters in a present that is the consequence of past events, and she gives them the intellect to recognize how those events continue to influence and shape the future. Finally, she draws upon a rich histor-ical legacy of ethical problems and reasonable solutions to them.

Although, as I have argued, she develops a moral system that is largely Stoic in character, I hope to show that she embeds it within a new literary myth that displays a keen awareness of traditional patterns of heroism and ancient understandings of symbolism.

In taking up the first of these uses of the past, I need not belabor how aspects of history, legend, and myth simply give shape to Harry's world, since I already spent a good part of this chapter providing numerous examples of all three types. After all, it is an imagined world whose features correspond rather well with fantastic and familiar elements of the real human past. Nonetheless, as I argued earlier, these features are essential to Harry's stories as fantasy fiction. Even though fantastic plot developments within the books might often seem merely incidental to the larger moral questions I addressed earlier, their tremendous ability to entertain and to instruct should not be underplayed. As Byatt and Calasso might note, such "old tales" in "new forms" bring readers into contact with issues that have not only long histories but contemporary significance as well. Within the stories, it is true, the big problems confronting Harry derive from the existence of magical forces and the power of some individuals to manipulate them, but it is also true that the realistic setting of the tales reminds readers that his problems are not entirely unlike their own.

Rowling accomplishes this most obviously in the "realistic" feel of her books. Both the suburban qualities of Little Whinging and other-worldly depictions of magic are historically accurate, despite their inventive and parodic portrayals. At first glance, matter-of-fact historical allusions to such things as trials for witchcraft (real events) or goblin rebellions (made-up ones) might not seem to remind readers of their own circumstances, but upon reflection, these events do come to resemble forms of persecution and resistance against them in our own times. By employing the past in these ways, Harry's adventures may *gently* encourage readers to see both themselves and important contemporary issues in light of historical developments.

Turning to Rowling's second way of using the past, I'd like to note that the pronounced fatalism in Harry's adventures serves to communicate the same message. Having paid considerable attention to this issue in chapter 3 and chapter 4, once again, I need not overwork it at this point. The fact that Rowling's characters are so clearly the products of past events and display an acute awareness of them should suggest to readers how important a historical sensibility is to her stories. Each subsequent book in the series carries the central story not only forward but backward as well. The more readers learn about the future, the more they learn about the past. The various stories are interconnected. With regard to this tendency, real historical antecedents are far less important than the age-old "recurring themes and patterns" that Byatt and Calasso find so appealing in numerous tales. Rowling develops personal and collective histories for her characters, outlining the interplay of friendship and enmity, love and betrayal, wisdom and ignorance, and right and wrong. The more things change, the more they stay the same.

Because Rowling's vision of Harry's world is so fully realized, in a very basic way, significant events within it always emerge from earlier ones. For example, multiple hints and intimations serve to portray Voldemort's antagonistic struggle with Harry as only the most recent manifestation of similar animosities between Salazar Slytherin and the other founders of Hogwarts. What's more, Rowling shows that her characters are cognizant of the workings of historical forces. Harry's experiences with Dumbledore's thought-revealing Pensieve are particularly important in this regard. Within this magical data base, the headmaster stores his memories for later retrieval, when, upon reflection, he may more easily recognize connections and significant patterns. Once he reconsiders events and communicates his thoughts to Harry, memory becomes history. Again and again, Harry and other characters recognize the past's potential to make itself felt in the present. This trend, I will offer, is likely to continue and to intensify within subsequent volumes of Rowling's series. The author has already promised as much before the arrival of *The Order of the Phoenix* in bookstores, by allowing her publisher to release a brief passage: "Dumbledore lowered his hands and surveyed Harry through his half-moon glasses. 'It is time', he said, 'for me to tell you what I should have told you five years ago, Harry. Please sit down. I am going to tell you everything.'"[14]

If I turn now to Rowling's third way of using the past, her elaboration of a moral system with deep historical roots, I think we'll begin to see even more clearly the kind of thing Byatt and Calasso value most in old stories—their "endless repeatability." We do not, of course, find references to Zeno or Seneca, as we do to Ptolemy, Flamel, and Agrippa, but we must remember that Rowling has written a *moral tale* and not a *moral treatise*. She thus puts the metaphoric power of the past to work in a story whose morals an audience must infer. The most palpable aspect of this tendency emerges in the many resemblances Rowling's storytelling has to other, traditional forms, such as the folktale and fairy tale. But given the sheer scope of her project, we must conclude that she goes even further. In the final analysis, Rowling puts history, legend, and myth to work in what we might consider a literary myth, an epic fantasy conveying important moral lessons. I'd now like to spend some time outlining this third way that Rowling puts the past to use.

What is "literary myth"? In his study of J. R. R. Tolkien, literary scholar and fantasy author Richard L. Purtill introduces the notion of literary myth in order to elaborate on how readers might see Tolkien as its chief exemplar. Purtill distinguishes the notion from "original myth," which honors the gods and conveys moral and religious lessons through their stories, and "philosophical myth," which conveys philosophical ideas through allegory or metaphor. Both these forms of myth are "true," according to those espousing them, but the latter is also fictional, insofar as someone consciously invents a story. In contrast to both, literary myth makes use of fictional heroes in an openly literary endeavor in order to convey moral lessons. Neither authors nor audiences accept its story as "true," and its lessons have no special status beyond an implicit claim to wisdom. Viewed from this perspective, folktales, fairy tales, and epic fantasies might all qualify as forms of literary myth.[15]

We may certainly read the Harry Potter books in this way. More than a few scholars have chosen to interpret the books as an updated folktale, fairy tale, or myth. Those who prefer to comprehend them in terms of epic fantasy invariably note their similarities to those popular genres. Regardless, Harry is often likened to Moses, Oedipus, King Arthur, Superman, or other manifestations of the hero of myth, which noted author Joseph Campbell reintroduced to the public in the popular reprint of his book *The Hero with a Thousand Faces*. Some writers have even chosen to interpret Harry's stories as highly symbolic religious allegories on par with the best of Tolkien and Lewis. Thus, we can see why the books offer a good example of literary myth if we consider two of their chief features: they represent heroism in very traditional ways and they often employ historically significant symbolism.[16]

We can better assess the nature of heroism in the books if we rely upon M. Katherine Grimes's wonderful article, "Harry Potter: Fairy Tale Prince, Real Boy, Archetypal Hero." As her title suggests, Grimes frames her understanding of Harry as a "real boy" within parameters established by the hero of fairy tales and the hero of myth. In general, fairy tales present more optimistic notions of the world and answer the fears of younger children, while myths tend to be more pessimistic in outlook and reflect greater awareness of adult realities. In either case, heroes are poised and ready to overcome adversity in order to find security and assert their independence.

Putting the ideas of famed psychologist Bruno Bettelheim to work in her analysis of Harry as a fairy tale hero, Grimes notes that such tales offer children magic, optimism, and distance in both time and place in their portrayals of fictional events. Most fundamentally, fairy tales posit a clear distinction between good and evil through numerous dualities represented symbolically by various characters. Thus, Harry has good parents and bad parents, as well as protectors and enemies. Bettelheim understood fairy tales largely as means for children to overcome fears of abandonment, on the one hand, and to comprehend personal independence, on the other. In Harry's tales, like so many others, a number of stock characters—in both paternal and maternal forms—serve as surrogates for his dead parents and foster confidence and autonomy through both positive and negative behavior. Some, as "good" parents, allay fears of abandonment and nurture independence through protection and provision (e.g., Hagrid, Sirius, Dumbledore, McGonagall, and Molly Weasley). Others, as "bad" parents, allow for resistance and the assertion of individuality (e.g., Voldemort, Vernon, and Petunia Dursley). Within this context, fairy tale heroes behave and crave the ways most children do. They endure adult unfairness, satisfy their animal longings, and hope their mistakes will go unpunished; they also want to see evil vanquished, to find protectors, and to have their uniqueness recognized. Yet, central to their progress toward confidence and independence is how they meet death, or, at least, the threat of it through a series of metaphorical deaths and rebirths. Harry's quest thus involves fear, suffering, struggle, and triumph over adversity. He "dies" only to "rise" again. Ultimately, these features of his tales offer children, and adult readers, both vicarious pleasures and simple reassurances.

Turning to the darker aspects of the hero of myth, Grimes begins her analysis by assessing Harry against ten basic characteristics of the mythic hero identified by psychologist Otto Rank (a student of Freud) in his *Myth of the Birth of the Hero*. She finds that Harry possesses eight of them. He is born of special parents (a witch and a wizard); his life is threatened; he is separated from his parents; he is exposed (on the doorstep in Little Whinging); he is put in water to be "killed" and to be "saved" (taken from land by the Dursleys, then returned to it by Hagrid); he is rescued by an underling (Hagrid); he is raised by social inferiors (the Dursleys); and he is recognized as a hero because of a special mark (his scar, the result of a wound inflicted upon him). We do not yet know if difficulty preceded Harry's conception or if he will be reconciled with (or seek vengeance upon) his father, two additional hallmarks of the mythic hero, but I'd wager good money on both propositions. In fact, reconciliation may already have occurred in *The Prisoner of Azkaban* with Sirius, Harry's godfather, and "Prongs", the form taken by Harry's *Patronus* (Latin for "protector" from *pater*, meaning "father") and by his father as an animagus.

There is, of course, much more to the heroism on display in myth, which tends to reflect concerns befitting an adult hero. Although mythic heroes may begin their adventures as children, and while plenty of parental surrogates populate their tales, the stories themselves go beyond childhood concerns to take up issues such as mortality and immortality; the relation of human beings to the divine, the relation between body and spirit; the meanings of birth, life, and death; and the ambiguous nature of evil. Still, we find many of the same features associated with the hero of fairy tales: persistent threats, a series of tests and trials, the unfolding of a special destiny, and metaphorical deaths and rebirths. As Grimes points out, Rank saw myths as collective expressions of "retrograde childhood fantasies"—as the product of adult human desires to overcome life's difficulties and uncertainties. To our satisfaction, mythical heroes usually do.[17]

Since Harry's tales emphasize his transition to adulthood, we find a number of more mature themes being played out within them, including Harry's path to maturity itself. For this reason, although I have followed Grimes in presenting Harry as a hero, I am also impressed by the insights offered by Mary Pharr, a professor of English at Florida Southern College, in her essay, "In Medias Res: Harry Potter as Hero-in-Progress." She emphasizes that the hero's instinctual goodness must be accompanied by a growing consciousness and by cultivation of individual capacities to serve the needs of others. Heroes do not simply act on their own behalf. Thus, in each subsequent book, Harry progresses. He not only embodies the wisdom of countless earlier heroes but also gives expression to its refinement through a heightened awareness of choice, empathy, and responsibility, made possible by new knowledge. As a "hero-in-progress," he educates himself, just as others seek to guide him. In Pharr's reading of Harry as a mythical hero who remains an ordinary boy, he becomes a "deceptively simple emblem" of faith in individual human potential.[18]

Since Harry has so many of the traits associated with the heroes of fairy tale and myth, we can read his adventures as an extended and updated allegory on historical forms of heroism. Given the emphasis that fairy tales and myth place upon *cultivation of the self* and *service to others*, we should not be surprised that their themes often relate to the Stoic virtues that I outlined in chapter 3: constancy, endurance, perseverance, self-discipline, reason, solidarity, empathy, and sacrifice. Rowling's new version of an old story becomes a literary myth communicating these same morals.

Also important to our understanding of the Harry Potter books as literary myth is the symbolism at work in them. Once again, in the very old symbols Rowling deploys, we encounter another kind of "endless repeatability"—old ideas fashioned within a new context. Although it is tempting to view symbols as "universal," I want to emphasize that their meanings are context-dependent. If readers have already gone through the available volumes of Harry Potter without recognizing Rowling's many uses of symbolic meanings, they have already experienced what I'm talking about. In our own times, many symbols with impressive historical pedigrees go entirely unnoticed because they are unfamiliar. They take on new significance, however, within the context of Harry's stories, which ask readers to suspend their disbelief of the fantastic. Symbols can certainly reflect human ideals, but they do not exist independently of how they are used.[19]

If we turn our attention to the many legendary creatures in the Harry Potter works, we can begin to get a sense of how Rowling uses symbols to communicate important moral lessons. Often enough, she simply drops these creatures into her stories to add vibrancy—or, crucially, comic potential. They nearly always appear for the first time in episodes that are humorous, but upon closer examination, even the humor associated with incidental creatures functions within the texts in ways that are significant. For example, a host of lesser folkloric creatures populates Harry's day-to-day life. Rowling deploys, among still others, the English grindylow, the West Country hinkypunk, the Japanese kappa, the Cornish pixie, the German poltergeist, and the English red cap as only so many magical pests. Each is symbolic of the unexpected difficulties and uncertainties that life so indifferently places in an individual's way. They are potentially dangerous but mostly frustrating, easily dealt with if one remains patient and diligent and recognizes them for the mere nuisances they are. (A true Stoic would eat them for breakfast.)

In contrast, other legendary creatures carry more symbolic weight—even when humor is present in their deployment. Let me briefly describe a few examples from the symbol-rich third volume, *Harry Potter and the Prisoner of Azkaban*. The boggart Harry encounters well suits Rowling's development of her hero's growing maturity—a central theme in the book. A well-known figure within northern English folklore, the boggart adopts the form of what individual people most fear. Upon learning that Harry most fears the dementors, Professor Lupin responds, "Well, well . . . I'm impressed. . . . That suggests that what you fear most of all is—fear. Very wise, Harry."[20] The boggart thus becomes a symbol for fear itself, and something the hero must overcome. (Rowling has also admitted that the purely fictional dementors symbolize the debilitating effects of depression.[21]) Significantly, laughter renders the boggart harmless. A similar moral is conveyed by the grim, a common omen of death in the British Isles, which Harry repeatedly sees in the same book. The grim turns out to be Sirius, again, as a kind of ironic joke, but before Harry realizes this fact, he must come to grips with the threat of his own demise (repeated often enough by the fraudulent Professor Trelawney). True to form, he meets it with poise, having already done so on numerous occasions. In her portrayals of the boggart and grim, Rowling thus puts fear and the threat of death into symbolic form. Harry, of course, greets both with their opposites, courage and a life-affirming resolve. Of course, not all legendary creatures symbolize negative aspects of the human condition. The hippogriff, invented by the Italian author Ludovico Ariosto in his epic poem *Orlando Furioso*, might be read as a symbol of human potential or the pursuit of dreams. Churlishly taunting human beings, the hippogriff becomes tame and loyal once mounted, capable of soaring quickly and to the highest altitudes. In the course of Harry's adventures, the standoffish Buckbeak literally becomes the vehicle upon which Harry and Hermione successfully pursue a hopeless cause. Eschewing faintheartedness, they need only dare to try.

Mythical creatures may also be read as symbols in the Potter books. Some ambiguously signal contrary tendencies and reflect the many tensions inherent within the human condition. We can certainly see this characteristic among the centaurs depicted, since they read the future in the stars except when they choose not to. They symbolize both instinct and wisdom, befitting their half-animal, half-human forms. Dragons are, perhaps, less ambiguous but still symbolize power in both its creative and destructive forms. It is telling that Harry must rescue an egg (another symbol) in the face of an extremely violent Hungarian Horntail. Hagrid likewise obtains a dragon's egg, only to have the baby nearly set him and his hut on fire. In mythology, mermaids (especially) and mermen (less so) symbolize enchantment, temptation, and death. Again, it is telling that, under the lake, Harry avoids all three. He ultimately ignores the instructions of the merpeople, shows his "moral fiber" by refusing to leave any of the captives, and successfully escapes with Ron, Fleur's sister, and his own life. The sphinx Harry encounters during the Triwizard Tournament rather unambiguously signals enigma and wit (as well as their danger), but the same creature in ancient mythology could also symbolize royalty, fertility, and immortality (in Egypt) or death and destruction (in Mesopotamia). Less ambiguous creatures include manticores, which symbolize evil and malevolence, as well as unicorns, which symbolize innocence and the sacred. Fluffy, the three-headed dog that guards the forbidden corridor in *The Sorcerer's Stone*, is an allusion to Cerberus, the dog that guarded the gates of the underworld. He symbolizes evil genius, as well as death and decay. In Greek mythology, Hercules overcame him through physical strength alone in pursuit of immortality. Orpheus, in contrast, soothed him with music. Each of these creatures enrich Rowling's tales (and offer Potter-maniacs ample opportunities to follow fresh leads). In an important sense, they also contribute to our understanding of her work as literary myth. They resurrect old ideas about the human condition for those who care to look.[22]

Even more significant, however, are two additional creatures drawn from legend and myth: the snake and the lion. Rowling uses the snake, along with its relative the basilisk, in a number of ways in her stories, most prominently as the symbol of Slytherin House and as the monster Harry must confront in *Harry Potter and the Chamber of Secrets*. The lion, in contrast, appears only obliquely on the crest of Gryffindor House. Significantly, however, the lion's relative, the half-eagle, half-lion griffon appears in the name of Godric Gryffindor and on the knocker to Dumbledore's office. Although the meanings associated with snakes are many and contradictory, both positive and negative, when used symbolically, they tend to represent evil more often than not. Lions, in contrast, despite a reputation as violent and rapacious beasts, usually carry more positive associations. In mythology, the basilisk and the griffin share many similarities. They are both guardians of treasure, they are "kings" of their respective realms, and they are equally dangerous. Nonetheless, the similarities end there, for they are also mortal enemies of one another. The basilisk is the deadliest of all creatures, while the griffin is the most noble. Of the basilisk, an English gentleman named John Guillim writes in his seventeenth-century *Display of Heraldry*:

> He seemeth to be a little king amongst serpents, not in regard to his quantity [size], but in respect of the infection of his pestiferous and poysonfull aspect, wherewith he poisoneth the aire.

Of the griffin, in contrast, he writes:

> By reason he uniteth force and industry together . . . having attained his full growth, [he] will never be taken alive; wherein he doth adumbrate [exhibit] or rather lively set forth the property of a valorous souldier, whose magnanimity is such as he had rather expose himselfe to all dangers, and even to death itself, than to become captive.[23]

If we apply Guillim's observations to the Potter books, we can see why Rowling generally uses the snake or the basilisk to symbolize evil and the lion or the griffin to symbolize good. By placing the two related pairs in conflict, she structures the epic struggle at the core of Harry's adventures. Salazar Slytherin and the school house that bears his name represent one set of values, while Godric Gryffindor (the "golden griffin") and the house that bears his name, along with its lion crest, represent quite another. We already know that Voldemort is the heir of Slytherin; I think we might learn that Harry is the heir of Gryffindor. Yet, Rowling is not wholly unaware of the ambiguities surrounding the snake and the lion, the basilisk and the griffin, or the many similarities that they share. After all, on the one hand, Harry is a Parselmouth who can speak with serpents, and the Sorting Hat did consider placing him in Slytherin; on the other, Snape, head of Slytherin House, has acted with courage, and Dumbledore trusts him completely.

Complicating matters is an additional mythical creature, the phoenix, which symbolizes, through its immolation at death and its rebirth from the ashes, both destruction and recreation. We can therefore understand Fawkes, Dumbledore's pet phoenix, as a mediating symbol, one situated (in a sense) between good and evil to serve as a reminder that, in the midst of devastation, hope may be found. In this sense, the immortal Fawkes represents the dual realities of never-ending change and similarly persisting continuities. We can see this type of symbolism at work in *The Metamorphoses*, when the Roman poet Ovid reflects upon the ceaseless transformations of nature and the seeming permanence of the phoenix:

> How many creatures walking on this earth
> Have their first being in another form?
> Yet one exists that is itself forever,
> Reborn in ageless likeness through the years.

The fourth-century Egyptian Horapollo describes how his ancestors used the phoenix to symbolize both transformation and permanence ("a long-enduring restoration") in human endeavors: "When they wish to indicate a long-enduring restoration, they draw the phoenix. For when this bird is born, there is a renewal of things." The symbolism of the phoenix, therefore, implies the reconciliation of counterbalancing realities: death and rebirth, destruction and recreation, change and continuity. It should not surprise us, therefore, that the phoenix is also a symbol of individual constancy, a symbol of the countless readjustments and renewals required to survive so many setbacks and disappointments. No less a person than Leonardo da Vinci interpreted the phoenix as such: "For constancy, the phoenix serves as a type; for understanding by nature its renewal, it is steadfast to endure the burning flames which consume it, and then it is reborn anew." Throughout Harry's adventures, Rowling has portrayed her hero as possessing such constancy. I will hazard to guess that in her next volume, she will have him meet likeminded individuals, the members of the "Order of the Phoenix," dedicated to a long-lasting restoration in the aftermath of devastation.[24]

If we turn our attention to the alchemical symbolism at work in Rowling's books, we can view the mediating quality of the phoenix in another light. For within alchemy the phoenix represents the philosopher's stone itself, the result of a "chemical wedding" that achieves the reconciliation of opposites through destruction and recreation. The production of the stone involves repeated cycles of chemical dissolutions and coagulations. Through this process, base matter is transformed into "prime matter" (prima materia), the original stuff of creation, which is then transformed into ever purer forms. Each stage represents the successful chemical reconciliation of opposite states and qualities (such as sulfur and mercury, hot and cold, dry and moist, fixed and volatile, spirit and body, form and matter, active and receptive, and male and female), which eliminates differences between them and unites their contrary attributes. The ultimate coagulation is the stone itself, capable of transmuting base metals into gold and humans into the divine.

Alchemists always present this process in highly metaphorical language, which Rowling has adopted and adapted in her work. If my reading of the alchemical symbolism of the phoenix is correct, it suggests that Rowling has chosen to depict it as the reconciler of the snake, on the one hand, and the lion and the griffin, on the other. Often, in alchemical writings, the snake represents the matter with which work is begun, as well as the prime matter. It is highly volatile: "The poisonous dragon or serpent . . . is a dark, destructive, chthonic [primitive] force with the power to kill the corrupt metal or matter for the Stone and dissolve it into its first matter or prima materia." In contrast, the lion symbolizes sulfur, and the griffin symbolizes mercury. Thus, the lion represents the hot, dry, solar, active, and male principle, while the griffin represents the cold, moist, lunar, receptive, and female principle. When the lion and the griffin are united and brought to bear against the snake, the phoenix is reborn.

Always described in ornately metaphorical language, as I have shown, this physical "wedding" of opposites is also a metaphysical union. Its explication begins with the Platonic assumption that humanity is divided against itself, separated into two sexes. Often enough, it is depicted as the marriage of the masculine sun and the feminine moon. Invariably, it unites willful power (the active male force) and wisdom (the receptive female force) to produce pure love (the "philosophical child," or stone). This metaphysical union leads to death, as the soul leaves the body to unite with the spirit, but out of this death emerges new life. For the soul's departure cleanses the body, and its return, now united with the spirit, resurrects the body. Dissolution and coagulation take place simultaneously. The body dissolves into spirit, and the spirit coagulates into form.[25]

In a very important sense, we can understand Harry's trials and tribulations as a metaphorical pursuit of the philosopher's stone—not for gold and eternal life, but for moral and, perhaps, spiritual virtue. In setting the values of Gryffindor (the lion and the griffin) against the values of Slytherin (the snake), Harry emerges as the exemplar of constancy (the phoenix). Furthermore, Dumbledore himself *is* an alchemist (his wizard card says so) and he has been carefully guiding Harry's development. Dare I say through metaphorical cycles of dissolution and coagulation? Many years ago, Pierre Vincenti Piobb, a French student of the occult, described the metaphysical process of dissolution and coagulation in the following way: "analyze all the elements in yourself, dissolve all that is inferior in you, even though you may break in doing so;

then, with the strength acquired from the preceding operation, congeal." In this way, we can begin to view Harry himself as an alchemist. Although I don't want to press the point too hard, we may also view Harry, the mythic hero, as the philosopher's stone, as a phoenix, as a reconciler of opposites, who brings hope out of danger and devastation. I can only speculate at this point, but I think it likely that he will continue to undergo the kinds of transformations to which alchemical symbolism alludes—not literally, but metaphorically. By following the path of Stoic virtue, he has already begun to do so.[26]

Through highly inventive uses of the past, Rowling develops Harry's adventures as a literary myth promoting virtue and conveying moral lessons. She employs ancient symbols to structure an age-old struggle between good and evil, and constructs her hero according to traditional patterns of heroism. She makes him the product of a past, and gives him the intellect to recognize its shaping influence upon the future. And she places him in a near-contemporary world, resembling our own, which combines numerous elements, both familiar and fantastic, drawn from history, legend, and myth.

If we return, at long last, to Rowling's critics, we can better assess the nature of their complaints. The social critics see her as not imaginative enough and too accepting of the status quo. The religious critics see her as too imaginative and hostile to the status quo. If we presume that the critics are right, we must conclude that Rowling fails in her uses of the past: she has created an imaginary world that is simultaneously too ordinary and too outrageous. She has violated the basic ground rules of fantasy. I clearly do not believe that Rowling has failed in her uses of the past, but she has successfully combined the familiar and the fantastic to create something new. In this sense, we should see Rowling herself as a kind of literary alchemist. In what follows, I'll attempt to illustrate how she reconciles social realism with a fanciful exploration of the problem of evil to produce a literary myth rich in Stoic morality.

SOCIAL REALISM

Some literary critics note that Harry Potter appeared just as a vogue for social realism in children's literature reached its peak. This trend, emerging in about the mid-seventies, exemplified the views of many in the field that real children should be encouraged to confront real problems in what they read. Children's authors thus provided works depicting greater social variation and a richer racial or ethnic mix. With more controversy, they also began to touch upon themes such as poverty, pregnancy, and drug use.[27]

Most of the secular critics of Harry Potter implicitly fault the series for not only bucking the trend toward social realism but also exploding it altogether. Here, as should be clear by now, I think they're only half right. They're only half right because Rowling's literary myth does take up "realist" themes, even if it does so in an inventive manner, one that, I shall grant, makes the issues more fantastic, if not exactly more mysterious. Let me sketch a few observations in response to the critics.

Much has been made of the boarding school setting of Rowling's novels and its association with conventional—and, indeed, reactionary—social values and structures of authority. But as Andrew Blake points out, the books, because of their ambivalence, do not exactly replicate this view. Nonetheless, the setting of the books contributes to the notion that Hogwarts students encounter only traditional moral values and disciplinary systems. Its structure, despite its ultra-unorthodox curriculum and the seemingly constant dangers facing students, communicates formality, order, and reassurance. The same claims may be made about representations of the institution Hogwarts replaces for much of the year, the family.[28]

As I already made clear in chapter 2 and chapter 3, Rowling does essentially update an old-fashioned virtue in her portrayal of Harry's constancy. In fact, she reinvents many old-fashioned virtues. There is a kind of reassurance, as well, offered by the kind leadership of Albus Dumbledore or the loving relations of the Weasley family, and this is as it should be in books written primarily for children.

But Rowling's books do not offer children a utopian vision of the way things should be. Instead, to some extent, they reflect the way things are, and by doing so, they address some of the issues valued by proponents of social realism in children's literature. The books may not have the gritty texture of other works for adolescents, but they hardly return kids to the days of greater cultural conformity or overt bigotry and the nuclear family ruled by the stern paterfamilias. They also put on display the effects of economic disparity and a moribund, self-satisfied political administration.

Hogwarts is ethnically and racially diverse, despite a preponderance of "white" children, as one would expect in contemporary British society. No student is destined for anything by birth, despite their "sorting" into one of four school houses and some parody of national stereotypes. Lee Jordan is identified subtly as being of African-Caribbean descent by his dreadlocks. One of Gryffindor's chasers, Angelina Johnson is also of African descent, but this does not stop her from dating Fred Weasley, across racial boundaries. Likewise, Harry's romantic interests extend across race lines, with passion to Cho Chang, of East Asian descent, and then with resignation to Parvati Patil, of South Asian descent. And, of course, Seamus Finnigan wears his Irish identity proudly—metaphorically, at first, but quite literally at the Quidditch World Cup.

There isn't much of a gender divide at the school, with both men and women on the faculty and a coed student body consisting (apparently) of an equal number of girls and boys. Slytherin's thuggish Quidditch team, it is pointedly noted, has no females among its members. Taking Hermione for granted—seeing her as "one of the guys"—exposes Ron as a fool. And honors and distinctions—as well as punishments—are awarded equitably. We might see some gender stereotyping, but, as I argued earlier, this cuts both ways and allows Rowling to lampoon particularly egregious examples, whether the girls fawn over Gilderoy Lockhart, or the boys over Fleur Delacour.

Families are also somewhat diverse. It is true that most students come from two-parent families, as far as we know, but some do not.

Readers knew early on that Neville Longbottom lives with his grandmother, although the reason was revealed only later. Still other students come from "mixed race" families, as does Fleur Delacour, whose grandmother was a Veela, and Seamus Finnigan, whose Muggle father is pointedly absent at the Quidditch World Cup. Likewise, Harry might end up with a single-father, in the (unlikely) event that Sirius's innocence is proven before the conclusion to the final book. Divorced parents are not represented, nor are many less traditional caretakers, but there are, in fact, plenty of dysfunctional families, starting with Harry's own in Little Whinging. Rowling does illustrate what a good family life could look like, but she also depicts how it can go awry. We need only remember the Crouches.

Family dynamics also play a role in the way Rowling addresses the disparities of wealth in the wizarding world. While she offers little in the way of solutions to the problem, she nonetheless makes clear that family finances shape (if not exactly determine) access to political and economic power. She neither valorizes nor demonizes the relative fortunes of the Weasley and Malfoy families, but she does implicitly question through their juxtaposition a system that produces economic injustices. Harry's discomfort in relation to his own wealth, inherited from his parents, serves to underscore the problem of inequality.

This issue is developed further in the way Rowling depicts Harry's relationship to the Ministry of Magic, the "political administration" of the wizarding world. On its surface, we see a superficial similarity to the parliamentary system of the United Kingdom (whose government cooperates with the ministry), even though democratic components are never expressly portrayed. Harry becomes privy (increasingly, as his stories progress) to the fact that not all is well within the ministry. Special treatment, unfair access, and abandonment of the rule of law are all depicted as parts of the system. Its head, Cornelius Fudge, is emblematic of the willful ignorance and bureaucratic sclerosis that shape its implementation of policy. At times, it seems to be the source, rather than a defense against, unfairness and injustice. If events at the end of *Harry Potter and the Goblet of Fire* are any indication, the ministry might continue to act in this capacity. Little doubt is left that it is a system in need of reform.

Although it is possible to denounce Rowling's portrayals of diversity and injustice as mere tokenism, I believe that she's up to something else. In each of her texts, depictions of diversity serve, on the one hand, to illustrate the ideal of peaceful coexistence and mutual respect, but they also serve, on the other, as gentle reminders to young readers that the ideal does not yet exist in their own world. Her depictions of injustice, prejudice, and outright bigotry in the wizarding world—whether directed against "mudbloods," house-elves, giants, or werewolves— serve to emphasize this point. Class antagonisms and elitism, in contrast, are portrayed directly, without the mediating influence of magical races and wizarding categories of descent. Will these depictions of diversity and injustice solve real-world problems? Certainly not, but they do serve to remind children of their existence.[29]

I'd like to take up one final example of Rowling's use of "social realism," one that at first glance might not seem pertinent: her portrayal of Severus Snape. Several critics have pointed to Snape's depiction in stereotypical ways and then sought to assess it. In *J. K. Rowling's Harry Potter Novels*, Philip Nel writes:

> Snape, another villainous sort, bears an unfortunate resemblance to the stereotype of the Jew: cunning, greasy-haired, and sallow-skinned.

Julia Eccleshare echoes this opinion in her *Guide to the Harry Potter Novels*:

> In her first description of him in *Harry Potter and the Philosopher's Stone*, Snape's physical characteristics of greasy dark hair, sallow skin and a hooked nose are an example of Rowling's sometimes clichéd use of expression which immediately casts Snape as a stereotyped villain.

Both observations are valid and disturbing (especially Nel's), but both authors go on to explain how Snape functions within Rowling's texts. In brief, both authors see Snape as Rowling's most complex and ambiguous character, used to full effect in order to show how appearances can be deceiving.

The explanations of Nel and Eccleshare are not apologies for Rowling's use of stereotype, but they can help us understand, I think, how careful readers should think about the portrayal of all characters in her series. They should be judged ultimately by their actions, rather than by their appearances. Throughout the books, the characters we identify with the most (Harry, Ron, and Hermione) are often guilty of prejudice when it comes to Snape. He has given them ample reason to dislike him, but he has not been guilty of any greater offence. In fact, he has acted as a double-agent providing important information and service to Dumbledore and the Ministry of Magic. He's been a "good guy," even if he is not likable. We can read in Snape's portrayal a central theme about the relationship between appearances and reality. Rowling does not consistently use physical characteristics, regardless of how disturbing they may be, to distinguish good from evil. This inconsistency, I contend, contributes to the "realistic" ways she chooses to depict the wizarding world—a world, as I have been saying, unlike our own, but very similar to it nonetheless.[30]

THE PROBLEM OF EVIL

Even more deeply embedded in Rowling's literary myth than contemporary social ills is a serious consideration of the problem of evil. We can begin by simply dismissing several facile claims made about her novels, which I addressed previously. They are not satanic, and they do not glorify rule-breaking. More important, even though we do not find in the books any overt definition of evil or descriptions of its ultimate source, we do find it displayed in two different ways that are highly suggestive. On the one hand, we see it personified in Voldemort, his followers, and a number of beings who seem genuinely evil by nature. They are, in other words, simply evil, and very little suggests why they are that way. Their evil, in a sense, drives the plot of the entire series.

On the other hand, we see evil depicted in mundane ways, such as mischievous behavior, indifference, or bigotry, which seem to be the result of immaturity, ignorance, or prejudice. In other words, this type of evil emerges from a failure to make the right choices rather than any inherent personal quality. This type of evil is also central to the plot of the series, because consciousness of it motivates the reactions of some characters to those depicted as naturally inclined toward malevolence.

But what precisely do I mean by "the problem of evil"? In Western cultures, it has been cast traditionally in religious terms. God is all-powerful, all-knowing, and all-good; yet, within the world he created, evil is clearly manifest in pain and suffering, as well as in numerous evident causes such as anger, hatred, and cruelty. Even if the problem is cast in secular terms, as many have done more recently, the need for a coherent explanation of the existence of good and evil remains. Different thinkers, of course, have addressed this exceptionally complex issue in different ways, but two general approaches do present themselves, which I shall simplify to the extreme. One emphasizes providence and holds that good and evil are the by-products of a larger design unfolding in nature. The other emphasizes free will and holds that good and evil are the by-products of human pursuits and choices.

Rowling has chosen to depict the *nature of evil* ambiguously, by drawing upon each of these approaches. Throughout Harry's adventures, she portrays both *intrinsic evil* (things evil by nature) and *instrumental evil* (things evil by choice). Yet, I must point out, she has also chosen to depict the *difference* between good and evil rather straightforwardly. In other words, her fiction does not tell us the source of evil directly, but it does display its cruel and destructive effects and suggest proper responses to it. I think these observations are important to our understanding of the Harry Potter books as literary myth, because even the best philosophical understandings of the nature of evil do little justice to real pain and suffering. As literary myth, the Potter books suggest that evil is part of the human condition; it exists both intrinsically, in things that cannot be controlled, and instrumentally, in actions and decisions that can be.[31]

In taking up these issues within a work of fantasy, Rowling follows several authors, particularly J. R. R. Tolkien and C. S. Lewis, whose best-known works create alternative worlds menaced by powerful and evil characters. Tolkien's Middle Earth is wholly other than our own world (despite some ironies and anachronisms that signal otherwise), while Lewis's Narnia is parallel to it (although clearly connected, since characters can travel back and forth.) Both Tolkien and Lewis are hailed as Christian authors, but both chose, at times, to consider evil through fantasy rather than expressly religious commentary. Tolkien's *The Lord of the Rings* makes no mention of religion, but its author claims to have written a book that is "fundamentally religious and Catholic." *The Silmarillion*, in contrast, is more overtly religious in tone but veils its ideas in mythic symbolism. Lewis's *Chronicles of Narnia* is an overtly Christian allegory, and other works by him tend in the same direction. Still, at other times, both Tolkien and Lewis wrote openly of their Christianity and its relation to their fiction. In comparison, Rowling's fantasy world is set in our own, even though parts of it are off-limits to Muggles, and it offers few allusions to religion or the divine, even though some commentators suggest that it, too, offers forms of Christian allegory. Rowling has identified herself as a Christian, but to date hasn't chosen to explain her faith's relation to the Harry Potter series.[32]

A brief examination of Tolkien's depiction of evil might be in order, since, I believe, it closely resembles Rowling's. In *The Lord of the Rings*, he presents views on the nature of evil that draw heavily from two different traditions. As Tom Shippey, the English professor of philology (and a successor of Tolkien's at Oxford), puts it in his book, *J. R. R. Tolkien: Author of the Century*, there is a "running ambivalence" throughout *The Lord of the Rings* on the nature of evil. At times, Tolkien presents evil as the absence of good—the failure to make the will conform to it; at other times he presents it as a force in its own right—a corrupting presence that can't be resisted. Both positions are presented with equal force. In this way, Tolkien's fantasy conveys a strong sense of the way things feel in the real world. Life is chaotic and uncertain for his characters, the result of things beyond their control, but they never abandon their power to choose how to respond. As Shippey notes, they are guided by both chance and courage in accord with an ambivalent portrayal of the nature of evil. He continues:

> It may not be possible to draw any certain *correct* conclusion from the confusions and bewilderments of Middle-earth, but it is possible to see one always marked as unequivocally and permanently *wrong*: which is, that there is no point in trying any further.

Given this portrayal of evil in Tolkien's fantasy, we can view it at work in both its intrinsic and instrumental forms. Some things seem to be evil by nature, while others are merely evil by choice. Both views have implications for understanding the workings of fate and free will. In a particularly significant series of passages in *The Lord of the Rings*, Sam Gamgee (of all people) muses that he and Frodo are characters in a *very* long story, begun in ages long past and continuing beyond their own parts in it. He also notes that characters never know what lies ahead and must simply do the best they can. I think the parallels to Rowling's consideration of evil are striking.

Tolkien has also provided his thoughts on how fantasy relates to the Christian faith that he shared with Rowling. He saw his own works as a form of "sub-creation," so many variations on the themes of the original creation of God, clearly subsidiary, but in accord with the lesser creative capacities that God placed in humanity. In taking this stance, Tolkien implied that any number of human philosophical views could be compatible with religious truth, though clearly many were incompatible as well. He expressly defended fairy tales—and, by extension, myth and fantasy—as worthy of "secondary belief." Only the Gospels, as the word of God, were worthy of "primary belief." Furthermore, I should note, Tolkien spent his entire academic career studying non-Christian works or, at best, ambiguously Christian works, such as *Beowulf*, the *Elder Edda*, a compilation of Norse mythology, or the Viking sagas. These works, as well as others, then found new life in his fiction—the literary myths, or sub-creations, for which he is justly renowned. He clearly did not see them as a threat to his faith and, indeed, was quite skeptical of overprotective religious practices. Rowling likewise employs non-Christian or ambiguously Christian elements in her works, in ways that are fundamentally consistent with her faith's moral teachings.[33]

It is possible to see religion as having a subterranean life in otherwise radically secular literature. As I suggested above, the problem of evil does not go away, even if it is removed from a religious context. For this reason, familiar religious archetypes, such as alienation and reunion, fall and redemption, death and rebirth, hell and heaven, paradise lost and paradise regained, surface repeatedly in books with hardly a mention of God. We also find sacrifice and Christ imagery in unexpected places without having to look very hard. In fact, almost any attention to morality and, therefore, the problem of evil in works of fiction implicitly summons comparisons to religious issues because religion is so deeply concerned with ethical problems.[34]

For these reasons, a number of authors have come to see the Harry Potter books as a form of Christian allegory, and to some extent, they make a valid point. Harry is alienated from the wizarding world only to be reunited with it. Some characters have clearly fallen, some have already achieved a type of redemption, and a few more will likely experience the same. In each book, Harry metaphorically dies and descends into hell (the Forbidden Corridor, the Chamber of Secrets, the Shrieking Shack, the cemetery), only to be metaphorically reborn and ascend into heaven (when order is restored). And it requires little effort to see Harry as a Christ figure. I have the feeling that these themes are likely to increase in number and intensity, as things turn even darker in subsequent volumes in Rowling's series. The question remains, however, how many of these developments are of an exclusively Christian nature. I have my doubts, because the problem of evil is not structured within his adventures in traditionally religious ways.[35]

If we adopt a Christian perspective, for the moment, we can read both mythical creatures and alchemical allusions in Harry Potter from a Christian perspective. Mythical creatures were used to symbolize evil, as well as Jesus Christ's triumph over it. Alchemy, too, could function as a religious metaphor. Within the Judeo-Christian tradition, serpents, snakes, and basilisks have long been associated with sin and evil. Many Christian writers also invoked the unicorn, the lion, the griffin, and the phoenix as symbols of Christ (despite the pagan origins of their meanings). In the first century, Jesus' resurrection was compared to the rebirth of the phoenix by Clement of Rome. In the fourth century, St. Basil likened him to the unicorn, and St. Ambrose followed Clement in again comparing him to the phoenix. In the sixth century, Pope Gregory I identified the leviathan of the Book of Job as a basilisk. Still other authors chose to liken Jesus to a griffin, and many medieval artists used the beast symbolically to communicate the same idea. Likewise, many alchemists chose to see their endeavors as a means of achieving mystical union with God, and as completely consistent with orthodox doctrine.[36]

In a book titled *The Hidden Key to Harry Potter*, John Granger takes up issues such as these and argues that Harry Potter is a Christian set of works. He makes the point rather emphatically:

> Joanne Rowling is a Christian novelist of the Inkling School [that is, like Tolkien and Lewis] writing to "baptise the imagination" and prepare our hearts and minds for the conscious pursuit of the greater life in Jesus Christ. Harry Potter is a Christian Hero.

In considering both the mythical and the alchemical symbols at work in the books (in ways not wholly, but generally, consistent with my reading of them), he finds both forms to be essentially Christian. The books therefore reflect an imaginative vision consistent with orthodox doctrine.[37]

I don't want so much to disagree with Granger as to sound a word of caution. The symbols *are* there to be interpreted, but symbols *are also* multivalent. In other words, they communicate multiple and even contradictory meanings. If we return to the Christian tradition, we find evidence that symbolic religious meanings were often disputed in the past, because while some saw them as beneficial to faith, others saw them as unbiblical, misguided, or even indicative of evil. (This is clearly also the case nowadays.) This claim is as applicable to the meanings of mythical creatures as it is to understandings of alchemy. Dante Alighieri (1265–1321) puts a griffin to work in paradise pulling the chariot of the church in a passage from his *Divine Comedy* ("A car triumphal: on two wheels it came/Drawn at a Griffon's neck"), even though Isidore of Seville (ca. 560–636) had a rather different understanding of the creatures ("they tear men to pieces"). Although, as I noted above, the griffin could symbolize the savior in medieval art, it was also used by many artists to symbolize the antichrist. In fact, Albertus Magnus, the famed teacher of St. Thomas Aquinas, challenged the whole notion that animals symbolically taught moral lessons, preferring to see them purely as part of the natural world. In addition, challenges to alchemy were common during the late medieval and early modern periods, when many theologians and philosophers viewed it not only with skepticism, seeing alchemists as scoundrels or fools, but also with some alarm, seeing the art as potentially demonic along with other forms of occult science. In the final analysis, we must keep in mind that both mythological creatures and alchemy *predate* Christianity. Some Christians certainly adopted and adapted pagan or noncanonical symbolism for religious uses, but they did not do so without resistance, at times, from others who did not share their views.[38]

More important, we must briefly assess the role of faith in confronting evil in the Harry Potter books. We find faith in one's self, faith in one's friends, and faith in the power of love, but we find relatively little expression of faith in a higher being who secures and guarantees victory over evil. In his thoughtful defense of the books from a religious perspective, the Anglican theologian Francis Bridger voices an important reservation, which I share, about reading the books as Christian allegory. He notes that the books are most at odds with Christianity when it comes to their depictions of an afterlife: "With no ostensible God, Potterworld has little in the way of traditional ideas about 'heaven' and 'hell' let alone resurrection." Further, several features of Rowling's creation suggest that something does follow death, which may not correspond entirely to Christian understandings: Dumbledore's claim that death is but the "next great adventure," the existence of ghosts, souls that can be sucked from one's body, and the "echoes" of Cedric and Harry's parents. Simply, Rowling never systematically describes a transcendent spiritual realm, let alone a Christian one. Its attributes remain the great unknown. To Bridger's credit, he finds nothing demonic about Harry's adventures and sees within them an implicit theology and metaphysics, worthy of what Tolkien might call "secondary belief," as well as a message of friendship, goodness, and love.[39]

Ultimately, I have no strong objections to reading the Harry Potter books as a form of Christian allegory, but on the basis of the books available to date, I can only conclude that the stories need not be read in that way. What I do not find in the books is a call to spiritual transcendence through faith, even if their message of love and tacit alchemical symbolism might hint in that direction. What I do find in such symbolism is a portrayal of personal development largely consistent with traditional patterns of heroism found in many cultures, on the one hand, and a largely secular Stoic moral philosophy, on the other. As literary myth, the Harry Potter works do not offer an expressly religious message, even if the moral system on display is largely consistent with religious moral teaching. In the last analysis, the books cast the problem of evil in secular terms. Evil is part of the human condition, but faith in a higher being does not guarantee victory over it. One's own virtue does—even if that victory implies making the ultimate sacrifice on behalf of others. But I might be wrong. I shall have to wait and see. After all, "Godric" (as in Godric Gryffindor) does mean "the rule of God." And Harry, as far as we can tell, was born in Godric's Hollow, the site of his parents' home.

STOICISM AND RELIGION

New York Times media critic A. O. Scott links Harry's morality to the supernatural workings of fate in his claim that "Dumbledore's benevolent but strict theology, involving the operations of free will in a supernaturally determined world, is classically Miltonian." In other words, even though events unfold on their own, characters cannot know their ultimate fate and must choose how to order their thoughts and actions. Scott's allusion, of course, is to John Milton's *Paradise Lost*, and it provides me a good place to begin a brief discussion of the relationship between Stoicism and religion. For Milton was clearly influenced by Stoic thinking, as were many of his contemporaries, and it shows in his epic poem. History is the unfolding of God's plan, but individual humans, lacking the omniscience of God, must make their will conform to it as best they can, given their more limited knowledge. In a way, Milton's epic poem adopts a view consistent with *The Book of Constancy* by Justus Lipsius: Lucifer's great sin is to set his own will against God's.[40]

As I suggested in chapter 3, the god of the Stoics was nature, or the divine inherent within. In this respect, nature was greater than humanity, though humans did have the capacity to understand how it shaped and influenced their lives. Their duty was to conform to it. Commenting on the Stoics, Cicero describes their theological views as presented in a text, Chrysippus, now lost to us:

> For if, says Chrysippus, there is something in nature which man's mind, reason, strength, and power cannot make, that which makes it must be better than man. But the things in the heavens and all those whose regularity is everlasting cannot be created by man. Therefore, that by which these things are created is better than man. But what more suitable name for this is there than "god."

This view is not entirely inconsistent with Christianity's understanding of God, and, in fact, many Christian proofs of the existence of God (namely those of Aquinas) follow the same basic logic. Yet Stoicism is not the same as religion, as it is most commonly understood, for it places far greater emphasis upon the active reason than upon faith in a higher being.[41]

For these reasons, as well as others, we should not be surprised to learn that different Christian thinkers both criticized and espoused

Stoic philosophy. St. Augustine soundly condemned Stoic calls to extirpate the passions as inducing stupor and standing in the way of virtuous love (*agapē*), despite finding much else to admire. A thousand years later, Martin Luther and John Calvin sounded similar themes, seeing normative Stoicism within Christianity as leading to a dangerous spiritual perfectionism and as insufficiently aware of the true depths of human depravity and sin. (Remember, however, that earlier in life, Calvin took the time to write a treatise on Seneca's *De Clementia*, so he at least saw the Stoics as worthy of study.) Yet, other Christians, Lipsius and Milton among them, saw little downside to *adapting* Stoic ideas for Christian purposes. The historian Gerhard Oestreich succinctly describes the attraction and uses of Stoic thinking in the early modern period:

> In the triad *constantia, patientia, firmitas* (steadfastness, patience, firmness) Lipsius gave to his age, an age of bloody religious strife, the watchword for resistance against the external ills of the world. His moral philosophy acquired a leading position in European thought and exercised an obvious influence on scholarship, poetry, and art right up to the Enlightenment of the eighteenth century.

Neither Stoicism nor Christianity stands still. Over the past two thousand years, each has adapted, at times, to the other.[42]

If I am right about the Stoic nature of morality portrayed in Rowling's Potter books, Christian parents of Potter-struck children should have nothing to worry about. Catholic authors Catherine Jack Deavel and David Paul Deavel lay out the case in defense of Harry's morality in "Character, Choice, and Harry Potter," and see it as consistent with their own Catholic faith. Although they do not identify Harry's virtues as Stoic, they do describe them in ways consistent with my claims. As their title suggests, they note that moral character is important above all else in the books. Further, they observe, Rowling's stories consistently emphasize choice over destiny and the deeper magic of love. This emphasis may not reflect the normative Stoicism of the ancient Greeks and Romans at work, but it does reflect an updated version consistent with profound religious faith. All books are a "mixed bag," they concede near the end of their essay, but ultimately, they conclude, "The Harry Potter books advance many Christian moral principles, even if these principles are not named as Christian." I think they're right.[43] But it must also be understood that many of the same moral principles are shared by non-Christian religions and by non-believers alike.[44]

BEING ENCHANTED

Let me conclude where J. K. Rowling, in a sense, began—with Nicolas Flamel and the discovery of the philosopher's stone. In my brief parable of "enchantment," you'll encounter the alchemy of the magician and the alchemy of the historian. You'll also find one last rumination on the relationship between imagination and the past to bring you a better appreciation of the alchemy of the novelist.

Early in September of 2001, my wife, Stephanie, and I vacationed in Paris. High on my list of things to do (if not exactly at the top) was a visit to L'Auberge Nicolas Flamel for lunch or dinner. I had learned about this restaurant while preparing for our trip, and when I realized it was located in a residence once owned by *the* Nicolas Flamel—medieval scribe, notary, and alchemist—well, my mind was made up. Stephanie needed little convincing. Upon being seated in the restaurant a few weeks later, I let my mind wander and pictured Flamel at work in the room, meeting with customers, copying important documents, or directing his assistants. I also pictured him busy at work in the cellar, engaged in experiments related to his legendary discovery of the philosopher's stone. The restaurant's proprietor, Nathan Hercberg, teasingly assured us that not even the secret cellar, discovered under the first, contained any remnants of the stone or the elixir of life. The cellars now housed another elixir of sorts, the many excellent wines the house offered. We were pleased, for our lunch proved outstanding. A photograph now memorializes that encounter of mine with the past and the enchantment and flights of historical imagination it occasioned.

What historians "know" of Flamel's alchemical work comes from *Hieroglyphica*, an early seventeenth-century book attributed to him. It takes its title from the alchemical symbols or "hieroglyphics"—really elaborate pictures—that he found in a strange book that came into his possession one day, and it recounts, in his own words, his fortuitous discovery of the philosopher's stone. Although Flamel tells us that he was not particularly interested in alchemy early in life, he nonetheless became convinced that the book, authored by someone identified only as Abraham the Jew, contained the secret of the philosopher's stone.

Unfortunately, Flamel could not decipher Abraham's writings. Unwilling to show the actual book to anyone other than his wife Perenelle, he copied its drawings, hung them in his shop, and waited many long years for help in understanding them. Eventually, he tells us, he decided to seek divine guidance and left Paris on a pilgrimage to Santiago in Spain, hoping to encounter a scholar wise in the lore of the Jews who could help him unravel the book's secrets. He found such a person in Master Canches, a Jewish physician of Leon, who explained the workings of the book to him and embarked with him to his shop in Paris. Although Flamel's fast friend died from illness along the way, by the time the scribe returned home, he had come to understand enough of the book's principles, with Canches's help, that he could begin to prepare the stone. According to his own account, he accomplished the feat at noon on Monday, January 17, 1382. Although he used it to make gold on only three occasions, he produced such an abundance that he and Perenelle were never in need again. Putting the money to use, they founded fourteen hospitals, built three chapels, supported seven churches, and provided generously to the needy. In addition, Flamel had Abraham's hieroglyphics carved and painted on an arch in the Churchyard of the Holy Innocents in Paris.

If we turn to other historical sources, we learn other interesting things about Flamel. From contemporary medieval sources, we learn that Perenelle died in 1397, and that Nicolas met the same fate twenty years later. Reports from the late sixteenth and seventeenth centuries tell us that their reputations continued to grow after their deaths. We learn that upon Flamel's burial, some of his contemporaries ransacked his properties in pursuit of the philosopher's stone, convinced it was the magical source of his wealth. They even opened his tomb, finding neither the alchemist nor the stone. The truth, some came to believe, was that neither Perenelle nor Nicolas was really dead. As his book became a best-seller in the seventeenth century, Flamel-sightings were reported on numerous occasions. The alchemist, sometimes along with his wife, was spotted in India during the seventeenth century, in Greece around 1700, in Paris at the opera in 1761, and once again in India a few years before 1832.[45]

Among students of alchemy, including scholars working on the topic today, Flamel enjoys a reputation as the first discoverer of the philosopher's stone, but different interpreters do different things with his reputation. Many seventeenth- and eighteenth-century commentators saw the discovery as the source of Nicolas and Perenelle's extraordinary acts of charity and used it to sustain the notion that both were still alive and well. Most historians today, in contrast, completely discount claims of supernatural accomplishments as legendary, and most even question whether Flamel actually authored the texts attributed to him. Still, they do believe that both Nicolas and Perenelle lived in Paris and accept the reality of their generosity.

A fifteenth-century tombstone housed in the Musée de Cluny in Paris is testament to Flamel's existence and generosity, but little else. Although it displays the sun and the moon, which might symbolize gold and silver or the alchemical reconciliation of opposites, the inscription upon it, along with depictions of Christ and Sts. Peter and Paul, hardly support the conclusion that Flamel was an alchemist:

> The late scribe Nicolas Flamel, according to his will, left to the corporation of this church certain incomes and properties, which he received as marital property and bought during his lifetime, in order to provide for divine service and the distribution of funds each and every year as alms, at the hospital for the blind and other churches and hospitals in Paris. Let the dead be remembered in prayer.

Still other facts call Flamel's reputation as an alchemist into question. No medieval document, beyond the equivocal tombstone, links him to alchemy, and no alchemical treatise written before the late sixteenth century makes any mention of him.

Nonetheless, we do know that alchemy was a fairly common practice in the late medieval period. And the sun and the moon on Flamel's tombstone remain suggestive of alchemical associations. In addition, a small number of documents seem to attest to the existence of an arch in the Churchyard of the Holy Innocents that was destroyed in the eighteenth century but might have had sculptures upon it whose designs were attributed to Flamel. The arch's images are preserved in a seventeenth-century etching, published with the *Hieroglyphica*. Although they might not depict alchemical symbols (a more traditional, Christian iconography will do), they are indeed strange. Furthermore, Flamel's reputation had to originate somewhere. Why not with local rumor that became legend? Ultimately, we cannot know for sure if the historical Flamel engaged in alchemical work, though it strikes me as possible that he did. Particularly compelling for my own understanding of Flamel, however, is a sentiment attributed to the notary that was apparently written upon the façade of a residence he and Perenelle occupied for many years. How unanticipated was my discovery that it espouses an essentially Stoic point of view: "Let each be content with what he has/Whoever has not this ease, has nothing." To my mind, if Flamel was indeed an alchemist, greed clearly did not motivate him. As for his legendary exploits, well, they remain precisely that.[46]

Although I had already known about Flamel's reputation as an alchemist before reading the *The Sorcerer's Stone*, when I returned from Paris, I grew increasingly intrigued by his role in the book. I decided to look once more at what historians had to say about him, hoping to see how it might influence my understanding of him in Harry's fictional adventures. As I went about my business, I became increasingly aware of the uncertain state of historical knowledge about him. With rare exception, it seemed mostly to be dependent upon informed speculation. I was not surprised by this insight (I've experienced it before), but it reminded me of the importance of imagination to the historical enterprise (another common insight). As historians interpret documents or seek to fill gaps in the historical record, they must use their imaginations, much as I had done in Paris, though usually in a more systematic fashion. In other words, historians do not let their imaginations run free and prefer to keep them constrained by the documentary record—and by reason and the rules of evidence—as a matter of professional obligation.[47]

In light of this responsibility, I feel compelled to point out how unlikely (but not impossible) it is that Flamel engaged in alchemical work at the site now occupied by L'Auberge Nicolas Flamel. Indeed, if I even accept that he was an alchemist, I ought to imagine him at work at other sites in Paris, which I am free to visit, even if the buildings once occupied by him no longer exist. After all, Flamel leased the site of the restaurant to several shopkeepers and ran the upper floors as a boarding house for the poor and indigent. These facts do not entirely invalidate my imaginative thoughts in September of 2001, but they do refine and constrain them.[48]

Novelists, of course, as we already know, operate under no such constraints in deploying historical figures in fictional works. Where I have found a mortal, late-medieval scribe who probably dabbled in alchemy and promoted some Stoic views, Rowling has found an immortal, six-hundred-sixty-five-year-old character who lives a quiet life in Devon with his wife. As historians have discovered, Flamel is a figure of both history and legend. As Rowling has discovered, he also makes an enchanting fictional character.

Although Flamel is not the only example of Rowling's use of history, in this case, she takes a person whose existence can be proven and then puts the "facts" of his life to work in a new story. By extrapolating from verifiable accounts of both historical and legendary incidents, she brings a character from the past into a largely imagined future. Her fiction asks readers to assume that the activities attributed to him really happened for the sake of her art. Of course, Rowling makes similar use of other historical figures, events, and themes, as well as numerous traditional (if sometimes unfamiliar) legends and myths. In each case, she carries important aspects of the human past—real persons, real events, real beliefs—into a new fictional story. She asks readers to suspend their disbelief of certain fantastic claims made in and about the past, so that they might lose themselves within an imagined plot unfolding within an imagined world.

But, as I argued before, Rowling is up to something else as well. Because her imagined world is set in a very real historical period, and because it relies upon verifiable aspects of the historical record beyond the purely fanciful, it resembles our own in more than a few significant ways. Rowling's fictional universe exists recognizably as part of our own in terms of its material qualities and moral attributes. She ensures that readers—both children and adults—do not entirely lose themselves within the product of her imagination and, more important, asks them to assess its problems in light of their own. Rowling's fanciful tales pose problems the solutions for which turn out to be not so unusual after all.

Rowling's literary alchemy combines both the familiar and the fantastic through the inventive use of history, legend, and myth to create a moral tale. Some critics are disturbed by the resulting literary myth, but it is safe to say most readers are enchanted. There is no single explanation for this enchantment, but I believe a good one resides in understanding how Rowling's fiction reconciles fantasy and real-world experiences for her young audience. Her books entertain through magical plots, fanciful settings, and offbeat characters, but they also instruct through their portrayal of an archetypal hero meeting the various challenges confronting him and through their deployment of vibrant moral symbolism. The fact that the books are set in the "real world" contributes enormously to children's ability to identify with a hero and to comprehend the symbolism at work in his tales. J. K. Rowling's inventive uses of history, legend, and myth allows children's imaginations to play, so they might put their imaginations to work. The wonderful literary magic of her tales goes a long way toward explaining her hero's Stoic appeal.

Afterword:
Harry Potter
and the
Order of the Phoenix

Harry Potter has had it. He's had it with the Dursleys keeping him captive. . . . He's had it with being lied to about his past. And in self-defense, he's turned himself into the nastiest creature imaginable. A troubled teen.
— Jackie Loohauis, in the *Milwaukee Journal-Sentinel*

The *Sunday Mail* of Scotland reported that on the day of its release, Saturday, June 21, 2003, J. K. Rowling's *Harry Potter and the Order of the Phoenix* sold at a rate of twenty-three copies per second. That's about eighty-three thousand books every hour, or nearly 2 million in the course of one day. Did I mention that those figures are for Great Britain alone? The *New York Times* estimates that 5 million copies sold in the United States within twenty-four hours of the book's release. Sales worldwide have been just as brisk. Needless to say, no other book has ever sold as quickly. Potter-mania is alive and well, and showing little sign of abating anytime soon.[1]

As fate would have it, on Friday, June 20, a few hours before this historic release at 12:01 A.M., the page proofs for my own book reached me. The corrected versions would be going to the printer in a few weeks, so I still had time to write a quick afterword, but I could not rethink or rework any of my arguments in light of revelations contained within Rowling's newest installment of Harry's adventures. You can imagine my trepidation later that evening, when at 12:07 A.M. a clerk at Conkey's Bookstore in Appleton handed me a copy of *The Order of the Phoenix*.

I turned to my son, Lukas, who had insisted that I rouse him from bed to accompany me to the bookstore. His eager first words were, "Can I see it?" I thought, You can only imagine. I gave him the book, and we set off for home, arriving there about ten minutes later. Looking at the quiet neighborhood around us, I joked that we were likely "the first on our block" to have it (and then amused myself by imagining what Harry's social critics would make of that egregious example of consumer sentiment). Once inside the house, we scanned the book's ominous, dark blue cover (which is sure to affront Harry's religious critics), and Lukas quickly identified the characters depicted there, save an apparently new one that stumped both of us. I returned my very tired young son to bed and then sat down to begin reading. The thought that I had been repressing all day finally escaped my lips, heard only by myself and a perplexed, yet attentive, orange tabby: "What will I do if Rowling has thrown me a curve?" Ten minutes and eleven pages later, I decided she had, but the pitch was still within the strike zone.

Rowling begins her portrayal of Harry Potter's fifth year of adventures as readers might expect, with her hero coping with the Dursleys. Flat on the ground in the sweltering heat, he surreptitiously listens to the television news in Little Whinging for any indication of Voldemort's return. Because his uncle Vernon has soundly denounced

Harry's interest in the news, Harry lies behind several hydrangea bushes, under the open living room window. Suddenly, a loud *crack* breaks the silence of the evening, startling Harry in the bushes, the Dursleys inside their home, and a cat hiding under a car. Leaping to his feet, Harry nearly splits his head in two on the bottom of the open window. A quick tussle and an argument with his aunt and uncle follow, and Harry heads off for a walk, nearly convinced the sound had a magical origin, and ruminating over the feeling of hopelessness that has engulfed him all summer.

As Harry heads off into the night, he bitterly wonders about what's happening in the wizarding world. The *Daily Prophet* had made no mention of Voldemort's return all summer. Ron and Hermione had cryptically hinted of ongoing activities against the villain, but they had provided no details in case their letters were intercepted. Rembering their vague hints and their promises that they would see him soon makes Harry even angrier and leads him to feel sorry for himself:

> And what were Ron and Hermione busy with? Why wasn't he, Harry, busy? Hadn't he proved himself capable of handling much more than they? Had they all forgotten what he had done? Hadn't it been *he* who had entered the graveyard and watched Cedric being murdered and been tied to that tombstone and nearly killed ... ?[2]

Dreams of those events still haunt Harry, and he reminds himself, yet again, not to think about them. Messages from Sirius had at least acknowledged Harry's increasing frustration, but they did little more than counsel patience: "'*Keep your nose clean and everything will be okay. . . .*' '*Be careful and don't do anything rash. . . .*'"[3] All this is rather rich, Harry thinks, as it comes from Sirius, whose own past actions run counter to his current advice.

Harry enters a nearby park and considers his plight. Alone in Little Whinging, he has nothing to look forward to other than another restless night, filled with visits to the cemetery where Cedric was killed and to long, dark corridors ending in locked doors. Feeling trapped, and concerned by the periodic pain in his scar, Harry grows more and more incensed over the injustice of it all. He needs to *do* something. And what about Dumbledore? Why had he so thoroughly abandoned Harry? "Furious thoughts whirled around in Harry's head, and his insides writhed with anger as a sultry, velvety night fell around him."[4]

Sitting in my living room, reading this portrayal of Harry Potter, I found myself growing uncomfortable as well. Harry seemed mostly to have abandoned the path of Stoic virtue. By page eleven, as he surveys Dudley Dursley and his bullying friends from a distance, I encountered a Harry whom I barely recognized:

> Harry watched the dark figures crossing the grass and wondered whom they had been beating up tonight. *Look round,* Harry found himself thinking as he watched them. *Come on ... look round ... I'm sitting here all alone ... Come and have a go. ...*
>
> ... It would be really fun to watch Dudley's dilemma; to taunt him, watch him, with him powerless to respond...and if any of the others tried hitting Harry, Harry was ready—he had his wand ... let them try. ... He'd love to vent some of his frustration on the boys who had once made his life hell—[5]

Who is this kid? I thought to myself. Harry doesn't go looking for fights! Where was the young adolescent resigned to his fate at the end of *Harry Potter and the Goblet of Fire*? I found him again in the next few lines:

> But they did not turn around, they did not see him. ... Harry mastered the impulse to call after them. ... Seeking a fight was not a smart move. ... He must not use magic. ... He would be risking expulsion again. ...[6]

An emotionally spent Harry thus manages to master his anger in order to remain true to himself. Yet his resignation in the face of difficulty doesn't last for long.

Having finished reading all 870 pages of *The Order of the Phoenix* some forty-eight hours later, I decided that the book largely depicted Harry as usually *failing* to subordinate his emotions to reason. Bullying, impulsive, angst-ridden, perpetually angry with his friends and mentors, and sick and tired of their keeping him in the dark, Harry does anything but live up to the Stoic ideals so prominent in the first four books detailing his adventures. Turning at last, in the following days, to early reviews of the book, I soon discovered that I was not alone in seeing Harry this way. In the *Milwaukee Journal-Sentinel*, Jackie Loohauis humorously but perceptively put it this way:

> Harry Potter has had it. He's had it with the Dursleys keeping him captive. . . . He's had it with being lied to about his past. And in self-defense, he's turned himself into the nastiest creature imaginable: A troubled teen.[7]

Still other critics reacted to Harry's behavior in a similar fashion, but they also hailed Rowling's authorial voice, the story it tells, and the psychological tensions it portrays as more mature than what her earlier books offer. In addition, despite this volume's darkening tone, Rowling's cleverness, humor, and pacing are better than ever. To fans and critics alike, Harry, despite all his most recent rottenness, remains an endearing and enduring hero.[8]

But even though Harry thoroughly fails to remain constant in *The Order of the Phoenix*, those around him largely do not, and a key aspect of the book is its elaboration of themes related to the importance of emotional control—and the extreme difficulty of maintaining it. Relatively early in the book, Professor Dumbledore muses in a passage whose import will become clear only later, "even the best wizards cannot always control their emotions."[9] Later on, while Harry is taking special lessons with Professor Snape, he hears the potions master also warn of the dangers of emotion in dealing with Voldemort:

> "Fools who wear their hearts proudly on their sleeves, who cannot control their emotions, who wallow in sad memories and allow themselves to be provoked easily—weak people in other words—they stand no chance against his powers! He will penetrate your mind with absurd ease, Potter!"[10]

And throughout the book, still other characters encourage Harry to maintain control. Although Harry remains virtuous in the final analysis (he's never really in danger of turning to evil), he allows his emotions to run wild and fails to live up to the ideals that he knows to be right and that his mentors seek to foster. Although critics have noted this change, none (to date) has remarked upon just how significant it is to Harry's unfolding quest as a hero within a literary myth.

In earlier volumes, Harry is certainly testy at times and acts in less-than-admirable ways, but within this fifth book, in failing to remain constant, he fails not only himself but others as well. In failing to exercise self-discipline, Harry places himself and his friends in jeopardy, leads some of them to serious injury, and occasions the death of someone very close to him, the very person whose life his rash actions were intended to save. This is the most significant point of all: Whereas Harry usually finds himself in difficulties through no real fault of his own, at the end of his fifth year at Hogwarts, he actually creates the extremely dangerous predicament in which he and others find themselves. In allowing Lord Voldemort to play upon his emotions and to dupe him into acting rashly, Harry finds himself paralyzed, despite earlier displays of courage, before the superior power of his enemy. He survives only because of the timely intervention of the Order of the Phoenix, a band of witches and wizards dedicated to resisting Voldemort's designs. Wielding his awesome powers against the Dark Lord, Albus Dumbledore must rescue Harry, for the first time, really, from a situation completely beyond his control. Although in the midst of Dumbledore's attack, Harry is able, on his own, to keep Voldemort from possessing him, he does so only—but also significantly—by embracing death out of an emotional desire (out of love?) to rejoin the friend he has lost. The book concludes with the restoration of order, but readers hoping for a truly happy ending will not find it.

Nonetheless, *The Order of the Phoenix* still advances the basic Stoic ethic I outlined previously, even if it tends to do so more by way of negative example than did earlier books. Here, Harry is hardly a role model to be emulated, but his moral education continues apace, punctuated by a lesson learned the hard way, yet a lesson very much in keeping with Rowling's decisions to depict adolescent behavior realistically and to present making moral choices as an emotional and intellectual process afflicted by uncertainty and ambiguity. Cultivation of the self while paying due attention to others remains its central, essentially Stoic, moral theme. Fate hounds Harry, and although he is not always successful in responding to it, he is reminded that endurance, perseverance, self-discipline, reason, solidarity, empathy, and sacrifice are the best means available for meeting its demands. In this most recent volume, however, readers must keep in mind that Harry's periodically reprehensible behavior occludes, at times, these otherwise present Stoic virtues. Without Harry as a secure guide, we must be more attentive to the insights offered by other characters.

For in this fifth book of Harry's adventures, although our hero *feels* alone most of the time, he is *not*. All summer, his supporters place a secret guard around him, even though they must shield him from their activities as well. This fact is made clear to Harry early in the book, but his knowledge of it does little to alleviate his anxiety and resentment.

Following Harry's anguished ruminations in the park in Little Whinging, he assuages his feelings by taunting Dudley mercilessly, as they both walk back home. Suddenly, complete darkness falls and a cold chill fills the air. Two dementors attack, and Harry barely repels them by summoning a *Patronus*, when he emotionally remembers his friends. Appearing out of nowhere, Mrs. Figg, a doddering old women who has periodically invited Harry to tea, warns him to keep his wand at the ready in case more dementors should appear. While stunned to learn that Mrs. Figg knows of the wizarding world, Harry does as instructed. Mrs. Figg reports that Mundungus Fletcher had left Harry alone, disapparating and causing the loud crack that had so startled everyone earlier, even though he was supposed to be guarding Harry. Fortunately, Mrs. Figg had positioned one of her cats to keep an eye on Mundungus. Still, as a squib—a witch incapable of performing magic—there is little she alone can do against dementors. A thoroughly confused Harry presses Mrs. Figg for information:

"Why didn't you tell me you're a squib?" Harry asked Mrs. Figg. . . . "All those times I came round your house—why didn't you say anything?"

"Dumbledore's orders. I was to keep an eye on you but not say anything, you were too young. . . . But oh my word," she said tragically, wringing her hands once more, "when Dumbledore hears about this—how could Mundungus have left, he was supposed to be on duty until midnight—*where is he?* How am I going to tell Dumbledore what's happened, I can't Apparate—"[11]

Upon Harry's return to the Dursleys' home, events become even more chaotic, as a flurry of owls arrives bearing messages from both the Ministry of Magic and Harry's defenders. The ministry threatens Harry with sanctions for improperly using magic as an underage wizard, while Arthur Weasley and Sirius Black insist that Harry stay put and resist the ministry's efforts to destroy his wand. Uncle Vernon rages at Harry and insists that he leave the house immediately. At that moment, however, a letter sent anonymously to Harry's aunt, a Howler that actually shouts its message at the recipient, is heard to thunder, "REMEMBER MY LAST, PETUNIA," and she insists that Harry remain.

For the next four days, Harry stews in resentment, since no one has bothered to inform him about what is really going on. At last, on the evening of the fourth day, a group of wizards, including Remus Lupin and Alastor Moody, arrives to whisk Harry to London. They are all members of the Order of the Phoenix, and their secret headquarters is Number Twelve, Grimmauld Place, the mansion inherited by Sirius, sole heir of the noble and ancient house of Black. Here, protected from Voldemort and the Ministry of Magic, Harry is to stay in hiding with Hermione and Ron, his godfather, and other members of the Order until the beginning of term at Hogwarts in four weeks' time.

Thus, in her early chapters, Rowling sets the basic parameters of this fifth book. On one side, the Ministry of Magic, its officials seriously in denial over Voldemort's rumored return, distrusts Harry and will bend or break its own rules in order to discredit both him and his headmaster at Hogwarts. On the other, the Order of the Phoenix reassembles under the leadership of Dumbledore, after a fourteen-year hiatus following Voldemort's demise, to protect Harry and to resist the rise of his archenemy. Harry, of course, finds himself in the middle without realizing just how low the ministry will stoop and without understanding why his defenders, and especially Dumbledore, refuse to reveal their activities to him. Of course, the threat of Voldemort hovers like a storm cloud over Harry's entire year at Hogwarts.

The ministry's persecution of Harry is embodied in the school's new Defense Against the Dark Arts teacher, Dolores Umbridge (whose name, by the way, loosely translates as "painful resentment"). She teaches a particularly vapid course that, in keeping with the ministry's willful denial, conveys the idea that the best defense is no defense. She refuses to allow students to practice counter-curses (or any magic at all) in her classroom and will not tolerate any mention of Voldemort's return. She gladly labels as liars any students who do bring it up and subjects them to a particularly malicious form of punishment, having them write *I must not tell lies* on parchment with a quill that also magically cuts the words onto the back of their hands. As a result, Harry is forced to undergo hours of this excruciating torture, which he bears in insolent silence.

But if Harry is able to endure the ministry's outrages with resignation, the reticence of his mentors proves a more difficult burden to carry. Harry comes to realize that he often dreams Voldemort's thoughts, and he soon recognizes that his dreams of dark corridors ending in locked doors pertain to his enemy's pursuit of what might be a secret weapon, hidden deep within the Ministry of Magic. What Harry fails to realize is that his own thoughts might be open to Voldemort and that he might fall under his enemy's control. This possibility has occurred to Dumbledore, and for that reason, he, Professors McGonagall and Snape, and other members of the Order of the Phoenix must keep Harry ignorant of the full dimensions of their efforts. Yet what appears to Harry as their abandonment and distrust of him is really a key feature of their unswerving loyalty. The headmaster's avoidance of Harry is particularly troubling to the fifteen-year-old, who must take Occlumency lessons with a still-hostile Snape (who is an indispensable member of the Order) to learn to shield his thoughts and emotions from Voldemort.

It's no wonder, therefore, that Harry feels a wreck during most of his fifth year at Hogwarts, caught, as he is, between the tyranny of governmental authorities and the silence of his adult mentors. Yet Harry takes heart over other developments. He experiences his first kiss with Cho Chang. Ron becomes Gryffindor's Quidditch keeper. Hermione forms Dumbledore's Army, a secret group of students that Harry teaches defensive magic. Rita Skeeter willingly publishes a legitimate interview with Harry about Voldemort's return, which gains Harry a lot of support in the wizarding world. And Harry successfully completes most of his Ordinary Wizarding Level examinations (O.W.L.s), without too much difficulty. Still, the pleasures of these events are far outweighed by additional disappointments. Professor Umbridge is appointed Hogwarts High Inquisitor and proceeds to ban many student activities and to censor their speech. Hagrid is long absent from school without explanation. Mr. Weasley is nearly killed while guarding the ministry from Voldemort's agents, an event vividly experienced by Harry in one of his dreams. Dumbledore's Army is discovered by Umbridge, but the headmaster dissembles, taking responsibility for its illegal formation to protect its student members, and flees Hogwarts to avoid arrest. And worst of all, Harry learns some troubling truths about his father. When Snape is called away from Occlumency lessons, Harry is able to enter his tutor's memories, which have been stored within a Pensieve. He witnesses his father, as a student, behaving with a level of arrogance and cruelty toward Snape that he wouldn't have imagined possible.

It is with these depressing thoughts in mind that Harry enters the final weeks of the term. Although Black and Lupin seek to assure Harry that his father did indeed mature, they nevertheless largely confirm what Harry had witnessed in Snape's memories. Soon thereafter, Harry and Hermione learn that Hagrid had returned from a mission to the giants with his dangerous half-brother Grawp, who can barely be controlled. A bit later, while taking his astronomy examination, Harry sees Hagrid barely escape an attempt by the ministry to arrest him outside his cabin. When Professor McGonagall arrives to object, ministry Aurors stun her, leaving her seriously injured and sent off to St. Mungo's Hospital for Magical Maladies and Injuries. If things were not bad enough, during his final O.W.L., Harry falls into a dream state and witnesses Voldemort cruelly tormenting Sirius in an attempt to obtain the secret locked within the bowels of the Ministry of Magic. Unable to consult any of his absent mentors, Harry surreptitiously attempts to contact Sirius at Grimmauld Place, carelessly forgetting out of ill will that he might first inform Snape, and makes use of the fireplace in Umbridge's office, the only one she has not placed under surveillance. Sirius's resentful and bitter house-elf Kreacher gleefully informs Harry that Sirius had left for the ministry and would not be coming back. Shocked to learn that his vision was true, Harry quickly finds himself and the students who were standing guard for him discovered by an irate and out-of-control Umbridge. Harry, along with Hermione, Ron, Ginny, Neville, and Luna Lovegood, a Ravenclaw member of Dumbledore's Army, manages to escape from Umbridge and her student assistants (with a little help from Grawp, as it turns out). After encountering several thestrals that live in the forbidden forest, Harry and his friends ride these serpentlike flying horses (visible only to humans who have witnessed death) to London in order to rescue Sirius from Voldemort's clutches in the Ministry of Magic.

So begins the climax to Harry's fifth adventure. It is important to take note, however, of *how* Rowling has chosen to structure this climax. As I pointed out earlier, it results from Harry's failure to remain constant. For Voldemort tricks Harry, and Kreacher lies to him. Sirius was safely at Grimmauld Place all along, but he will be killed during the Order's rescue of Harry. Furthermore, what Harry believes to be a secret weapon turns out to be a prophecy uttered by Sybill Trelawney to Albus Dumbledore some fifteen years earlier:

*"THE ONE WITH THE POWER TO VANQUISH THE DARK LORD
APPROACHES. . . . BORN TO THOSE WHO HAVE THRICE DEFIED HIM,
BORN AS THE SEVENTH MONTH DIES . . . AND THE DARK LORD WILL
MARK HIM AS HIS EQUAL, BUT HE WILL HAVE THE POWER THE DARK
LORD KNOWS NOT...AND EITHER MUST DIE AT THE HAND OF THE
OTHER FOR NEITHER CAN LIVE WHILE THE OTHER SURVIVES. . . . THE
ONE WITH THE POWER TO VANQUISH THE DARK LORD WILL BE BORN
AS THE SEVENTH MONTH DIES. . . ."[12]*

Certainly useful information, but hardly anything that Voldemort
hasn't already acted upon. Harry's efforts to protect Sirius's life, and in
defense of the secret, have all been wasted. In the cold light of his
failure, Harry discusses the truth of the night's events with Dumbledore with a heavy heart and an inconstant rage, both induced by
exceptionally strong feelings of guilt roiling inside him.

But it would be unfair for readers to place all the blame for this
story's tragic events upon Harry, since Dumbledore, too, had miscalcu-
lated terribly in deciding not to tell Harry the full truth about his past
and about events unfolding around him. This choice leads to a particularly cruel twist of fate and makes Harry its victim. In response to
Harry's sadness and anger, the headmaster concedes that he is to blame:

> "It is *my* fault that Sirius died," said Dumbledore clearly. "Or I should
> say almost entirely my fault—I will not be so arrogant as to claim
> responsibility for the whole. . . . If I had been open with you, Harry,
> as I should have been, you would have known a long time ago that
> Voldemort might try to lure you to the Department of Mysteries, and
> you would never have been tricked into going there tonight. And
> Sirius would not have had to come after you. That blame lies with me,
> and with me alone."[13]

Dumbledore, in attempting to shield Harry from further hurt, had forgotten the impetuousness of youth. He forgot that it can be harnessed
best through honesty and trust:

"Harry, I owe you an explanation," said Dumbledore. "An explanation of an old man's mistakes. For I see now that what I have done and not done, with regard to you, bears all the hallmarks of the failings of age. Youth cannot know how age thinks and feels. But old men are guilty if they forget what it was to be young . . . and I seem to have forgotten lately. . . ."[14]

For Harry deserved the truth, but Dumbledore had chosen, incorrectly, not to provide it.

Yet, because of Trelawney's prophecy, Dumbledore had set into motion a plan to protect Harry at all costs. He had secured Harry's safety by placing him with the Dursleys—by employing an ancient magic dependent upon his mother's love and the blood of her sister, Aunt Petunia. In accepting Harry, she sealed the protective charm that Dumbledore had placed upon him. It would remain in effect for as long as he returned to the Dursleys and made their home his own. Furthermore, Dumbledore carefully mentored him at Hogwarts, watching him surmount difficulties few could bear, and desiring not to add to them. Thus did Dumbledore fall into a trap that he had foreseen years earlier:

> "Yet there was a flaw in this wonderful plan of mine," said Dumbledore. "An obvious flaw that I knew, even then, might be the undoing of it all. And yet, knowing how important it was that my plan should succeed, I told myself that I would not permit this flaw to ruin it."[15]

The headmaster was initially tested during Harry's first year at Hogwarts, when Harry asked him why Voldemort had tried to kill him as a baby. In not revealing the truth then, Dumbledore failed the test. And he did so as well during each subsequent year that he remained silent:

> "Do you see, Harry? Do you see the flaw in my brilliant plan now? I had fallen into the trap I had foreseen, that I told myself I could avoid, that I must avoid."
>
> "I don't—"

"I cared about you too much," said Dumbledore simply. I cared more for your happiness than your knowing the truth, more for your peace of mind than my plan, more for your life than the lives that might be lost if the plan failed. In other words, I acted exactly as Voldemort expects we fools who love to act.

"Is there a defense? I defy anyone who has watched you as I have—and I have watched you more closely than you can have imagined—not to want to save you more pain than you have already suffered."[16]

Out of compassion for Harry, Dumbledore had chosen not to reveal the prophecy stored in the Ministry of Magic because of its central implication: either Voldemort or Harry would have to die at the hand of the other.

In showing such compassion toward Harry, Dumbledore fails to live up to the basic Stoic value of radical egalitarianism—he falls victim to the power of love. Harry, as well, has become a victim of its power. Dumbledore draws attention to another feature of Trelawney's prophecy, its claim that Harry would have *the power the Dark Lord knows not*, and hints cryptically of what it might be:

"There is a room in the Department of Mysteries . . . that is kept locked at all times. It contains a force that is at once more wonderful and more terrible than death, than human intelligence, than forces of nature. It is also, perhaps, the most mysterious of the many subjects for study that reside there. It is the power held within that room that you possess in such quantities and which Voldemort has not at all. That power took you to save Sirius tonight. That power saved you from possession by Voldemort, because he could not bear to reside in a body so full of the force he detests. In the end, it mattered not that you could not close your mind. It was your heart that saved you."[17]

Although Dumbledore never precisely names this power, the implication of his observation is clear. Love, the source of Harry's power, is both his greatest weakness and his greatest strength. Readers will have to wait to find out if it proves to be his undoing or his salvation.

But Harry has seen death and he has accepted it, as Lord Voldemort has not, because he possesses love in such large measure. Even though Harry remains grief-stricken over Sirius's death, it helps, once again, to remind him of an important lesson: Some things are worse than death. Thus, in *The Order of the Phoenix*, Rowling returns to the theme of death, and what might come after it, first touched upon in *Harry Potter and the Sorcerer's Stone*. There, she constructs her villain as someone who rejects the ultimate reality of death and portrays her hero as someone willing to risk it in pursuit of greater good. She also has Dumbledore remark, following the destruction of the Stone, "to the well-organized mind, death is but the next great adventure."[18]

In *The Order of the Phoenix*, both love and death are revealed as life's great mysteries, as mysteries to be either accepted or feared. In order to make the point, Rowling has Harry, tormented by the loss of Sirius, seek one of the Hogwarts ghosts for solace and enlightenment. He hopes that Sirius might come back, at least as a ghost. Nearly Headless Nick sadly informs Harry that Sirius will not be coming back; he will have "gone on":

> "What d'you mean, 'gone on'?" said Harry quickly. . . .
> "I cannot answer," said Nick.
> "You're dead, aren't you?" said Harry exasperatedly. "Who can answer better than you?"
> "I was afraid of death," said Nick. "I chose to remain behind. I sometimes wonder whether I oughtn't to have. . . . Well, that is neither here nor there. . . . In fact, *I* am neither here nor there. . . ." He gave a small sad chuckle. "I know nothing of the secrets of death, Harry, for I chose my feeble imitation of life instead."[19]

Harry loses hope only to find it again in the words of Luna Lovegood, who lost her mother some years earlier. She speaks of her lost mother, of the archway located in the Department of Mysteries into which Sirius had fallen, and of the whispers both she and Harry had heard issuing from it:

"Yes, it was rather horrible," said Luna conversationally. "I still feel very sad about it sometimes. But I've still got Dad. And anyway, it's not as though I'll never see Mum again, is it?"

"Er—isn't it?" said Harry uncertainly.

She shook her head in disbelief. "Oh, come on. You heard them, just behind the veil, didn't you?"

"You mean . . ."

"In that room with the archway. They were just lurking out of sight, that's all. You heard them."

They looked at each other. Luna was smiling slightly. Harry did not know what to say, or to think. Luna believed so many extraordinary things . . . yet he had been sure he had heard voices behind the veil. . . .[20]

Rowling thus hints more directly of some kind of existence beyond death and introduces spiritual issues in more detail than she has done previously. It remains to be seen how she will resolve them, but it is likely that she will have Harry confront, yet again, the strange power of love, along with its dangers and its advantages, and that she will have him assess its relation to the great mystery of death.

For ultimately, the central moral of the book is the implacable and ambiguous nature of love—its undisputed powers both to create and to destroy. It is telling that, within the book, love both leads to Harry's predicament and serves also to resolve it. It must be the *ancient magic* of which Professor Dumbledore so often speaks. In Harry, it must be the alchemical *phoenix*, the reconciler of opposites that brings restoration out of destruction—and life out of death. If the truth is *a beautiful and terrible thing to be treated with caution*, as Dumbledore tells Harry during his first year at Hogwarts, then so too must love, *a force that is at once more wonderful and more terrible than death*, be understood and handled in the same way.

There is much more, of course, on display in *Harry Potter and the Order of the Phoenix*. Reflecting upon the book barely a week after its historic release, I can only conclude that it presents a Stoic ethic of individual self-fashioning in ways consistent with earlier Harry Potter books, even if it elaborates upon moral responsibility in increasingly challenging ways. Although it pays greater attention to emotional and spiritual uncertainties than do earlier books, it nevertheless continues to develop their central moral themes: the workings of fate, the significance of inborn proficiencies and shortcomings, the nature of moral ambiguity, and the importance of virtuous intentions. In addition, even though we witness within the book less endurance and perseverance in Harry's actions, as well as little self-discipline or reason motivating them, we nonetheless find these virtues given ample attention in Harry's recognition of his own failures and in the advice given to him by his friends and mentors. His inability to live up to ideals does not imply that he has abandoned them. Equally important, we find the book placing greater emphasis upon solidarity, empathy, and sacrifice, as people of goodwill—both children and adults—band together in the face of radical evil. It also continues to explore social issues such as inequality, injustice, prejudice, and bigotry, and to interrogate the nature of authority and the exercise of political power. Likewise, it takes up the problem of evil in ways consistent with earlier books and presents evil as an inescapable aspect of the human condition. In the end, my trepidation upon receiving the book proved unjustified, for in the last analysis, its plot suggests that moral constancy remains the best way to confront fate and the evils that it may bring.

Notes

CHAPTER 1: IMAGATIVELY UPDATING AN OLD-FASHIONED VIRTUE

1. Daniel Handler, "Frightening News," *New York Times* (October 30, 2001): 17.

2. Ibid.

3. Larry Fine, "Director Gives All to Second Harry Potter Film," *Entertainment Tonight* (Reuters) [online], www.etonline.com/reuters/N04327104.htm [November 4, 2002] (175 million copies); "Potter Breaks UK Box Office Records," *Guardian Unlimited* [online], www.film.guardian.co.uk/harrypotter/news/0,10608,842586,00.html [November 18, 2002] ($90 million); "New Harry Potter Movie Premieres in London," *Fox News* (Associated Press) [online], www.foxnews.com/story/0,2933,68876,00.html [November 3, 2003] ($975 million); "All about Harry Potter," *Entertainment Weekly* [online], www.ew.com/ew/allabout/0,9930,37629~11~0~harrypotterandchamber,00.html [December 21, 2002] ($222.6 million); and "Potter Film Moves Rowling into Billionaire League,"

Guardian Unlimited [online], www.film.guardian.co.uk/News_Story/Exclusive/ 0,4029,606205,00.html [November 26, 2001] (royalties from merchandise).

4. Text and interview with Ray Suarez available at *NewsHour* [online], www.pbs.org/newshour/conversation/july-dec00/bloom_8-29.html [August 29, 2000]. Jamie Allen reports comments made to Charlie Rose in "'Harry' and Hype," CNN.com [online], www.cnn.com/2000/books/news/07/13/potter. hype/ [July 13, 2000].

5. Peggy Tibbets, "Release Your Inner Editor" [online], www.word weaving.com/articlemay08_00.html; Julia Eccleshare, *A Guide to the Harry Potter Novels* (New York: Continuum, 2002), p. 3; Jack Zipes, "The Phenomenon of Harry Potter, Or Why All the Talk?" in his book *Sticks and Stones: The Troublesome Success of Children's Literature from Slovenly Peter to Harry Potter* (New York: Routledge, 2000), pp. 170–89; Christine Schoefer, "Harry Potter's Girl Trouble," Salon.com [online], www.dir.salon.com/books/feature/2000/01/13/potter/ index.html [January 13, 2000]; and Farah Mendlesohn, "Crowning the King: Harry Potter and the Construction of Authority," in *The Ivory Tower and Harry Potter: Perspectives on a Literary Phenomenon*, ed. Lana A. Whited (Columbia: University of Missouri Press, 2002), pp. 159–81, quoted at pages 159 and 181.

6. Phone interview with Beverley Becker, associate director of the Office for Intellectual Freedom, American Library Association, August 27, 2001; "Purging Flame: Pa. Church Members Burn Harry Potter, Other Books 'Against God,'" ABCNews.com [online], www.more.abcnews.go.com/sections/us/daily news/book_burning010326.html [March 26, 2001].

7. J. K. Rowling, *Harry Potter and the Sorcerer's Stone* (New York: Scholastic Press, 1998), pp. 1–2 and 5. All quotations will be cited from the American editions of the Harry Potter books. Throughout, I shall refer to the first volume using the American title that incorporates the term "Sorcerer's Stone" (in order to avoid confusion for a mostly American audience). It is unfortunate that the historically nonsensical "Sorcerer's Stone" replaced the more accurate "Philosopher's Stone" found in the title of the British edition, *Harry Potter and the Philosopher's Stone* (London: Bloomsbury, 1997). The "philosopher's stone" is a key feature of medieval alchemy, and Scholastic has denied American readers this historical allusion. *The Sorcerer's Stone* also did away with dozens of wonderful British idioms, "translating" them for the trans-Atlantic audience and compromising much of the charm of Rowling's prose. Some small consolation may be found in the less frequent "translation" perpetrated by American editors in later volumes of the series. For a full account, please see Philip Nel, "You

Say 'Jelly, I Say 'Jell-O'? Harry Potter and the Transfiguration of Language," in *The Ivory Tower and Harry Potter*, ed. Whited, pp. 261–84.

8. Rowling, "Interviews and Essays" [online], www.search.barnesand noble.com/booksearch/isbninquiry.asp?btob=Y&isbn=0590353403&display only=authorInterview [March 19, 1999].

9. Rowling, *Harry Potter and the Sorcerer's Stone* (see note 7); *Harry Potter and the Chamber of Secrets* (New York: Scholastic Press, 1999); *Harry Potter and the Prisoner of Azkaban* (New York: Scholastic Press, 1999); and *Harry Potter and the Goblet of Fire* (New York: Scholastic Press, 2000).

10. Rowling, *The Goblet of Fire*, p. 84.

11. Mark Twain, *The Adventures of Tom Sawyer* (New York: Washington Square Press, 1950 [1875]), "Preface"; Kenneth Grahame, *The Wind in the Willows* (Chicago: Contemporary Books, 1988 [1908]), p. viii; J. R. R. Tolkien, "[Letter] To Milton Waldman" (1951), in *The Letters of J. R. R. Tolkien*, ed. Humphrey Carpenter (Boston: Houghton Mifflin Company, 1981), p. 159; and C. S. Lewis, "On Three Ways of Writing for Children" (1952), in *Of Other Worlds: Essays and Stories* (London: Geoffrey Bles, 1966), pp. 22–34, especially pages 26–28.

12. Philip Pullman, *The Golden Compass* (New York: Dell Yearling, 2001), p. 40.

13. Dav Pilkey, *The Adventures of Captain Underpants* (New York: Little Apple, 1997).

14. Rowling, *The Sorcerer's Stone*, p. 111.

15. See, for example, Roger Sutton, "Potter's Field" and "When Harry Met Dorothy," *The Horn Book Magazine* [online], www.hbook.com/editorial_sep99.shtml [September/October 1999] and www.hbook.com/editorial_jan01.shtml [January/February 2001].

16. Rowling, *The Sorcerer's Stone*, p. 103.

17. William J. Bennett and Michael Hague, *The Children's Book of Virtues* (New York: Simon and Schuster, 1995).

18. Rowling, *The Sorcerer's Stone*, p. 298.

19. Rowling, *The Goblet of Fire*, pp. 718–19.

20. Justus Lipsius, *Two Bookes of Constancie*, 1594 translation of *De Constantia* by Sir John Stradling (New Brunswick, N.J.: Rutgers University Press, 1939), p. 79. One may also follow the links at The Stoic Place, maintained by Dr. Jan Garrett, www.wku.edu/~jan.garrett/stoa.htm for an electronic version.

21. The sketch of Stoicism in the preceding paragraphs is drawn from many sources. To find out more about the topic, readers are encouraged to start

with any encyclopedia entry, but they might wish to consult in particular "Stoicism," in *The Encyclopedia of Philosophy*, ed. Paul Edwards, 8 vols. (New York: The Macmillan Company & The Free Press, 1967), 8:19–22. An especially useful online resource is The Stoic Place (see note 20). The best, detailed, recent treatments of the Stoics, both for what they argued in their works and for how they still speak to us today, are to be found in the works of Martha C. Nussbaum: *The Therapy of Desire: Theory and Practice in Hellenistic Ethics* (Princeton, N.J.: Princeton University Press, 1994), and *Upheavals of Thought: The Intelligence of Emotions* (New York: Cambridge University Press, 2001).

22. Alain de Botton, *The Consolations of Philosophy* (New York: Pantheon Books, 2000); Nussbaum, *Upheavals of Thought*, p. 5 and throughout; and (on the renaissance of Stoicism) William O. Stephens, "The Rebirth of Stoicism," *Creighton Magazine* (Winter 2000): 34–39 [online], www.puffin.creighton.edu/phil/Stephens/rebirth_of_stoicism.htm [updated, May 18, 2001].

23. Rowling, *The Sorcerer's Stone*, p. 297.

24. Nussbaum, *Upheavals of Thought*, p. 6.

25. Lawrence Kohlberg, *The Philosophy of Moral Development: Moral Stages and the Idea of Justice*, vol. 1 of *Essays on Moral Development* (San Francisco: Harper and Row, 1981), and *The Psychology of Moral Development: The Nature and Validity of Moral Stages*, vol. 2 of *Essays on Moral Development* (San Francisco: Harper and Row, 1984). Although I had been thinking for some time about the application of Kohlberg's thought to my analysis of morality in the Potter books, I was pleasantly surprised by the appearance of Lana A. Whited and M. Katherine Grimes's excellent article, "What Would Harry Do? J. K. Rowling and Lawrence Kohlberg's Theories of Moral Development," in *The Ivory Tower and Harry Potter*, ed. Whited, pp. 182–208.

26. Phone interview with Linda DeNell, Children's Librarian, Appleton Public Library, August 27, 2001.

CHAPTER 2: PLOT THREADS AND MORAL FIBERS

1. J. K. Rowling, *Harry Potter and the Sorcerer's Stone* (New York: Scholastic Press, 1998), pp. 2, 3, 4, 5, and 17. To my knowledge, Alison Lurie is the first critic to take note of the punning name "Little Whinging" in print, though she does not relate it to Harry's Stoic demeanor. See "Not for Muggles," *The New York Review of Books* (December 19, 1999): 6–8.

2. On psychological harm, see Farah Mendlesohn, "Crowning the King: Harry Potter and the Construction of Authority," in *The Ivory Tower and Harry Potter: Perspectives on a Literary Phenomenon*, ed. Lana A. Whited (Columbia: University of Missouri Press, 2002), p. 162. For more positive (or, at least, mixed) assessments of how Rowling uses the Dursleys, see John Kornfeld and Laurie Prothro, "Comedy, Conflict, and Community," pp. 188 and 197, and Deborah De Rosa, "Wizardly Challenges to and Affirmations of the Initiation Paradigm in *Harry Potter*," pp. 168–69, both in *Harry Potter's World: Multidisciplinary Critical Perspectives*, ed. Elizabeth E. Heilman (New York: Routledge Falmer, 2003); as well as Mary Pharr, "In Medias Res: Harry Potter as Hero-in-Progress," pp. 56–57; Jann Lacoss, "Of Magicals and Muggles: Reversals and Revulsions at Hogwarts," pp. 78, 80, and 81; and Roni Natov, "Harry Potter and the Extraordinariness of the Ordinary," pp. 125–27, all in *The Ivory Tower and Harry Potter*, ed. Whited. Scholarly treatments of Harry Potter and the heroic paradigm include De Rosa (above), Maria Nikolajeva, "Harry Potter—A Return to the Romantic Hero," pp. 125–40, and Anne Hiebert Alton, "Generic Fusion and the Mosaic of *Harry Potter*," pp. 141–62, in *Harry Potter's World*, ed. Heilman; as well as Pharr (above) and M. Katherine Grimes, "Harry Potter: Fairy Tale Prince, Real Boy, and Archetypal Hero," pp. 89–122, in *The Ivory Tower and Harry Potter*, ed. Whited.

3. Rowling, *The Sorcerer's Stone*, p. 13.

4. Ibid., p. 118.

5. Ibid., p. 295.

6. Ibid., p. 291.

7. Ibid., p. 297.

8. Ibid., p. 220.

9. Ibid., pp. 300–301.

10. J. K. Rowling, *Harry Potter and the Chamber of Secrets* (New York: Scholastic Press, 1999), p. 338.

11. Ibid., p. 333.

12. J. K. Rowling, *Harry Potter and the Prisoner of Azkaban* (New York: Scholastic Press, 1999), p. 28.

13. Ibid., p. 90.

14. Ibid., p. 435.

15. Ibid., pp. 392–93.

16. Ibid., p. 284.

17. Ibid., p. 290.

18. Ibid.

19. Ibid., p. 376.

20. Ibid., p. 393.

21. J. K. Rowling, *Harry Potter and the Goblet of Fire* (New York: Scholastic Press, 2000), pp. 632–33.

22. Ibid., p. 734.

23. Ibid., p. 724.

Chapter 3: Harry Potter's Morality on Display

1. Alain de Botton, *The Consolations of Philosophy* (New York: Pantheon Books, 2000), pp. 75–112, quoted at pages 80–81.

2. Ibid., pp. 80–81.

3. On the uses of emotion, see Martha C. Nussbaum, *Upheavals of Thought: The Intelligence of Emotions* (New York: Cambridge University Press, 2001), pp. 1–7 and throughout.

4. De Botton, *The Consolations of Philosophy*, pp. 82–109, quoted at pages 82–83 and 90.

5. Ibid., pp. 108 and 109.

6. J. K. Rowling, *Harry Potter and the Sorcerer's Stone* (New York: Scholastic Press, 1998), pp. 213–14.

7. Ibid., p. 297.

8. Catherine Atherton, *The Stoics on Ambiguity* (New York: Cambridge University Press, 1993), pp. 3, 502–504, quoted at page 502.

9. Rowling, *The Sorcerer's Stone*, p. 298.

10. Julia Eccleshare, *A Guide to the Harry Potter Novels* (New York: Continuum, 2002), pp. 63-64 and 90-91; Philip Nel, *J. K. Rowling's Harry Potter Novels* (New York: Continuum, 2001), pp. 29 and 39–41; Joan Acocella, "Under the Spell," *The New Yorker* (July 31, 2000): 77–78; Lana A. Whited and M. Katherine Grimes, "What Would Harry Do? J. K. Rowling and Lawrence Kohlberg's Theories of Moral Development," in *The Ivory Tower and Harry Potter: Perspectives on a Literary Phenomenon*, ed. Lana A. Whited (Columbia: University of Missouri Press, 2002), pp. 182–208; and Rebecca Skulnick and Jesse Goodman, "The Civic Leadership of *Harry Potter*: Agency, Ritual, and Schooling," in *Harry Potter's World: Multidisciplinary Critical Perspectives*, ed. Elizabeth E. Heilman (New York: Routledge Falmer, 2003), pp. 268–69.

11. Rowling, *The Sorcerer's Stone*, p. 270.

12. Eccleshare, *Guide*, pp. 60–62.

13. Lindsey Fraser, *Conversations with J. K. Rowling* (New York: Scholastic, 2000), p. 40; see also, Nel, *Harry Potter Novels*, pp. 15–16.

14. Eccleshare, *Guide*, pp. 77–82 and 92; Nel, *Harry Potter Novels*, pp. 44–45; Alan Jacobs, "Harry Potter's Magic," *First Things: The Journal of Religion and Public Life* 99 (2000): 35–38; and Peter Appelbaum, "Harry Potter's World: Magic, Technoculture, and Becoming Human," pp. 48–49, and Charles Elster, "The Seeker of Secrets: Images of Learning, Knowing, and Schooling," pp. 211–12, both in *Harry Potter's World*, ed. Heilman.

15. Joan Acocella, "Under the Spell," pp. 74–78, quoted at page 78.

16. Nel, *Harry Potter Novels*, pp. 50–51; and C. S. Lewis, "On Three Ways of Writing for Children," in *Of Other Worlds: Essays and Stories* (London: Geoffrey Bles, 1966), pp. 22–34.

17. On adolescent rebellion, see Robert Coles, *The Moral Intelligence of Children* (New York: Random House, 1997), pp. 136–38, 147, and 165. On independence and parental involvement in children's lives, see Carol Gilligan, "Adolescent Development Reconsidered," in *Approaches to Moral Development: New Research and Emerging Themes*, ed. Andrew Garrod (New York: Teachers College Press, 1993), pp. 103–32.

18. Eccleshare, *Guide*, pp. 34–37; Alison Lurie, *Boys and Girls Forever: Children's Classics from Cinderella to Harry Potter* (New York: Penguin Books, 2003), p. 117; and Fraser, *Conversations with J. K. Rowling*, p. 38.

19. Deborah De Rosa, "Wizardly Challenges to and Affirmations of the Initiation Paradigm in *Harry Potter*," in *Harry Potter's World*, ed. Heilman, pp. 163–84, especially pages 163–62, 171, and 182–83. See also Gilligan, "Adolescent Development Reconsidered" (note 17 above), who makes similar claims about adolescent development.

20. Sharon Moore, ed., *We Love Harry Potter! We'll Tell You Why* (New York: St. Martin's Griffin, 1999), p. 33 (Charlie Johnson), as well as p. 25 (Kyle Sargent), p. 32 (Catherine Gannascoli), and p. 42 (Harrison Weis Monsky). Phone interview with Linda DeNell, Children's Librarian, Appleton Public Library, August 27, 2001.

21. Nussbaum, *Upheavals of Thought*, p. 6 (on children), and *Therapy of Desire*, pp. 344–47 and 353–54 (on education), quoted at page 344. Also see Nussbaum, *Cultivating Humanity: A Classical Defense of Reform in Liberal Education* (Cambridge, Mass.: Harvard University Press, 1997), pp. 28–35. A number of authors have described the nature of learning in Harry Potter, without relating it to Stoic ideals. Their claims nevertheless resemble, at times, Nussbaum's description of

Stoic education. See, for example, Nel, *Harry Potter Novels*, pp. 29–30; Elster, "The Seeker of Secrets"; and Pat Pinsent, "The Education of a Wizard: Harry Potter and his Predecessors," in *The Ivory Tower and Harry Potter*, ed. Whited, pp. 27–50.

22. "Stoicism," in *The Encyclopedia of Philosophy*, ed. Paul Edwards (New York: Macmillan/Free Press, 1967), vol. 8, p. 20.

23. Rowling, *Sorcerer's Stone*, p. 86.

24. Eccleshare, *Guide*, p. 40. Worth noting, as well, is the frequency with which the adjective "stoic" is used in online fan fiction based on Rowling's stories.

25. On constancy and fatalism: Nussbaum, *Therapy of Desire*, pp. 29–32, 333, 464–71, and 497–99. Seneca, "On Providence," in *The Stoic Philosophy of Seneca*, trans. Moses Hadas (Garden City, N.J.: Doubleday, 1958), p. 41, and "De Constantia Sapientis," in *Moral Essays*, trans. John W. Basore (New York: G. P. Putnam's Sons, 1928) 1:61; Epictetus, *The Enchiridion*, trans. Thomas W. Higginson (Indianapolis: Bobbs-Merrill, 1955), pp. 20 and 30.

26. Rowling, *The Sorcerer's Stone*, pp. 259 and 293.

27. On endurance and perseverance: Nussbaum, *Therapy of Desire*, pp. 363–64, 395–96, and 419–38. Epictetus, *Enchiridion*, p. 18; Marcus Aurelius Antoninus, *The Meditations*, trans. G. M. A. Grube (Indianapolis: Hackett Publishing, 1983), pp. 118 and 84; Chrysippus, [original text lost] quoted by Cicero, *Tusculan Disputations*, in *The Hellenistic Philosophers*, trans. and ed. A. A. Long and D. N. Sedley (New York: Cambridge University Press, 1987) 1:192.

28. On self-discipline and reason: Nussbaum, *Therapy of Desire*, pp. 344–48, 353–54, 357–58, and 504–505. Epictetus, *Enchiridion*, pp. 28 and 33; and Cicero, Stobaeus, Plutarch, and Seneca, *Letters*, all in *The Hellenistic Philosophers*, ed. Long and Sedley, pp. 323, 378, 394, and 395.

29. J. K. Rowling, *Harry Potter and the Goblet of Fire* (New York: Scholastic Press, 2000), p. 717.

30. Nussbaum, *Therapy of Desire*, pp. 318, 341–53, 426–29, 437–38, 482, and 504–506; *Upheavals of Thought*, pp. 301–303, 309–10, 324–35, 359–80, 386–91, and 398. Hierocles [quoted by Stobaeus], in *The Hellenistic Philosophers*, ed. Long and Sedley, p. 349; Marcus Aurelius, *Meditations*, p. 116; and Epictetus, *Enchiridion*, pp. 30–31. On Seneca and Socrates, see de Botton, *Consolations of Philosophy*, pp. 3–8 and 75–79.

31. J. K. Rowling, *Harry Potter and the Prisoner of Azkaban* (New York: Scholastic Press, 1999), pp. 274–75.

32. Nussbaum, *Cultivating Humanity*, pp. 28–35 and 59–66; *Upheavals of Thought*, throughout.

33. Deborah J. Taub and Heather L. Servaty, "Controversial Content in Children's Literature: Is *Harry Potter* Harmful to Children?" in *Harry Potter's World*, ed. Heilman, pp. 53–72.

34. Lawrence Kohlberg, *The Philosophy of Moral Development: Moral Stages and the Idea of Justice*, vol. 1 of *Essays on Moral Development* (San Francisco: Harper and Row, 1981), pp. xxviii and 17–28. In presenting Kohlberg's model, I have largely followed the lead and employed some of the useful shorthand of Whited and Grimes, "What Would Harry Do?"

35. Kohlberg, *The Philosophy of Moral Development: Moral Stages and the Idea of Justice*, pp. 17–28; Whited and Grimes, "What Would Harry Do?" pp. 185, 188, 192, and 195–97.

36. Kohlberg, *The Philosophy of Moral Development: Moral Stages and the Idea of Justice*, pp. 141–47; Whited and Grimes, "What Would Harry Do?" pp. 204 and 206.

37. Whited and Grimes, "What Would Harry Do?" pp. 205–206.

38. Ibid., pp. 194–95, 197, 204, and 206.

39. Robert E. Grinder, *Adolescence*, 2nd ed. (New York: Wiley, 1978) p. 288. Whited and Grimes, "What Would Harry Do?" pp. 201–202.

40. Carol Gilligan, *In a Different Voice: Psychological Theory and Women's Development* (Cambridge, Mass.: Harvard University Press, 1982), and "Adolescent Development Reconsidered," pp. 107–109; Whited and Grimes, "What Would Harry Do?" 191–92.

41. Andrew Garrod and Carole R. Beal, "Voices of Care and Justice in Children's Responses to Fable Dilemmas," pp. 59–71, and Joseph Reimer, "The Case of the Missing Family: Kohlberg and the Study of Adolescent Moral Development," pp. 91–102, both in *Approaches to Moral Development*, ed. Garrod.

42. Fraser, *Conversations with J. K. Rowling*, pp. 39–40.

CHAPTER 4: GREED, CONVENTIONALITY, DEMONIC THREAT

1. Philip Nel, *J. K. Rowling's Harry Potter Novels* (New York: Continuum, 2001), pp. 53–63, quoted here at page 56: "By the time *Prisoner of Azkaban* was published (July 1999 in Great Britain, September 1999 in America), most opinions of *Harry Potter* fell into one of four categories: (1) praise for the books, because they either entice children to read or prove that children's literature is

worthy of adult attention; (2) scorn directed at people in the first group and, by extension, at the Harry Potter phenomenon, for a variety of reasons; (3) conservative U.S. Christians suggesting that the books should be removed from school libraries; and (4) the debate over whether the novels deserved to be ranked with classic children's fiction."

2. Forum on morality and Harry Potter, University of Wisconsin-Parkside, Kenosha, December 5, 2002. Speakers included Zach Tutlewski, the Rev. Todd Peperkorn of Kenosha's Messiah Lutheran Church, Kelly Salazar of Martha Merrell's Bookstore in Racine, Mary Jordan of the Kenosha Public Library, and Prof. Mary Lenard of the University of Wisconsin-Parkside English Department (who organized the event), as well as myself. Zach and his parents kindly provided me a copy of his comments in private correspondence.

3. Don Ward, age thirteen, in *We Love Harry Potter! We'll Tell You Why*, ed. Sharon Moore (New York: St. Martin's Griffin, 1999), p. 65. For additional children's commentary, see the "Harry Potter Discussion Chamber Archive" hosted by Scholastic [online], www.scholastic.com/harrypotter/reading/archive. htm, or any of the countless fan postings to Web sites dedicated to Harry Potter.

4. Rebecca Sutherland Borah, "Apprentice Wizards Welcome: Fan Communities and the Culture of Harry Potter," in *The Ivory Tower and Harry Potter*, ed. Lana A. Whited (Columbia: University of Missouri Press, 2002), pp. 343–64, quoted at page 344. Also see Kathleen F. Malu, "Ways of Reading *Harry Potter*: Multiple Stories for Multiple Reader Identities," pp. 75–95, Hollie Anderson, "Reading *Harry Potter* with Navajo Eyes," pp. 97–107, and Ernie Bond and Nancy Michelson, "Writing Harry's World: Children Coauthoring Hogwarts," pp. 109–22, all in *Harry Potter's World*, ed. Elizabeth Heilman (New York: Routledge Falmer, 2003).

5. Stanley Fish, "Literature in the Reader: Affective Stylistics," in *Is There a Text in This Class? The Authority of Interpretive Communities* (Cambridge, Mass.: Harvard University Press, 1980), pp. 21–67. His "Introduction, or How I Stopped Worrying and Learned to Love Interpretation," in the same volume, pp. 1–17, goes further by questioning even the "independence and stability" of the text and the reader. For an example of reader response theory applied to the Harry Potter books, see Malu, "Ways of Reading *Harry Potter*," pp. 75–95.

6. Nel, *Harry Potter Novels*, pp. 25–26; Linton Winks, "Charmed, I'm Sure," *Washington Post* (October 20, 1999): C1, [online] http://www.washingtonpost. com/wp-srv/style/books/features/rowling1020.htm; and Joanna Carey, "Who Hasn't Met Harry," *Guardian Unlimited* (Manchester) [online], www.guardian.co.

uk/Archive/Article/0,4273,3822242,00.html [February 16, 1999]. The proceeds from two short books, written under pseudonyms by Rowling, have gone to the British charity, Comic Relief: J. K. Rowling, as Newt Scamander, *Fantastic Beasts and Where to Find Them* (New York: Scholastic, 2001), and as Kennilworthy Whisp, *Quidditch through the Ages* (New York: Scholastic, 2001).

7. Alison Lurie, *Boys and Girls Forever: Children's Classics from Cinderella to Harry Potter* (New York: Penguin Books, 2003), p. xi; Deborah J. Taub and Heather L. Servaty, "Controversial Content in Children's Literature: Is *Harry Potter* Harmful to Children?" in *Harry Potter's World*, ed. Heilman, pp. 53–54 and throughout; and P. L. Travers, "On Not Writing for Children," *Children's Literature* 5 (1975): 18.

8. Rex Murphy, "All Hail Frankenpotter," *The Globe and Mail* (Toronto) (July 10, 2000) [online], www.radio.cbc.ca/programs/checkup/potter.html; and Roger Sutton, "Potter's Field," *The Horn Book Magazine* (September/October 1999). On Michael Gerber's *Barry Trotter and the Unauthorized Parody* (New York: Fireside, 2002), see Emma Yates, "Harry Potter and the Fight against Global Capitalism," *Guardian Unlimited* [online], www.books.guardian.co.uk/news/articles/0,6109, 621826,00.html [December 19, 2001].

9. Jack Zipes, "The Phenomenon of Harry Potter, Or Why All the Talk?" in *Sticks and Stones: The Troublesome Success of Children's Literature from Slovenly Peter to Harry Potter* (New York: Routledge, 2000), pp. 170–89, quoted at page 172.

10. Ibid., pp. 171–72.

11. Ibid., p. 176.

12. Ibid., p. 178.

13. Ibid., p. 188.

14. Tammy Turner-Vorbeck, "Pottermania: Good, Clean Fun or Cultural Hegemony?" in *Harry Potter's World*, ed. Heilman, pp. 13–24, quoted at page 13.

15. Ibid., pp. 13 and 19.

16. Andrew Blake, *The Irresistible Rise of Harry Potter* (London: Verso, 2002), pp. 8–9, 112–13, 74, and 87.

17. Ibid., pp. 74 and 87.

18. Eli Lehrer, "Why the Left Hates Harry Potter," *FrontPageMagazine.com* [online], www.frontpagemag.com/Articles/ReadArticle.asp?ID=4891 [December 5, 2002].

19. Terence Blacker, "Why Does Everyone Like Harry Potter?" *The Independent* (London) (July 13, 1999): 4; Pico Iyer, "The Playing Fields of Hogwarts," *The New York Times Book Review* (October 10, 1999): 39; and Richard Adams, "Harry

Potter and the Closet Conservative," *The Voice of the Turtle* [online], www.voiceof theturtle.org/printer/reviews/books/richard_potter.shtml [May 2001].

20. Christine Schoefer, "Harry Potter's Girl Trouble," *Salon.com* [online], http://dir.salon.com/books/feature/2000/01/13/potter/index.html [January 13, 2000].

21. Ibid.

22. Ibid.

23. Elizabeth E. Heilman, "Blue Wizards and Pink Witches: Representations of Gender Identity and Power," pp. 221–39; John Kornfeld and Laurie Prothro, "Comedy, Conflict, and Community: Home and Family in *Harry Potter*," pp. 187–202, quoted at page 191; Heilman and Anne E. Gregory, "Images of the Privileged Insider and Outcast Outsider," pp. 241–59, quoted at page 242; and Rebecca Skulnick and Jesse Goodman, "The Civic Leadership of *Harry Potter*," pp. 261–77, quoted at page 263; all in *Harry Potter's World*, ed. Heilman.

24. Farah Mendlesohn, "Crowning the King: Harry Potter and the construction of Authority," in *The Ivory Tower and Harry Potter*, ed. Whited, p. 159. On the role of ideology in Rowling's work, note the following from pages 159–60: "The ideological structures of Rowling's work focus on a manipulation of this uncritical construction of 'fairness'. The denial of ideology, which forms a significant element of the text, promotes a willing suspension of intellectual rigor. This contributes to promoting a particular understanding of authority while simultaneously undermining the coherence of the texts. Further, it leads to a rejection of the subversive opportunities available to the fantasist, exemplified in the works of Lewis Carroll and others: if a world is fundamentally fair and rational, subversion is politically unnecessary."

25. Ibid., p. 160.

26. Ibid., pp. 171 and 176.

27. Ibid., p. 181.

28. J. K. Rowling, *Harry Potter and the Sorcerer's Stone* (New York: Scholastic Press, 1998), pp. 298–99.

29. Mendlesohn, "Crowning the King," p. 163.

30. Karin E. Westman, "Specters of Thatcherism: Contemporary British Culture in J. K. Rowling's Harry Potter Series," in *The Ivory Tower and Harry Potter*, ed. Whited, pp. 305–28.

31. *Luther's Works*, Vol. 2, *Lectures on Genesis, Chapters 6–14*, ed. Jaroslav Pelikan (St. Louis: Concordia Publishing House, 1960), p. 160.

32. Stephen Dollins, *Under the Spell of Harry Potter* (Topeka, Kan.: The

Prophecy Club, 2001); Richard Abanes, *Harry Potter and the Bible: The Menace behind the Magick* (Camp Hill, Pa.: Horizon Books, 2001); and *Fantasy and Your Family: Exploring* The Lord of the Rings, Harry Potter, *and Modern Magick* (Camp Hill, Pa.: Christian Publications, Inc., 2002); and Gene Edward Veith, "Good Fantasy and Bad Fantasy," *Christian Research Journal* 23, no. 1 (2000) [online], Christian Research Institute, www.equip.org/free/DF801.htm.

33. Chuck Colson, "Witches and Wizards: The Harry Potter Phenomenon," *Breakpoint Commentary*, no. 91102, November 2, 1999 [online], www.pfmonline. net/transcripts.taf?_function=detail&ID=183&site=BPT&userreference argument>; Ted Olson, "Positive about Potter," *Christianity Today* (December 13, 1999) [online], www.christianitytoday.com/ct/1999/150/12.0.html; and "Why We Like Harry Potter," *Christianity Today* (January 10, 2000) [online], www. christianitytoday.com/ct/2000/001/29.37.html.

34. Kimbra Wilder Gish, "Hunting Down Harry Potter: An Exploration of Religious Concerns about Children's Literature," *The Horn Book Magazine* 76 (2000): 262–71; and Taub and Servaty, "Controversial Content," pp. 53–72. Deuteronomy 18:9–12, New Revised Standard Version with Apocrypha.

35. Dollins, *Under the Spell*, pp. 7, 34, and 95.

36. For only some examples, see Dollins, *Under the Spell*, and consider that: the covers to the American editions use occult symbols; the books introduce children to killings and murders; they depict prejudice; because Harry was entered into the Triwizard Tournament by cheating the moral is that cheating is okay (half-truths, pp. 16, 21, and 27); throughout the books "evil is referred to as 'good'"; speaking to snakes is "spirit communication"; Harry is "constantly in rebellion and defiance of authority" (factual errors, pp. 42, 54, and 57); Rowling dresses as a witch and embraces an image of a demon (photographs, pp. 35 and 36); and child readers describe how they're drawn to evil (quotations without attribution, pp. 96–97). On Web sites, see Taub and Servaty, "Controversial Content," pp. 54–55.

37. Abanes, *Harry Potter and the Bible*, pp. 7, 260–61, as well as pp. 173, 186–87, 205, 209, 213, 215–16, 230, and 247. The long account of the seventeen-year-old Satanist can be found on pages 177–86. Supporting the view that interest in the occult can be associated with criminal behaviors are (1) a short study by one psychologist claiming that occult involvement is a "warning sign" of potential violence in children and (2) a quotation from a philosopher suggesting occult practitioners have doubts about conventional values (see pages 186–87). Taub and Servaty, "Controversial Content in Children's Literature," advances argu-

ments and cites studies that demolish Abanes's claims. See the authors cited in note 44 (below) as well.

38. Abanes, *Harry Potter and the Bible*, p. 21, quoting J. K. Rowling, interview, *The Diane Rehm Show*, WAMU, National Public Radio (October 20, 1999) [online], www.wamu.org; and "Harry Potter 'Strolled into My Head,'" Reuters (July 17, 2000).

39. Abanes, *Fantasy and Your Family*, p. 193, quoting me in "Harry Potter, Stoic Boy Wonder," *The Chronicle Review*, a supplement to *The Chronicle of Higher Education* (November 16, 2001): B18–B19. Readers will find the same claim, in the proper context, in the first chapter of the present volume. (I'm a bit concerned that my assessment of Abanes's *presentation* in this work will someday be used to imply that I support his *ideas*.)

40. Abanes, *Harry Potter and the Bible*, pp. 22–23, quoted at 23; *Fantasy and Your Family*, pp. 293–94, n. 19, and p. 136. J. K. Rowling, interviews with Barnes and Noble, March 19, 1999 (available at *Hogwarts* [online], magichogwarts. com/book/interviews/mar19-99.html), and September 8, 1999 (available at *Arabella Figg's Hogwarts Express* [online], www.angelfire.com/mi3/cookarama/barnobintsep99.html). Rowling makes similar points in her interview on *The Diane Rehm Show* (see note 38).

41. Abanes, *Fantasy and Your Family*, pp. 193–235, quoted at 193, 194, 196, 201, 206, 222, and 235.

42. Abanes, *Harry Potter and the Bible*, p. 232.

43. J. R. R. Tolkien, *The Hobbit* (London: George Allen & Unwin, 1937), and *The Lord of the Rings* (London: George Allen & Unwin, 1954–1955).

44. T. M. Luhrmann, *Persuasions of the Witch's Craft: Ritual Magic in Contemporary England* (Cambridge, Mass.: Harvard University Press, 1989); Loretta Orion, *Never Again the Burning Times: Paganism Revived* (Prospect Heights, Ill.: Waveland Press, 1995); Ronald Hutton, *The Triumph of the Moon: A History of Modern Pagan Witchcraft* (New York: Oxford University Press, 1999); Kenneth V. Lanning, "Investigator's Guide to Allegations of 'Ritual' Child Abuse," Behavioral Science Unit, National Center for the Analysis of Violent Crime, Federal Bureau of Investigation, FBI Academy, Quantico, Virginia 22135 (1992) [online], www. religioustolerance.org/ra_rep03.htm; Gail Goodman, *Characteristics & Sources of Allegations of Ritual Child Abuse*, Clearing House on Child Abuse and Neglect Information, Suite 350, 3998 Fair Ridge Dr., Fairfax, Virginia 22033 (1994) [summary online], www.religioustolerance.org/ra_rep00.htm; and Malcolm McGrath, *Demons of the Modern World* (Amherst, N.Y.: Prometheus Books, 2002).

45. Veith, "Foreword," in *Fantasy and Your Family*, pp. ix–xii; and "Good Fantasy and Bad Fantasy" (unpaginated).

46. Colin Manlove, *Christian Fantasy: From 1200 to the Present* (Notre Dame, Ind.: University of Notre Dame Press, 1992), pp. 1–11; H. C. Erik Midelfort, "Social History and Biblical Exegesis: Community, Family, and Witchcraft in Sixteenth-Century Germany," in *The Bible in the Sixteenth Century*, ed. David C. Steinmetz (Durham, N.C.: Duke University Press, 1990), pp. 7–20; Edmund M. Kern, "An End to Witch Trials in Austria: Reconsidering the Enlightened State," *Austrian History Yearbook* 30 (1999): 159–85; and T. A. Shippey, *J. R. R. Tolkien: Author of the Century* (Boston: Houghton Mifflin Company, 2001), pp. 180–81, 187, and 293.

47. Connie Neal, *What's a Christian to Do with Harry Potter?* (Colorado Springs: Waterbrook Press, 2001); and *The Gospel According to Harry Potter: Spirituality in the Stories of the World's Most Famous Seeker* (Louisville, Ky.: Westminster John Knox Press, 2002); John Killinger, *God, the Devil, and Harry Potter: A Christian Minister's Defense of the Beloved Novels* (New York: St. Martin's Press, 2002); Francis Bridger, *A Charmed Life: The Spirituality of Potterworld* (New York: Image Books, 2002); John Granger, *The Hidden Key to Harry Potter: Understanding the Meaning, Genius, and Popularity of Joanne Rowling's* Harry Potter *Novels* (Port Hadlock, Wash.: Zossima Press, 2002); and Catherine Jack Deavel and David Paul Deavel, "Character, Choice, and Harry Potter," *Logos* 5, no. 4 (2002): 49–64, quoted at page 62.

48. C. S. Lewis, *The Discarded Image: An Introduction to Medieval and Renaissance Literature* (Cambridge: Cambridge University Press, 1964), quoted at pages 216 and 222.

CHAPTER 5: IMAGINATION, HISTORY, LEGEND, AND MYTH

1. Edmund M. Kern, "Harry Potter," *Conversations with Kathleen Dunn*, Wisconsin Public Radio, 5:00–6:00 P.M. (Wednesday, November 21, 2001). Alison Lurie, "Not for Muggles," *New York Review of Books*, December 19, 1999, pp. 6–8.

2. Philip Nel, *J. K. Rowling's Harry Potter Novels* (New York: Continuum, 2001), p. 33.

3. Allan Zola Kronzek and Elizabeth Kronzek, *The Sorcerer's Companion: A Guide to the Magical World of Harry Potter* (New York: Broadway Books, 2001), pp. 39–40, 132–45, 164–67, and 172–74, provide wonderful discussions of these figures; also see the less detailed but instructive entries in David Colbert, *The Magical Worlds of Harry Potter: A Treasury of Myths, Legends, and Fascinating Facts* (New

York: Berkley Books, 2001), pp. 53–54, 71–73, 183–93. For scholarly treatments of these figures, see, for example, Richard Kieckhefer, *Magic in the Middle Ages* (New York: Cambridge University Press, 1990); E. M. Butler, *The Myth of the Magus* (New York: Cambridge University Press, 1993 [1948]); and Stuart Clark, *Thinking with Demons: The Idea of Witchcraft in Early Modern Europe* (Oxford: The Clarendon Press, 1997). On Alberich, see *The Nibelungenlied*, trans. A. T. Hatto (New York: Penguin, 1982), p. 28. On Cliodna, see Miranda J. Green, *Dictionary of Celtic Myth and Legend* (New York: Thames & Hudson, 1997), p. 56.

4. Nel, *Harry Potter Novels*, pp. 7, 21, 30–36, and 51, and throughout. Also see entries in *Bulfinch's Mythology* (New York: Avenel Books, 1979) or other guides to mythology.

5. Kieckhefer, *Magic in the Middle Ages*, pp. 56–94 and 116–50.

6. Kronzek and Kronzek, *Sorcerer's Companion*, offers a useful guide to situating these practices in a historical context.

7. Kieckhefer, *Magic in the Middle Ages*, pp. 56–94 and 116–201. Also see Robin Briggs, *Witches and Neighbors: The Social and Cultural Context of European Witchcraft* (New York: Viking, 1996); Darren Oldridge, ed., *The Witchcraft Reader* (New York: Routledge, 2002); Bengt Ankarloo and Stuart Clark, eds., *The Athlone History of Witchcraft and Magic in Europe*, 6 vols. (London: The Athlone Press, 1999–2002); and Edmund M. Kern, "An End to Witch Trials in Austria," *Austrian History Yearbook* 30 (1999): 159–85. The most comprehensive account of attitudes toward magic is Stuart Clark's magisterial book, *Thinking with Demons* (note 3 above).

8. Again, Kieckhefer's *Magic in the Middle Ages* (pp. 56–94 and 116–201, and throughout, especially pages 151–201) is a useful guide to historical forms of demonic magic. On neo-paganism and Satanism, T. M. Luhrmann's *Persuasions of the Witch's Craft* (Cambridge, Mass.: Harvard University Press, 1989) is essential, and Ronald Hutton's *Triumph of the Moon* (New York: Oxford University Press, 1999) is definitive: "Like Tanya Luhrmann before me, I have never encountered anything remotely resembling Satanism in my entire experience of pagan witches. To do so would, indeed, be something of a conceptual impossibility, as belief in the Devil itself requires a Christian cosmology, and modern Pagans of all kinds do not perceive any inherently evil forces to exist in the non-human world" (p. 407).

9. Both Kronzek and Kronzek, *Sorcerer's Companion*, and Colbert, *Magical Worlds*, provide admirable treatments of the legendary and mythical creatures found in Harry Potter. Readers might want to turn to additional reference works. Richard Barber and Anne Riches, *A Dictionary of Fabulous Beasts* (New

York: Walker and Company, 1971), offer especially useful introductions to legendary and mythical creatures, combining short entries with clear references to source material. Joe Nigg, *Wonder Beasts: Tales and Lore of the Phoenix, the Griffin, the Unicorn, and the Dragon* (Englewood, Colo.: Libraries Unlimited, 1995), provides extensive analysis of several creatures mentioned frequently in Harry's tales. By the same author, *The Book of Fabulous Beasts: A Treasury of Writings from Ancient Times to the Present*, ed. Joseph Nigg (New York: Oxford University Press, 1999), reproduces passages from numerous historical sources. Carol K. Mack and Dinah Mack, *A Field Guide to Demons, Fairies, Fallen Angels, and other Subversive Spirits* (New York: Arcade Publishing, 1998), is also useful, though sources are identified only in a bibliography.

10. Andrew Blake makes similar observations in *The Irresistible Rise of Harry Potter* (London: Verso, 2002), even though he erroneously places Harry's stories in the late 1990s (p. 1). Also see Karin E. Westman, "Specters of Thatcherism: Contemporary British Culture in J. K. Rowling's Harry Potter Series," in *The Ivory Tower and Harry Potter*, ed. Lana A. Whited (Columbia: University of Missouri Press, 2002), pp. 305–28.

11. Blake, *Irresistible Rise*, pp. 71 and 113; Nel, *Harry Potter Novels*, pp. 36–41. Others elaborating upon the attractions of what I have labeled the familiar and the fantastic in Harry Potter include Amanda Cockrell, "Harry Potter and the Secret Password: Finding Our Way in the Magical Genre," pp. 15–26; M. Katherine Grimes, "Harry Potter: Fairy Tale Prince, Real Boy, and Archetypal Hero," pp. 89–122; and Roni Natov, "Harry Potter and the Extraordinariness of the Ordinary," pp. 125–39, all in *The Ivory Tower and Harry Potter*, ed. Whited.

12. John Pennington, "From Elfland to Hogwarts, or the Aesthetic Trouble with Harry Potter," *The Lion and the Unicorn* 26 (2002): 78–97, quoted at pages 79 and 96, n.8.

13. A. S. Byatt, *On Histories and Stories* (Cambridge, Mass.: Harvard University Press, 2001), pp. 5–11, 36–38, 41–45, 107, 118–32, and throughout, quoted at pages 10, 45, 54, 100, 124, 129, and 132. Roberto Calasso, *The Marriage of Cadmus and Harmony*, trans. Tim Parks (New York: Vintage Books, 1994), p. 10.

14. "Potter Book Five," *BBC Newsround* [online], http://news.bbc.co.uk/cbbcnews/hi/uk/newsid_2661000/2661257.stm [January 15, 2003].

15. Richard L. Purtill, *J. R. R. Tolkien: Myth, Morality, and Religion* (San Francisco: Harper & Row, 1984), pp. 1–3 and 111–14.

16. On heroism in all its guises, see Joseph Campbell, *The Hero with a Thousand Faces*, 2d ed. (Princeton, N.J.: Princeton University Press, 1968).

17. Grimes, "Harry Potter: Fairy Tale Prince, Real Boy, and Archetypal Hero," pp. 90–99 (fairy tales) and 106–20 (myth), especially pages 107 and 117, citing and quoting Otto Rank, *The Myth of the Birth of the Hero*, trans. F. Robbins and Smith Ely Jelliffe, in *In Quest of the Hero*, ed. Robert Segal (Princeton, N.J.: Princeton University Press, 1990), pp. 57, 62, and 70–71.

18. Mary Pharr, "In Medias Res: Harry Potter as Hero-in-Progress," in *The Ivory Tower and Harry Potter*, ed. Whited, p. 66.

19. See, for example, J. E. Cirlot, *A Dictionary of Symbols*, trans. Jack Sage (New York: Barnes & Noble Books, 1993), "Symbolism and Historicity," pp. xiii–xvi, with which I do not entirely agree, but which lays out the central issues.

20. J. K. Rowling, *Harry Potter and the Prisoner of Azkaban* (New York: Scholastic, 1999), p. 155.

21. Ann Treneman, "J. K. Rowling: The Interview," *The Times* (London) (June 30, 2000), available at *TimesOnline* [online], www.timesonline.co.uk/article/0,, 927-79520,00.html.

22. See the entries for each creature in Kronzek and Kronzek, *Sorcerer's Companion*, and Colbert, *Magical Worlds*. For discussions unrelated to Harry Potter, see entries in Mack and Mack, *Field Guide*; Barber and Riches, *Fabulous Beasts*; and Cirlot, *Symbols*. On the hippogriff, see Nigg, *Book of Fabulous Beasts*, pp. 223–24.

23. See the entries in the works cited in note 22, as well as Nigg, *Book of Fabulous Beasts*, pp. 42, 90, 111–12, 121, 144–45, 164–68, and 203–10, which provides a wealth of information in passages from historical sources (quoted at pages 208 and 209).

24. Again, see works cited in note 22, as well as the sources in Nigg, *Book of Fabulous Beasts*, pp. 39, 55–56, 85–91, 105–107, 109–10, 119–20, 124–27, 144, 196–97, 223, and 225–26, quoted at pages 55, 91, and 223.

25. Lyndy Abraham, *A Dictionary of Alchemical Imagery* (New York: Cambridge University Press, 1998), pp. 35–39, 94, 141, 145–49, 152, and 181.

26. Cirlot, *Symbols*, p. 8, quoting P. V. Piobb, *Clef universelle des sciences secrètes* (Paris, 1950).

27. Julia Eccleshare, *A Guide to the Harry Potter Novels* (New York: Continuum, 2002), p. 47; Blake, *Irresistible Rise*, p. 7.

28. Blake, *Irresistible Rise*, p. 107. On the boarding school tradition, see Eccleshare, *Guide*, pp. 48–49, and Nel, *Harry Potter Novels*, pp. 27–28. On the highly conventional moral code, rules, and order, see Eccleshare, *Guide*, pp. 50 and 90. On the family, see Eccleshare, *Guide*, p. 73 and 101; Nel, *Harry Potter*

Novels, p. 47; and John Kornfeld and Laurie Prothro, "Comedy, Conflict, and Community," in *Harry Potter's World: Multidisciplinary Critical Perspectives*, ed. Elizabeth E. Heilman (New York: Routledge Falmer, 2003), pp. 189–91 and 196.

29. See, for example, the variety of comments on these issues in Eccleshare, *Guide*, pp. 52, and 73–88; Blake, *Irresistible Rise*, pp. 27–46 and 102–10; Elizabeth E. Heilman and Anne E. Gregory, "Images of the Privileged Insider and the Outcast Outsider," pp. 242–45; and Rebecca Skulnick and Jesse Goodman, "Civic Leadership," pp. 262–67 in *Harry Potter's World*, ed. Heilman.

30. Eccleshare, *Guide*, p. 92; and Nel, *Harry Potter Novels*, p. 34.

31. "Evil, Human" and "Evil, the Problem of," in *The Oxford Companion to Philosophy*, ed. Ted Honderich (New York: Oxford University Press, 1995); and "Evil," in *The Encyclopedia of Religion*, ed. Vergilius Ferm (Secaucus, N.J.: Poplar Books, 1945).

32. T. A. Shippey, *J. R. R. Tolkien: Author of the Century* (Boston: Houghton Mifflin Company, 2001), pp. 174–78, 213–21, and throughout, quoting Tolkien at page 293; Purtill, *Tolkien*, pp. 111–14 and passim; Gene Edward Veith, "Good Fantasy and Bad Fantasy," *Christian Research Journal* 23, no. 1 (2000) [online], Christian Research Institute, www.equip.org/ free/DF801.htm; Alison Lurie, *Boys and Girls Forever: Children's Classics from Cinderella to Harry Potter* (New York: Penguin Books, 2003), pp. 120–22; and "Christian Fantasy" in *The Encyclopedia of Fantasy*, ed. John Clute and John Grant (New York: St. Martin's Press, 1997).

33. Purtill, *Tolkien*, pp. 3, 12, 15, 27, 39–40, 111–14, and 115–18; Shippey, *Tolkien*, pp. 107–60, 174–82, 187, 193–94, 196, 200, 213–21, 238–42, 259, 293, and 328, quoted at pages 130 and 111.

34. "Literature," in *The Encyclopedia of Religion*, edited by Mircea Eliade, 16 vols. (New York: Macmillan Publishing Company, 1987), 8:558–80.

35. Each of these works, in ascending order of intensity, advance arguments in favor of reading the Harry Potter books as Christian allegory: Francis Bridger, *A Charmed Life: The Spirituality of Potterworld* (New York: Image Books, 2002); John Killinger, *God, the Devil, and Harry Potter: A Christian Minister's Defense of the Beloved Novels* (New York: St. Martin's Press, 2002); Connie Neal, *What's a Christian to Do with Harry Potter?* (Colorado Springs: Waterbrook Press, 2001); *The Gospel According to Harry Potter: Spirituality in the Stories of the World's Most Famous Seeker* (Louisville, Ky.: Westminster John Knox Press, 2002); and *especially* John Granger, *The Hidden Key to Harry Potter: Understanding the Meaning, Genius, and Popularity of Joanne Rowling's* Harry Potter *Novels* (Port Hadlock, Wash.: Zossima Press, 2002).

36. Nigg, *Book of Fabulous Beasts*, pp. 105–12, 124–27, and 164–68; Cirlot, *Symbols*, pp. 22–23, 133, 189–90, 253–54, 285–90, and 357–58.

37. Granger, *Hidden Key*, pp. xv, 138, 166, and throughout.

38. Nigg, *Book of Fabulous Beasts*, pp. 121, 142–46, 165–68, quoted at pages 121 and 166; Cirlot, *Symbols* (see note 26); Colbert, *Magical Worlds*, p. 95; and Kieckhefer, *Magic in the Middle Ages*.

39. Bridger, *Charmed Life*, p. 107 and throughout.

40. A. O. Scott, "Will There Be Trouble with Harry?" *Slate* [online], http://slate.msn.com/id/2000111/entry/1003477/ [August 24, 1999]. On Milton, see Gerhard Oestreich, *Neostoicism and the Early Modern State*, trans. David McLintock (New York: Cambridge University Press, 1982), pp. 116–17. Andrew Eric Shifflett, *Stoicism, Politics, and Literature in the Age of Milton: War and Peace Reconciled* (Cambridge: Cambridge University Press, 1998).

41. *The Hellenistic Philosophers*, trans. and ed. A. A. Long and D. N. Sedley (New York: Cambridge University Press, 1987) 1:323–33, quoted at page 323.

42. Martha C. Nussbaum, *Upheavals of Thought: The Intelligence of Emotions* (New York: Cambridge University Press, 2001), pp. 542–43 and throughout; Richard Strier, "Against the Rule of Reason: Praise of Passion from Petrarch to Luther to Shakespeare to Herbert," forthcoming in *Reading the Early Modern Passions*, ed. Mary Floyd-Wilson, Karen Rowe, and Gail Kern Pastor (Philadelphia: University of Pennsylvania Press); and Oestreich, *Neostoicism and the Early Modern State*, pp. 13–14.

43. Catherine Jack Deavel and David Paul Deavel, "Character, Choice, and Harry Potter," *Logos* 5, no. 4 (2002): 49–64, quoted at page 62.

44. See, for example, the extensive work by Thomas McEvilley, *The Shape of Ancient Thought: Comparative Studies in Greek and Indian Philosophies* (New York: Allworth Press, 2002).

45. For a brief account relating Flamel to Harry Potter, see Kronzek and Kronzek, *Sorcerer's Companion*, pp. 177–80. For a recent edition of Flamel's *Hieroglyphica* in English, see Laurinda Dixon, ed., *Nicolas Flamel: His Exposition of the Hieroglyphicall Figures* (New York: Garland, 1996). Dixon's introduction is the most up-to-date synthesis of scholarly opinion on Flamel. Other treatments of Flamel include: John Read, *Prelude to Chemistry* (Cambridge, Mass.: The M.I.T. Press, 1966 [1936]), pp. 59–67; E. J. Holmyard, *Alchemy* (New York: Dover, 1990 [1957]), pp. 239–49; Reinhard Federmann, *The Royal Art of Alchemy*, trans. Richard H. Weber (New York: Chilton, 1969 [1964]), pp. 104–11; and Allison Coudert, *Alchemy: The Philosopher's Stone* (Boulder, Colo.: Shambhala, 1980), pp. 14–16.

46. My translations from the medieval French in Holmyard, *Alchemy*, p. 248: "Feu Nicolas Flamel jadis escrivain a laissie par son testament a leuvre de ceste eglise certaines rentes et maisons quil avoit acquestees et achetees a son vivant pour faire certain service divin et distribucions dargent chascun an par aumosne touchans les quinze vins lostel dieu et autres eglises et hospitaux de paris Soit prie po les trespasses" (tombstone); and "Chacun soit content de ses biens/Qui n'a suffisance, il n'a rien" (inscription). Also see the works cited above (note 45), especially Dixon, *Nicolas Flamel*, pp. xii–xvii. For a discussion of scholarly approaches to alchemy, see Lawrence M. Principe and William R. Newman, "Some Problems with the Historiography of Alchemy," in *Secrets of Nature: Astrology and Alchemy in Early Modern Europe*, ed. William R. Newman and Anthony Grafton (Cambridge, Mass.: The M.I.T. Press, 2001), pp. 385–431.

47. The relationship between history and imagination is far more complex than my brief comments imply. Nonetheless, even historians reaching opposing conclusions about the discipline of history allow for the exercise of imagination. Compare, for instance, Alun Munslow, *Deconstructing History* (New York: Routledge, 1997), pp. 163–78 and throughout, and Richard J. Evans, *In Defense of History* (New York: Norton, 1999), pp. 210–20 and throughout. Carlo Ginzburg offers a practical guide to the imaginative interpretation of evidence in his essay, "Clues: Roots of an Evidential Paradigm," in *Clues, Myths, and the Historical Method*, trans. John and Anne Tedeschi (Baltimore: Johns Hopkins University Press, 1989), pp. 96–125; Inga Clendinnen also offers important insights in her essay, "Fellow Sufferers: History and Imagination," *Australian Humanities Review* [online], www.lib.latrobe.edu.au/AHR/archive/Issue-Sept-1996/clendinnen.html.

48. Historical Site—Harry Potter [online], nicolasflamel.parisbistro.net/default-uk.htm.

AFTERWORD: HARRY POTTER AND THE ORDER OF THE PHOENIX

1. Carmen Reid, "Yes, It's Magic," *Sunday Mail* (Scotland), June 22, 2003, p. 14; and David D. Kirkpatrick, "New 'Harry Potter' Book Sells Five Million on First Day," *New York Times*, June 23, 2003, p. A14.

2. J. K. Rowling, *Harry Potter and the Order of the Phoenix* (New York: Scholastic Books, 2003), p. 8.

3. Ibid., p. 9.

4. Ibid., p. 10.

5. Ibid., p. 11.

6. Ibid.

7. Jackie Loohauis, "A Wizard Rebels: Enchanting Potter Book Features an Angrier Harry—and a Deeper, Darker Tale," *Milwaukee Journal-Sentinel*, June 24, 2003, p. 6B.

8. For a selection of very early reviews highlighting Harry's teen angst, see: Michiko Kakutani, "For Famous Young Wizard, a Darker Turn," *New York Times*, June 21, 2003, p. 1; Phil Kloer, "Teenage Wizardry: In Which Our Hero Survives Not Only Villainy but Also Adolescent Angst," *Atlanta Journal-Constitution*, June 20, 2003, p. 1G; Rebecca Tyrrel, "What the Critics (of All Ages) Think of the New Book," *Sunday Telegraph* (London), June 22, 2003, p. 8; and Laura Miller, "Harry Potter, Teen Rebel," Salon.com [online], salon.com/books/feature/2003/06/23/harry_potter [June 23, 2003]. For a brief review of favorable reviews, see Hillel Italie, "Harry Potter Book a Hit with Critics, Too," *Washington Post* [online], washingtonpost.com/wp-dyn/articles/A24721-2003Jun23.html [June 24, 2003].

9. Rowling, *The Order of the Phoenix*, p. 149.

10. Ibid., p. 536.

11. Ibid., p. 22.

12. Ibid., p. 841.

13. Ibid., pp. 825–26.

14. Ibid., p. 826.

15. Ibid., p. 837.

16. Ibid., pp. 838–39.

17 Ibid., pp. 843–44.

18. J. K. Rowling, *Harry Potter and the Sorcerer's Stone* (New York: Scholastic Press, 1998), p. 297.

19. Rowling, *The Order of the Phoenix*, p. 861.

20. Ibid., p. 863.

Bibliography

Abanes, Richard. *Fantasy and Your Family: Exploring* The Lord of the Rings, Harry Potter *and Modern Magick*. Camp Hill, Pa.: Christian Publications, Inc., 2002.

———. *Harry Potter and the Bible: The Menace behind the Magick*. Camp Hill, Pa.: Horizon Books, 2001.

Abraham, Lyndy. *A Dictionary of Alchemical Imagery*. New York: Cambridge University Press, 1998.

Acocella, Joan. "Under the Spell." *The New Yorker*, July 31, 2000.

Adams, Richard. "Harry Potter and the Closet Conservative." *The Voice of the Turtle* [online]. www.voiceoftheturtle.org/printer/reviews/books/richard_potter.shtml [May 2001].

"All about Harry Potter." *Entertainment Weekly* [online]. www.ew.com/ew/allabout/0,9930,37629~11~0~harrypotterandchamber,00.html [December 21, 2002].

Allen, Jamie. "'Harry' and Hype." *CNN.com* [online]. www.cnn.com/2000/books/news/07/13/potter.hype/ [July 13, 2000].

Alton, Anne Hiebert. "Generic Fusion and the Mosaic of *Harry Potter*." In *Harry Potter's World*, edited by Elizabeth E. Heilman.

Anderson, Hollie. "Reading *Harry Potter* with Navajo Eyes." In *Harry Potter's World*, edited by Elizabeth E. Heilman.

Ankarloo, Bengt, and Stuart Clark, eds. *The Athlone History of Witchcraft and Magic in Europe*. 6 vols. London: The Athlone Press, 1999–2002.

Antoninus, Marcus Aurelius. *The Meditations*. Translated by G. M. A. Grube. Indianapolis: Hackett Publishing, 1983.

Appelbaum, Peter. "Harry Potter's World: Magic, Technoculture, and Becoming Human." In *Harry Potter's World*, edited by Elizabeth E. Heilman.

Atherton, Catherine. *The Stoics on Ambiguity*. New York: Cambridge University Press, 1993.

Barber, Richard, and Anne Riches. *A Dictionary of Fabulous Beasts*. New York: Walker and Company, 1971.

Becker, Beverly. Phone Interview. August 27, 2001.

Bennett, William J., and Michael Hague. *The Children's Book of Virtues*. New York: Simon and Schuster, 1995.

Berendt, Thomas. *Child Development*. Fort Worth, Texas: Harcourt Brace Jovanovich, 1991.

Blacker, Terence. "Why Does Everyone Like Harry Potter?" *The Independent* (London), July 13, 1999.

Blake, Andrew. *The Irresistible Rise of Harry Potter*. London: Verso, 2002.

Bloom, Harold. Conversation with Ray Suarez. *NewsHour* [online]. www.pbs.org/newshour/conversation/july-dec00/bloom_8-29.html [August 29, 2000].

Bond, Ernie, and Nancy Michelson. "Writing Harry's World: Children Coauthoring Hogwarts." In *Harry Potter's World*, edited by Elizabeth E. Heilman.

Borah, Rebecca Sutherland. "Apprentice Wizards Welcome: Fan Communities and the Culture of Harry Potter." In *The Ivory Tower and Harry Potter*, edited by Lana A. Whited.

Botton, Alain de. *The Consolations of Philosophy*. New York: Pantheon Books, 2000.

Bridger, Francis. *A Charmed Life: The Spirituality of Potterworld*. New York: Image Books, 2002.

Briggs, Robin. *Witches and Neighbors: The Social and Cultural Context of European Witchcraft*. New York: Viking, 1996.

Bulfinch's Mythology. New York: Avenel Books, 1979 [1855–1863].

Butler, E. M. *The Myth of the Magus*. New York: Cambridge University Press, 1993 [1948].

Byatt, A. S. *On Histories and Stories*. Cambridge, Mass.: Harvard University Press, 2001.

Calasso, Roberto. *The Marriage of Cadmus and Harmony*. Translated by Tim Parks. New York: Vintage Books, 1994.

Campbell, Joseph. *The Hero with a Thousand Faces*. 2nd ed. Princeton, N.J.: Princeton University Press, 1968.

Carey, Joanna. "Who Hasn't Met Harry." *Guardian Unlimited* [online]. www.guardian.co.uk/Archive/Article/0,4273,3822242,00.html [February 16, 1999].

Cirlot, J. E. *A Dictionary of Symbols*. Translated by Jack Sage. New York: Barnes & Noble Books, 1993.

Clark, Stuart. *Thinking with Demons: The Idea of Witchcraft in Early Modern Europe*. Oxford: The Clarendon Press, 1997.

Clendinnen, Inga. "Fellow Sufferers: History and Imagination." *Australian Humanities Review* [online]. www.lib.latrobe.edu.au/AHR/archive/Issue-Sept-1996/clendinnen.html [February 12, 2003].

Cockrell, Amanda. "Harry Potter and the Secret Password: Finding Our Way in the Magical Genre," in *The Ivory Tower and Harry Potter*, edited by Lana A. Whited.

Colbert, David. *The Magical Worlds of Harry Potter: A Treasury of Myths, Legends, and Fascinating Facts*. New York: Berkley Books, 2001.

Coles, Robert. *The Moral Intelligence of Children*. New York: Random House, 1997.

Colson, Chuck. "Witches and Wizards: The Harry Potter Phenomenon." *Breakpoint Commentary*, no. 91102 [online]. www.pfmonline.net/transcripts.taf?_function=detail&ID=183&site=BPT&userreferenceargument [November 2, 1999].

Coudert, Allison. *Alchemy: The Philosopher's Stone*. Boulder, Colo.: Shambhala, 1980.

De Rosa, Deborah. "Wizardly Challenges to and Affirmations of the Initiation Paradigm in *Harry Potter*." In *Harry Potter's World*, edited by Elizabeth E. Heilman.

Deavel, Catherine Jack, and David Paul Deavel. "Character, Choice, and Harry Potter," *Logos* 5, no. 4 (2002): 49–64.

DeNell, Linda. Phone Interview. August 27, 2001.

Dixon, Laurinda, ed. *Nicolas Flamel: His Exposition of the Hieroglyphicall Figures*. New York: Garland, 1996.

Dollins, Stephen. *Under the Spell of Harry Potter.* Topeka, Kan.: The Prophecy Club, 2001.

Eccleshare, Julia. *A Guide to the Harry Potter Novels.* New York: Continuum, 2002.

Elster, Charles. "The Seeker of Secrets: Images of Learning, Knowing, and Schooling." In *Harry Potter's World,* edited by Elizabeth E. Heilman.

Epictetus. *The Enchiridion.* Translated by Thomas W. Higginson. Indianapolis: Bobbs-Merrill, 1955.

Evans, Richard J. *In Defense of History.* New York: Norton, 1999.

"Evil, Human," and "Evil, the Problem of." In *The Oxford Companion to Philosophy,* edited by Ted Honderich. New York: Oxford University Press, 1995.

"Evil." In *The Encyclopedia of Religion,* edited by Vergilius Ferm. Secauscus, N.J.: Poplar Books, 1945.

Federmann, Reinhard. *The Royal Art of Alchemy.* Translated by Richard H. Weber. New York: Chilton, 1969.

Fine, Larry. "Director Gives All to Second Harry Potter Film." *Entertainment Tonight* (Reuters) [online]. www.etonline.com/reuters/N04327104.htm [November 4, 2002].

Fish, Stanley. *Is There a Text in This Class? The Authority of Interpretive Communities.* Cambridge, Mass.: Harvard University Press, 1980.

Fraser, Lindsey. *Conversations with J. K. Rowling.* New York: Scholastic, 2000.

Garrod, Andrew, ed. *Approaches to Moral Development: New Research and Emerging Themes.* New York: Teachers College Press, 1993.

Garrod, Andrew, and Carole R. Beal. "Voices of Care and Justice in Children's Responses to Fable Dilemmas." In *Approaches to Moral Development,* edited by Andrew Garrod.

Gerber, Michael. *Barry Trotter and the Unauthorized Parody.* New York: Fireside, 2002.

Gilligan, Carol. "Adolescent Development Reconsidered." In *Approaches to Moral Developments,* edited by Andrew Garrod.

———. *In a Different Voice: Psychological Theory and Women's Development.* Cambridge, Mass.: Harvard University Press, 1982.

Ginzburg, Carlo. "Clues: Roots of an Evidential Paradigm." In *Clues, Myths, and the Historical Method,* translated by John and Anne Tedeschi. Baltimore: Johns Hopkins University Press, 1989.

Gish, Kimbra Wilder. "Hunting Down Harry Potter: An Exploration of Religious Concerns about Children's Literature." *The Horn Book Magazine* 76 (2000): 262–71.

Goodman, Gail, director. *Characteristics & Sources of Allegations of Ritual Child Abuse*, Clearing House on Child Abuse and Neglect Information, Fairfax, Virginia (1994) [summary online]. www.religioustolerance.org/ra_rep00.htm [July 11, 2001].

Grahame, Kenneth. *The Wind in the Willows*. Chicago: Contemporary Books, 1988 [1908].

Granger, John. *The Hidden Key to Harry Potter*. Port Hadlock, Wash.: Zossima Press, 2002.

Green, Miranda J. *Dictionary of Celtic Myth and Legend*. New York: Thames & Hudson, 1997.

Grimes, M. Katherine. "Harry Potter: Fairy Tale Prince, Real Boy, and Archetypal Hero." In *The Ivory Tower and Harry Potter*, edited by Lana A. Whited.

Grinder, Robert E. *Adolescence*. 2nd ed. New York: Wiley, 1978.

Handler, Daniel. "Frightening News." *New York Times*, October 30, 2001: 17.

Harry Potter Discussion Chamber Archive. Scholastic [online]. www.scholastic.com/harrypotter/reading/archive.htm [December 15, 2002].

Heilman, Elizabeth E., ed. "Blue Wizards and Pink Witches: Representations of Gender Identity and Power." In *Harry Potter's World*, edited by Elizabeth E. Heilman.

Heilman, Elizabeth E., ed. *Harry Potter's World: Multidisciplinary Critical Perspectives*. New York: Routledge Falmer, 2003.

Heilman, Elizabeth E., and Anne E. Gregory. "Images of the Privileged Insider and Outcast Outsider." In *Harry Potter's World*, edited by Elizabeth E. Heilman.

Historical Site—Harry Potter [online]. nicolasflamel.parisbistro.net/default-uk.htm [December 15, 2002].

Holmyard, E. J. *Alchemy*. New York: Dover, 1990.

Hutton, Ronald. *The Triumph of the Moon: A History of Modern Pagan Witchcraft*. New York: Oxford University Press, 1999.

Italie, Hillel. "Harry Potter Book a Hit with Critics, Too." *Washington Post* [online]. washingtonpost.com/wp-dyn/articles/A24721-2003Jun23.html [June 24, 2003].

Iyer, Pico. "The Playing Fields of Hogwarts." *The New York Times Book Review*, October 10, 1999.

Jacobs, Alan. "Harry Potter's Magic." *First Things: The Journal of Religion and Public Life* 99 (2000): 35–38.

Jann Lacoss, "Of Magicals and Muggles: Reversals and Revulsions at Hogwarts." In *The Ivory Tower and Harry Potter*, edited by Lana A. Whited.

Kakutani, Michiko. "For Famous Young Wizard, a Darker Turn." *New York Times*, June 21, 2003, p. A1.

Kern, Edmund M. "An End to Witch Trials in Austria: Reconsidering the Enlightened State." *Austrian History Yearbook* 30 (1999): 159–85.

———. "Harry Potter." *Conversations with Kathleen Dunn*. Wisconsin Public Radio, 5:00–6:00 p.m., Wednesday, November 21, 2001.

———. "Harry Potter, Stoic Boy Wonder." *The Chronicle Review*. Supplement to *The Chronicle of Higher Education*, November 16, 2001.

Kieckhefer, Richard. *Magic in the Middle Ages*. New York: Cambridge University Press, 1990.

Killinger, John. *God, the Devil, and Harry Potter: A Christian Minister's Defense of the Beloved Novels*. New York: St. Martin's Press, 2002.

Kirkpatrick, David D. "New 'Harry Potter' Book Sells Five Million on First Day." *New York Times*, June 23, 2003, p. A14

Kloer, Phil. "Teenage Wizardry: In Which Our Hero Survives Not Only Villainy but Also Adolescent Angst." *Atlanta Journal-Constitution*, June 20, 2003, p. 1G.

Kohlberg, Lawrence. *The Philosophy of Moral Development: Moral Stages and the Idea of Justice*. Vol. 1. *Essays on Moral Development*. San Francisco: Harper and Row, 1981.

———. *The Psychology of Moral Development: The Nature and Validity of Moral Stages*. Vol. 2. *Essays on Moral Development*. San Francisco: Harper and Row, 1984.

Kornfeld, John, and Laurie Prothro. "Comedy, Conflict, and Community: Home and Family in *Harry Potter*." In *Harry Potter's World*, edited by Elizabeth E. Heilman.

Kronzek, Allan Zola, and Elizabeth Kronzek. *The Sorcerer's Companion: A Guide to the Magical World of Harry Potter*. New York: Broadway Books, 2001.

Lanning, Kenneth V. "Investigator's Guide to Allegations of 'Ritual' Child Abuse." Behavioral Science Unit, National Center for the Analysis of Violent Crime, Federal Bureau of Investigation, FBI Academy, Quantico, Virginia 22135 (1992) [online]. www.religioustolerance.org/ra_rep03.htm [July 11, 2001].

Lehrer, Eli. "Why the Left Hates Harry Potter." FrontPageMagazine.com [online]. www.frontpagemag.com/Articles/ReadArticle.asp?ID=4891 [December 5, 2002].

Lewis, C. S. *The Chronicles of Narnia*. New York: Macmillan, 1950–1956.

———. *The Discarded Image: An Introduction to Medieval and Renaissance Literature*. Cambridge: Cambridge University Press, 1964.

———. "On Three Ways of Writing for Children." In *Of Other Worlds: Essays and Stories*. London: Geoffrey Bles, 1966.

Lipsius, Justus. *Two Bookes of Constancie*. Translated by Sir John Stradling. New Brunswick, N. J.: Rutgers University Press, 1939 [1594].

"Literature." In *The Encyclopedia of Religion*, edited by Mircea Eliade. 16 vols. New York: Macmillan Publishing Company, 1987.

Long, A. A., and D. N. Sedley, eds. and trans. *The Hellenistic Philosophers*. Vol. 1. New York: Cambridge University Press, 1987.

Loohauis, Jackie. "A Wizard Rebels: Enchanting Potter Book Features an Angrier Harry—and a Deeper, Darker Tale." *Milwaukee Journal-Sentinel*, June 24, 2003, p. 6B.

Luhrmann, T. M. *Persuasions of the Witch's Craft: Ritual Magic in Contemporary England*. Cambridge, Mass.: Harvard University Press, 1989.

Lurie, Alison. *Boys and Girls Forever: Children's Classics from Cinderella to Harry Potter*. New York: Penguin Books, 2003.

———. "Not for Muggles." *The New York Review of Books*, December 19, 1999.

Luther, Martin. *Lectures on Genesis, Chapters 6–14*. Vol. 2, *Luther's Works*. Edited by Jaroslav Pelikan. St. Louis: Concordia Publishing House, 1960.

Mack, Carol K., and Dinah Mack. *A Field Guide to Demons, Fairies, Fallen Angels, and other Subversive Spirits*. New York: Arcade Publishing, 1998.

Malu, Kathleen F. "Ways of Reading *Harry Potter*: Multiple Stories for Multiple Reader Identities." In *Harry Potter's World*, edited by Elizabeth E. Heilman.

Manlove, Colin. *Christian Fantasy: From 1200 to the Present*. Notre Dame, Ind.: University of Notre Dame Press, 1992.

McEvilley, Thomas. *The Shape of Ancient Thought: Comparative Studies in Greek and Indian Philosophies*. New York: Allworth Press, 2002.

McGrath, Malcolm. *Demons of the Modern World*. Amherst, N.Y.: Prometheus Books, 2002.

Mendlesohn, Farah. "Crowning the King: Harry Potter and the Construction of Authority." In *The Ivory Tower and Harry Potter*, edited by Lana A. Whited.

Midelfort, H. C. Erik. "Social History and Biblical Exegesis: Community, Family, and Witchcraft in Sixteenth-Century Germany." In *The Bible in the Sixteenth Century*, edited by David C. Steinmetz. Durham, N.C.: Duke University Press, 1990.

Miller, Laura. "Harry Potter, Teen Rebel." Salon.com [online]. salon.com/books/feature/2003/06/23/harry_potter [June 23, 2003].

Moore, Sharon, ed. *We Love Harry Potter! We'll Tell You Why*. New York: St. Martin's Griffin, 1999.

Munslow, Alun. *Deconstructing History*. New York: Routledge, 1997.

Murphy, Rex. "All Hail Frankenpotter." *Globe and Mail* (Toronto) [online]. www.radio.cbc.ca/programs/checkup/potter.html [July 10, 2000].

Neal, Connie. *The Gospel According to Harry Potter: Spirituality in the Stories of the World's Most Famous Seeker*. Louisville, Ky.: Westminster John Knox Press, 2002.

———. *What's a Christian to Do with Harry Potter?* Colorado Springs: Waterbrook Press, 2001.

Nel, Philip. "You Say 'Jelly,' I Say 'Jell-O'? Harry Potter and the Transfiguration of Language." In *The Ivory Tower and Harry Potter*, edited by Lana A. Whited.

Nel, Philip. *J. K. Rowling's Harry Potter Novels*. New York: Continuum, 2001.

"New Harry Potter Movie Premieres in London." Fox News (Associated Press) [online]. www.foxnews.com/story/0,2933,68876,00.html [November 3, 2003].

Nigg, Joe. *Wonder Beasts: Tales and Lore of the Phoenix, the Griffin, the Unicorn, and the Dragon*. Englewood, Colo.: Libraries Unlimited, 1995.

Nigg, Joseph. *The Book of Fabulous Beasts: A Treasury of Writings from Ancient Times to the Present*. New York: Oxford University Press, 1999.

Nikolajeva, Maria. "Harry Potter—A Return to the Romantic Hero." In *Harry Potter's World*, edited by Elizabeth E. Heilman.

Nussbaum, Martha C. *Cultivating Humanity: A Classical Defense of Reform in Liberal Education*. Cambridge, Mass.: Harvard University Press, 1997.

———. *The Therapy of Desire: Theory and Practice in Hellenistic Ethics*. Princeton, N.J.: Princeton University Press, 1994.

Nussbaum, Martha C. *Upheavals of Thought: The Intelligence of Emotions*. New York: Cambridge University Press, 2001.

Oestreich, Gerhard. *Neostoicism and the Early Modern State*. Translated by David McLintock. New York: Cambridge University Press, 1982.

Oldridge, Darren. ed. *The Witchcraft Reader*. New York: Routledge, 2002.

Olson, Ted. "Positive about Potter." *Christianity Today* [online]. www.christianity-today.com/ct/1999/150/12.0.html [December 13, 1999].

Orion, Loretta. *Never Again the Burning Times: Paganism Revived*. Prospect Heights, Ill.: Waveland Press, 1995.

Pennington, John. "From Elfland to Hogwarts, or the Aesthetic Trouble with Harry Potter." *The Lion and the Unicorn* 26 (2002): 78–97.

Pharr, Mary. "In Medias Res: Harry Potter as Hero-in-Progress." In *The Ivory Tower and Harry Potter*, edited by Lana A. Whited.

Pilkey, Dav. *The Adventures of Captain Underpants*. New York: Little Apple, 1997.

Pinsent, Pat. "The Education of a Wizard: Harry Potter and His Predecessors." In *The Ivory Tower and Harry Potter*, edited by Lana A. Whited.

"Potter Book Five." BBC Newsround [online]. news.bbc.co.uk/cbbcnews/hi/uk/newsid_2661000/2661257.stm [January 15, 2003].

"Potter Breaks UK Box Office Records." *Guardian Unlimited* [online]. film.guardian.co.uk/harrypotter/news/0,10608,842586,00.html [November 18, 2002].

"Potter Film Moves Rowling into Billionaire League." *Guardian Unlimited* [online]. film.guardian.co.uk/News_Story/Exclusive/0,4029,606205,00.html [November 26, 2001].

Principe, Lawrence M., and William R. Newman. "Some Problems with the Historiography of Alchemy." In *Secrets of Nature: Astrology and Alchemy in Early Modern Europe*, edited by William R. Newman and Anthony Grafton. Cambridge, Mass.: The M.I.T. Press, 2001.

Pullman, Philip. *The Golden Compass*. New York: Dell Yearling, 2001.

"Purging Flame: Pa. Church Members Burn Harry Potter, Other Books 'Against God.'" ABCNews.com [online]. http://more.abcnews.go.com/sections/us/dailynews/book_burning010326.html [March 26, 2001].

Purtill, Richard L. *J. R. R. Tolkien: Myth, Morality, and Religion*. San Francisco: Harper & Row, 1984.

Read, John. *Prelude to Chemistry*. Cambridge, Mass.: The M.I.T. Press, 1966.

Reid, Carmen. "Yes, It's Magic." *Sunday Mail* (Scotland), June 22, 2003, p. 14.

Reimer, Joseph. "The Case of the Missing Family: Kohlberg and the Study of Adolescent Moral Development." In *Approaches to Moral Development*, edited by Andrew Garrod.

Roni Natov, "Harry Potter and the Extraordinariness of the Ordinary." In *The Ivory Tower and Harry Potter*, edited by Lana A. Whited.

Rowling, J. K, as Newt Scamander. *Fantastic Beasts and Where to Find Them*. New York: Scholastic, 2001.

———. "Harry Potter 'Strolled into My Head.'" Reuters, July 17, 2000.

———. *Harry Potter and the Chamber of Secrets*. New York: Scholastic Press, 1999.

———. *Harry Potter and the Goblet of Fire*. New York: Scholastic Press, 2000.

———. *Harry Potter and the Order of the Phoenix*. New York: Scholastic Books, 2003.

———. *Harry Potter and the Philosopher's Stone*. London: Bloomsbury, 1997.

———. *Harry Potter and the Prisoner of Azkaban*. New York: Scholastic Press, 1999.

———. *Harry Potter and the Sorcerer's Stone*. New York: Scholastic Press, 1998.

———, as Kennilworthy Whisp. *Quidditch through the Ages*. New York: Scholastic, 2001.

———. "Interviews and Essays" [online]. search.barnesandnoble.com/book search/isbninquiry.asp?btob=Y&isbn=0590353403&displayonly=author Interview [March 19, 1999].

———. Interview. *The Diane Rehm Show*, WAMU, *National Public Radio* [online]. www.wamu.org [October 20, 1999].

———. Interview. Barnes and Noble, March 19, 1999. *Hogwarts* [online]. magic hogwarts.com/book/interviews/mar19-99.html.

———. Interview. Barnes and Noble, September 8, 1999. *Arabella Figg's Hogwarts Express* [online]. www.angelfire.com/mi3/cookarama/barnobintsep99. html.

Schoefer, Christine. "Harry Potter's Girl Trouble." Salon.com [online]. dir.salon. com/books/feature/2000/01/13/potter/index.html [January 13, 2000].

Scott, A. O. "Will There Be Trouble with Harry?" Slate [online]. slate.msn.com/ id/2000111/entry/1003477/ [August 24, 1999].

Seneca. "De Constantia Sapientis." In *Moral Essays*, translated by John W. Basore. New York: G. P. Putnam's Sons, 1928.

Seneca. "On Providence" In *The Stoic Philosophy of Seneca*, translated by Moses Hadas. Garden City, N.J.: Doubleday, 1958.

Shifflett, Andrew Eric. *Stoicism, Politics, and Literature in the Age of Milton: War and Peace Reconciled*. Cambridge: Cambridge University Press, 1998.

Shippey, T. A. *J. R. R. Tolkien: Author of the Century*. Boston: Houghton Mifflin Company, 2001.

Skulnick, Rebecca, and Jesse Goodman. "The Civic Leadership of *Harry Potter*: Agency, Ritual, and Schooling." In *Harry Potter's World*, edited by Elizabeth E. Heilman.

Stephens, William O. "The Rebirth of Stoicism." *Creighton Magazine* (Winter 2000) [online]. puffin.creighton.edu/phil/Stephens/rebirth_of_stoicism. htm [May 18, 2001].

"Stoicism." In *The Encyclopedia of Philosophy*, edited by Paul Edwards. Vol. 8. New York: The Macmillan Company & The Free Press, 1967.

Strier, Richard. "Against the Rule of Reason: Praise of Passion from Petrarch to Luther to Shakespeare to Herbert." Forthcoming in *Reading the Early Modern Passions*, edited by Mary Floyd-Wilson, Karen Rowe, and Gail Kern Pastor. Philadelphia: University of Pennsylvania Press.

Sutton, Roger. "Potter's Field." *The Horn Book Magazine* [online]. www.hbook. com/editorial_sep99.shtml [September/October 1999].

———. "When Harry Met Dorothy." *The Horn Book Magazine* [online].

www.hbook.com/editorial_jan01.shtml [January/February 2001].

Taub, Deborah J., and Heather L. Servaty. "Controversial Content in Children's Literature: Is *Harry Potter* Harmful to Children?" In *Harry Potter's World*, edited by Elizabeth E. Heilman.

The Nibelungenlied. Translated by A. T. Hatto. New York: Penguin, 1982.

The Stoic Place [online]. www.wku.edu/~jan.garrett/stoa.htm [July 10, 2001].

Tibbets, Peggy. "Release Your Inner Editor" [online]. www.wordweaving. com/articlemay08_00.html [March 10, 2001].

Tolkien, J. R. R. *The Hobbit*. London: George Allen & Unwin, 1937.

Tolkien, J. R. R. "[Letter] To Milton Waldman." In *The Letters of J. R. R. Tolkien*, edited by Humphrey Carpenter. Boston: Houghton Mifflin Company, 1981.

Tolkien, J. R. R. *The Lord of the Rings*. London: George Allen & Unwin, 1954–1955.

Travers, P. L. "On Not Writing for Children." *Children's Literature* 5 (1975): 15–22.

Treneman, Ann. "J. K. Rowling: the Interview." *The Times* (London), June 30, 2000). *TimesOnline* [online]. www.timesonline.co.uk/article/0,,927-79520,00.html.

Turner-Vorbeck, Tammy. "Pottermania: Good, Clean Fun or Cultural Hegemony?" In *Harry Potter's World*, edited by Elizabeth E. Heilman.

Twain, Mark. *The Adventures of Tom Sawyer*. New York: Washington Square Press, 1950 [1875].

Tyrrel, Rebecca. "What the Critics (of All Ages) Think of the New Book." *Sunday Telegraph* (London), June 22, 2003, p. 8.

Veith, Gene Edward. "Good Fantasy and Bad Fantasy." *Christian Research Journal* 23, no. 1 (2000) [online]. www.equip.org/free/DF801.htm [December 29, 2002].

Westman, Karin E. "Specters of Thatcherism: Contemporary British Culture in J. K. Rowling's Harry Potter Series." In *The Ivory Tower and Harry Potter*, edited by Lana E. Whited.

Whited, Lana A, ed., *The Ivory Tower and Harry Potter: Perspectives on a Literary Phenomenon*. Columbia: University of Missouri Press, 2002.

Whited, Lana A., and M. Katherine Grimes. "What Would Harry Do? J. K. Rowling and Lawrence Kohlberg's Theories of Moral Development." In *The Ivory Tower and Harry Potter*, edited by Lana A. Whited.

"Why We Like Harry Potter." *Christianity Today* [online]. www.christianitytoday. com/ct/2000/001/29.37.html [January 10, 2000].

Winks, Linton. "Charmed, I'm Sure." *Washington Post* [online]. www.washingtonpost.com/wp-srv/style/books/features/rowling1020.htm [October 20, 1999].

Yates, Emma. "Harry Potter and the Fight against Global Capitalism." *Guardian Unlimited* [online]. books.guardian.co.uk/news/articles/0,6109,621826,00. html [December 19, 2001].

Zipes, Jack. *Sticks and Stones: The Troublesome Success of Children's Literature from Slovenly Peter to Harry Potter*. New York: Routledge, 2000.

Index